OFFICIAL

Cambridge English

Business BENCHMARK

Upper Intermediate
BULATS and Business Vantage

Teacher's Resource Book

Guy Brook-Hart with David Clark

2nd Edition

CAMBRIDGE
UNIVERSITY PRESS

University Printing House, Cambridge CB2 8BS, United Kingdom

Cambridge University Press is part of the University of Cambridge.

It furthers the University's mission by disseminating knowledge in the pursuit of education, learning and research at the highest international levels of excellence.

www.cambridge.org
Information on this title: www.cambridge.org/9781107632110

© Cambridge University Press 2013

This publication is in copyright. Subject to statutory exception and to the provisions of relevant collective licensing agreements, no reproduction of any part may take place without the written permission of Cambridge University Press.

First published 2006
Second edition published 2013

A catalogue record for this publication is available from the British Library

ISBN 978-1-107-63211-0 Upper Intermediate BULATS and Business Vantage Teacher's Resource Book
ISBN 978-1-107-68098-2 Upper Intermediate Business Vantage Student's Book
ISBN 978-1-107-63983-6 Upper Intermediate BULATS Student's Book
ISBN 978-1-107-68660-1 Upper Intermediate BULATS and Business Vantage Personal Study Book
ISBN 978-1-107-68003-6 Upper Intermediate BULATS Class Audio CDs (2)
ISBN 978-1-107-63315-5 Upper Intermediate Business Vantage Class Audio CDs (2)

Cambridge University Press has no responsibility for the persistence or accuracy of URLs for external or third-party internet websites referred to in this publication, and does not guarantee that any content on such websites is, or will remain, accurate or appropriate. Information regarding prices, travel timetables, and other factual information given in this work is correct at the time of first printing but Cambridge University Press does not guarantee the accuracy of such information thereafter.

Contents

Introduction

Who this course is for

Business Benchmark Second edition Upper Intermediate Business Vantage/BULATS is a completely updated and revised course at CEFR B2 level, reflecting contemporary international business in a stimulating way both for people already working and for students who have not yet worked in business.

It teaches the reading, speaking, listening and writing skills needed in today's global workplaces, together with essential business vocabulary and grammar.

Business Benchmark Upper Intermediate is also the most complete preparation material available for *Cambridge English:Business Vantage*, also known as *Business English Certificate (BEC) Vantage*, and for the Business Language Testing Service (BULATS) test, and is officially approved as an exam preparation course by Cambridge ESOL. It includes either one complete exam for Business Vantage supplied by Cambridge ESOL or selected tasks from the BULATS test.

What the course contains

Student's Book

- **24 units for classroom study** covering all four skills in a dynamic and integrated way, together with essential business vocabulary and grammar.
- Authentic listening and reading material, including interviews with real business people.
- Six **Grammar workshops** which explain and extend the grammar work covered in the units and which are informed by the Cambridge Learner Corpus (CLC) – see below.
- A nine-page **Writing reference** covering emails, memos, letters, reports and proposals and function bank.
- A fully-referenced **Word list** with definitions, covering key vocabulary from the units and the transcripts.
- An **Exam skills and Exam practice** section, which gives students detailed guidance on how to approach each exam task, the skills required and what the exam task is testing, together with exercises to build up students' exam skills. The Exam practice pages contain either **a complete past Business Vantage exam**, with answers, supplied by **Cambridge ESOL** or **selected tasks from the BULATS test**.
- A **full answer key** for all the exercises in the Student's Book, including **sample answers** to all the writing tasks.
- Complete **recording transcripts**.

New features in the 2nd edition

- **Updated grammar and vocabulary** exercises based on correcting common grammar and vocabulary mistakes made by Business English students at this level, as shown by the CLC (see below). Exercises based on the CLC are indicated by this symbol: ⊙
- New **Writing reference** section with guidance for each type of writing task and sample answers.
- New topics, texts and recordings reflecting the realities of contemporary international business.
- **Complete revision of all exam-style tasks**, making them closer to real exam tasks.

The Cambridge Learner Corpus (CLC)

The Cambridge Learner Corpus (CLC) is a large collection of exam scripts written by candidates taken from Cambridge ESOL exams around the world. It currently contains over 220,000 scripts, which translates to over 48 million words, and it is growing all the time. It forms part of the Cambridge International Corpus (CIC) and it has been built up by Cambridge University Press and Cambridge ESOL. The CLC currently contains scripts from over:

- 200,000 students
- 170 different first languages
- 200 different countries.

Find out more about the Cambridge Learner Corpus at www.cambridge.org/corpus.

Personal Study Book

The Personal Study Book contains:

- 24 units, each relating to the 24 units of the Student's Book. These units contain:
  - vocabulary revision and consolidation work
  - grammar revision and consolidation work.
- a 15-page Writing supplement covering spelling, punctuation, paragraphing, organisation and planning of writing tasks.
- a full answer key to all the exercises.

Recorded materials

The recordings for the Student's Book are available on two **audio CDs**, containing a variety of recorded material, including authentic interviews with real business people and exam listening tasks.

Teacher's Resource Book

The Teacher's Resource Book contains:

- information about how the activities in each unit relate to the Business Vantage exam and BULATS test

- step-by-step notes on each exercise in each unit in the Student's Book, with advice on how to handle activities in the unit and suggestions for alternative treatments and extension ideas for certain exercises

- answer keys to all exercises in the Student's Book, including the Exam skills and Exam practice section.

- additional photocopiable activities for every unit and six case studies, including further reading texts, discussion activities and games, intended to supplement and extend the work done in the Student's Book units and to provide a wider range of activities or a more in-depth study of certain business topics. The photocopiable activities also provide extra writing tasks, all with a step-by-step approach and a sample answer for students or teachers to refer to

- answers to all exercises in the photocopiable activities

Cambridge English: Business Vantage exam

The Business Vantage exam assesses language ability used in the context of business at the Council of Europe's Vantage Level (B2) for general language proficiency.

- In the Reading component, there are five tasks of the following types: multiple-choice, matching, sentence-level gap-filling, multiple-choice gap-filling and error identification. The Reading component contributes 25% of the total marks.

- In the Writing component, there are two tasks, both compulsory. Candidates produce a piece of internal company communication and a short report, proposal or piece of business correspondence. The Writing component contributes 25% of the total marks.

- In the Listening component, there are three tasks of the following types: gap-filling or note completion, matching and multiple-choice. Texts used are monologues and dialogues, including interviews, discussions, telephone conversations and messages. The Listening component contributes 25% of the total marks.

- The Speaking Test is conducted by two external examiners, and candidates are tested in pairs (or, if there is an uneven number of candidates, in groups of three). There are three tasks in which each candidate responds to the questions, gives a 'mini-presentation' lasting approximately six minutes and takes part in a collaborative task with the other candidate.

A single overall grade is awarded, based on the aggregate of marks gained in the four components indicated above.

Business Language Testing Service (BULATS) test

BULATS makes use of a number of specially designed tests:

- The Computer Test
- The Standard Test
- The Speaking Test
- The Writing Test

Each test can be used independently of the others, or they can be used in various combinations. All the tests aim to be relevant to people using the language at work. They cover areas such as descriptions of jobs, companies and products, travel, management and marketing, customer service planning, reports, phone messages, business correspondence and presentations. The tasks in the test are generally practical ones, e.g. taking a phone message, checking a letter, giving a presentation, understanding an article, writing a report.

All the tests aim to assess candidates across the six levels of the ALTE Framework, i.e. the same test is used for all candidates whatever their level. (0–5 of the ALTE Framework correspond to the Council of Europe framework levels A1–C2.)

Acknowledgements

The authors and publishers acknowledge the following sources of copyright material and are grateful for the permissions granted. While every effort has been made, it has not always been possible to identify the sources of all the material used, or to trace all copyright holders. If any omissions are brought to our notice, we will be happy to include the appropriate acknowledgements on reprinting.

Text on p.112 adapted from '"Cool Hunters" – next big job' by Sarah Rohner, http://rememberrohner1.wordpress. com/2011/09/02/cool-hunters-next-big-job/; Text on p.114 adapted from 'Fifteen ideas for promoting your company', BusinessFinance.com; Petpals (UK) Limited for the text on p.122 adapted from 'The Petpals pawprint for business success', http://www.petpals.com. Reproduced with permission; Radisson Blu Hotel Shanghai New World for the text on p.140 adapted from http://www.radisson.com/ shanghai-hotel-cn-200003/chnsghnw. Reproduced with permission; Text on p.147 adapted from 'Is traditional marketing dying?', Focus.com, http://www.focus.com/ questions/traditional-marketing-dying/#.

The authors and publishers acknowledge the following sources of photographs and are grateful for the permissions granted.

p.113 (T): Copyright © 2006 Centragon, Inc. dba PROSHADE, www.proshade.net. Graphic Design: Tom Donaldson. Photographer: Jim Bowen from Hope Mills, NC, US; p.113 (B): Glowimages/Pietro Scozzari; p.129 (T): Thinkstock; p.129 (B): Alamy/LBarnwell; p.140: Radisson Blu Hotel Shanghai New World; p.150: Shutterstock/ Fotoverkaeufer; p.154: Shutterstock/Gunnar Pippel.

Illustrations by Simon Tegg (pp.105 and 146) and Tim Oliver (p.151).

David Clark would like to thank Jane Coates and Catriona Watson-Brown for all their invaluable help and support throughout the writing of this book. It was a real pleasure working with you both.

Staff development and training

Unit objectives

Topic:	how companies encourage staff development and training
Reading:	skimming; a multiple-choice cloze; identifying the subjects of paragraphs; using reference devices to recognise organisation; replacing gapped sentences in a text
Listening:	a phone conversation; two students discussing a collaborative task
Speaking:	discussing training; agreeing/disagreeing; role-play deciding on a training course; making suggestions
Grammar:	countable and uncountable nouns;
Vocabulary:	perks and benefits; *ability, certificate*, etc.; *work, job, training, training course; tailor-made, learning goals*, etc.; *dedicated facilities*, etc.

Getting started

Warming up With books closed, ask students to work in small groups and make a list of things which they think are important when looking for or choosing a job.

When they have finished, round up with the whole class.

Tell them to look at the exercise in the book and ask them *Are there any ideas in the list which you didn't mention?*

Before they do the exercise, go through the Useful language box with them. Elicit complete sentences for each of the phrases.

Elicit other ways of agreeing and disagreeing.

Extension idea Ask: *Which of these things would you expect to be mentioned in a job advertisement in your country? Are there other things which are not mentioned here?*

Recruitment brochure

Reading

1 *Extension idea* Ask: *What do you think are the attractions of working for a travel company?*

BEC Reading part 4   BULATS Reading part 2 section 2

2 Tell students it is important to quickly skim the text (read quickly to get a general idea of what it is about) before choosing which option fills each gap. Skimming will give them an idea of how the text develops and, since they will then know the context, help them to choose the correct options.

Give students one minute for this task and be strict about the time limit. When they have finished, ask them to compare their answers in pairs, but without looking back at the text.

Answers

1 Advanced Sales, Goal Setting, Time Management
2 It gives staff the skills they need to succeed, they promote from within the company, they want to train their future leaders.

3 Business Vantage Reading Part 4 is a gapped text from an authentic source. The four options for each gap often form a lexical set of words with similar meanings. Students have to choose the correct option based on:
- meaning or usage of the word in the context
- grammatical context, e.g. is there a dependent preposition, or is the word followed by an infinitive or a verb + *-ing*, etc.?
- collocation (e.g. *financial advisor* not *financial helper*)
- whether it forms part of a fixed phrase or expression.

Tell students they should read around the gaps before choosing an option. To help them, you can elicit the answer to Question 1 (B *gain*) by eliciting that *gain* implies some advance or improvement.

You can also elicit why the other options are incorrect (*win* is used in the context of a competition, contest or prize; *earn* with salary in exchange for work; *collect* with physical things that form a collection).

Tell students that the best preparation for this type of task is to read business texts extensively. This builds up their language knowledge and their intuitive feel for which word fits correctly in the context.

Although it may be time-consuming, it is worth going through the wrong options, or asking students to look up the wrong options in a dictionary to see in what contexts they would be correct.

Note: In the Business Vantage exam, this task consists of 15 questions; in BULATS, five questions.

Answers

2 A 3 C 4 B 5 D 6 C 7 A 8 D 9 B 10 A

Speaking

Before students answer the questions, go through the Useful language box with them. To practise, you can make some contentious statements and invite students to agree/ disagree, e.g.

I think all employees in a company should be paid exactly the same salary.

All employees should be expected to study in their spare time.

Extension idea Ask students if companies in their country take the same attitude to training and staff development.

Vocabulary 1

Students can do this task in pairs. To check the meanings of the words, ask them to find out/explain the difference between *skill* and *ability; certificate, course, degree* and *qualifications*. If necessary, ask them to use dictionaries.

Answers

2 qualifications 3 degree 4 course; certificate; knowledge; experience 5 development

Extension idea Ask students to work in pairs and say what job-related skills, experience and qualifications they have.

Grammar workshop

Countable and uncountable nouns

Tell students that Business English students often make mistakes with countable and uncountable nouns, particularly by making uncountable nouns plural.

Go through the brief explanation at the beginning of this section with them before they do the exercise.

Now would be a good time to do the Grammar workshop on Countable and uncountable nouns on page 24.

Answers

2 U 3 C 4 C 5 U 6 U

Extension idea Ask students in pairs to think of five other countable and five other uncountable nouns which might be used in a business context.

Round up with the whole class, writing their suggestions in two columns – for countable and uncountable – on the board.

Vocabulary 2

After students have looked at the dictionary extracts, ask them to work in pairs and think of their own examples for each word/phrase.

Tell students that these words are frequently confused and that they should be especially careful to use them correctly.

When you go through the answers, elicit why each answer is correct.

Answers

1 work 2 job 3 work 4 job 5 training course 6 training
7 training course

Training course

Listening

BEC Listening part 1   BULATS Listening part 2

1 In these parts of the Business Vantage and BULATS exams, there will be three recordings to listen to; students will be expected to complete notes, a message or a form by writing one or two words in each gap.

This task focuses on factual information: students may need to copy down names and numbers and other facts correctly spelled. Point out to students that the task is in note form, i.e. incomplete sentences, and that they will not hear exactly the same words used when they listen as the words they read in the notes. However, they should write words they hear.

Tell students that they have some time before they listen to read the notes, and that in this time, they should decide what information they need to listen for and what type of word(s) (noun, adjective, etc.) they need.

Suggested answers

1 a name or type of company 2 *staff/employees*? 3 a length of time 4 something a Director of Studies can give

2 ①01 In the exams, candidates hear each recording twice. At the end, they have a short time to copy their answers to an answer sheet.

Play the recording twice.

Give students some time to check their answers: they should make sure the words they have written down are spelled correctly and fit the meaning of the notes.

Ask them to compare their ideas in pairs.

Answers

1 Forrest Insurance 2 graduate trainees 3 one/1 month
4 quotation

Extension idea If you and your students wish, you can play the recording again for them to check their answers, or you can refer them to the transcript at the back of the Student's Book.

3 *Alternative treatment* Ask students to find the phrases on the left in the transcript at the back of the Student's Book before doing the exercise.

Answers

2 f 3 d 4 a 5 b 6 c

Extension idea Ask students to choose three phrases and write three example sentences using the phrases. They can then round up by reading their sentences to the whole class.

Training at Deloitte in China

Reading

BEC Reading part 2

1 In this task, six sentences have been removed from an authentic business text and are listed after the text with one 'distractor'. Students have to decide which sentence to put in each gap. The first is done as an example.

This task tests students' ability to understand the structure and development of the text. They need to use clues within the text and the sentences to decide which sentences go where. These clues will include:

– the content of the paragraph and the sentences around the gap

– the content of the missing sentences

– cohesive devices around the gap and in the missing sentences, such as linking devices and pronouns.

It is important that students read through the whole article quite quickly, recognising the subject or main idea of each paragraph.

Extension idea Two of Deloitte's Chinese employees do not use quite standard English: *I was very emotional to see their concern* and *I don't need to change environment*. Ask students to rephrase them in more standard English (**suggested answer:** I felt very emotional when I saw their concern; I don't need to change the place where I work / my employer).

Suggested answers

paragraph 1: Deloitte's dedication to training
paragraph 2: support for employees from managers
paragraph 3: managers' interest in staff development
paragraph 4: managers' attention to staff
paragraph 5: counsellors

2 Tell students that in the Business Vantage exam, words will not be underlined; it has been done here to help them recognise connections and cohesive devices.

Use the example (1G) to show students how the task works. In this case, the meaning of a phrase in the text is repeated in the missing sentence.

Tell them to work through the text, reading before and after each gap, then choosing the correct sentence and crossing it off the list so they do not need to read it again when looking at the next gap.

They should pencil in possibilities for any gap where they are not sure of the answer.

When they have finished:

– tell them to quickly read the text again with the missing sentences in the correct places to check that the text reads coherently and logically. If anything seems not quite logical, they should check to see if there is a better choice.

– ask them to compare their answers in pairs and resolve any differences they have.

Answers

1 *Suggested answer*: The connection between *clear upward path* and *ascend to the top*.
2 2C 3A 4B 5F 6D

3 *Extension idea* Ask: *What other things can companies do to ensure loyalty from their employees?*
Do you agree that the success of a company depends on its people?

Vocabulary

Ask students to quickly find the words/phrases in the text before doing the exercise.

Answers

1 b 2 c 3 a 4 d 5 f 6 e

Extension idea If students have good business dictionaries, ask them to look up the words/phrases and copy them into their notebooks with an example from the dictionary.

Training scheme for new staff

Role-play

BEC Speaking part 3   BULATS Speaking part 3

1 In this part of the Business Vantage Speaking Test, which is done in pairs or groups of three, candidates are given 30 seconds to read the task and think before they start speaking. They then discuss the task for about three minutes (about four minutes if it is a group of three). The examiner will follow up with further questions on the same topic. The task tests a range of discussion strategies and functions, as well as effective turn-taking.

If you wish, you can get students started by asking them to suggest the type of company they work for.

2 ① 02 Elicit what function all the underlined phrases have (**answer:** making suggestions). Point out that this is a discussion activity, so it is important to suggest ideas and for other people in the discussion also to have a chance to suggest ideas and react to your ideas.

Answers

a 1, 3, 4, 6 b 2 c 5

Extension idea Ask: *What did the two people decide?*

3 *Extension idea* Tell students to look at the transcript at the back of the Student's Book and underline any other phrases they think would be useful when they discuss. Ask them to copy them to their notebooks.

4 Tell students that they have about three minutes for this discussion. Tell them to make sure they cover all the points in the task.

Round up by asking them what decisions they reached.

Job descriptions and job satisfaction

Topic:	job descriptions and feelings about the job
Writing:	an extract from a report
Listening:	interview with multiple-choice questions; matching short extracts
Speaking:	describing jobs; talking about what you like/dislike; answering interview questions
Grammar:	forming questions; present perfect and past simple
Vocabulary:	jobs and responsibilities; phrases to introduce responsibilities; *staff, employee, member of staff*

Getting started

1 *Warming up* With books closed, tell students they are going to work on describing jobs. Ask *In what situations might you have to describe the job you do?* (**Suggested answers:** when meeting a new client or colleague, when meeting new people in social situations, at job interviews, in letters of application.)

Alternative treatment If your students are working or have worked, ask *Which of these things do/did you do in your job?*

Ask students to add two more activities they would enjoy and two more they would dislike to the list.

2 If your students are working, ask if any of them have (or have had) these jobs.

Suggested answers

a 2, 6 b 1, 5, 6 c 1, 2, 4, 5, 6 d 1, 3, 4, 5, 6 e 1, 2, 3, 4, 6

Job responsibilities

Vocabulary

1 Tell students that in business, it is useful not just to be able to describe your own job, but also to understand what other people's work involves.

Ask them to notice verbs which go with nouns to form verb–noun collocations, e.g. *keep financial records*. They should write these phrases in their notebooks.

2 **Answers**

1 c 2 d 3 b 4 a 5 e

Extension idea Ask: *Which job sounds the most complicated? Which do you think is the easiest to do?*

3 **Answers**

2 recruit 3 evaluating 4 promoting 5 investment 6 funds 7 performance 8 deadlines

Extension idea Ask students to organise vocabulary in their notebooks in categories. You can suggest three categories to get them started: finance, human resources and marketing.

Ask students to categorise the words from this exercise in their notebooks. This will make the vocabulary easier to find and use, and will help students to remember new words. (**Answers**: finance: *investments, funds*; human resources: *recruit, evaluating, performance*; marketing: *promoting. Deadlines* does not fit in any of the categories.)

4 Before students write, go through the Useful language box with them. Ask them to suggest ways of completing the sentences.

5 In small classes, you can do this activity with the whole class.

6 Ask when someone might ask these questions in a business context (**answer**: at a job interview).

Answers

1 of; are 2 have; been; have; been 3 did 4 are; for

Extension idea Ask students to work in pairs and write two more questions like these that an employer might ask at a job interview.

BEC Speaking part 1   BULATS Speaking part 1

7 Before students speak, ask them to look back at the vocabulary they have studied during this unit and think how they could use some of it while answering the questions.

Tell students they should answer the questions with two or three sentences: the examiner will want to hear how fluently they speak, how well they can construct sentences and their range of vocabulary.

Extension idea If you did the extension idea in Exercise 6, tell students to use these questions, as well as any others they think of while speaking.

A human resources manager

Listening

BEC Listening part 3   BULATS Listening part 4

1 Many of the listening exercises in *Business Benchmark Vantage* use authentic recordings of real business people.

This type of exercise in the Listening Test consists of a monologue, interview or discussion and requires students to listen to a longer piece, where they need to listen for the main ideas as well as details, factual information, opinions and feelings.

Christina Bunt is an HR manager for Tesco in Cornwall in south-west England.

Tell students that they should make underlining the key idea in the questions a routine when doing multiple-choice questions. This helps them to focus on what each question is asking, rather than just reading through the questions, and is a quick way of reminding them what they are listening for.

Suggested underlining

2 makes managing people easy
3 How / become
4 doing in ten years' time
5 advice / for job candidates
6 know / good at the job

2 ① 03 Play the recording twice, as in the exam. Afterwards, ask students to compare their answers in pairs.

Alternative treatment Instead of checking answers with the whole class, ask students to read the transcript at the back of the Student's Book and find how each answer is expressed. This should reinforce the idea that the question and the correct option in multiple-choice questions will be a paraphrase of what the speaker says in the recording i.e. they have to listen for meaning rather than specific words.

Answers

1 A 2 B 3 C 4 C 5 B 6 B

Human resources

Speaking

Extension idea Ask students in small groups to answer this question: *Have you ever done a job interview? What was it like? Describe the experience.*

Vocabulary

1 Elicit that *staff* refers to the whole group and is therefore uncountable. *Member of staff* and *employee* are often interchangeable.

Answers

1 c 2 b 3 a

2 **Answers**

2 ~~staffs~~ staff/employees 3 ~~staff~~ member of staff / employee
4 ~~staffs~~ members of staff / employees

What I like about my job

Listening

1 Go through the Useful language box with students before they discuss. Elicit ways of completing the sentences. They can write these in their notebooks.

Alternative treatment Before they discuss, ask students to explain in their own words what each of the reasons means: for example, **a)** balancing working life with family life: *There's enough time for me to spend with my family; I don't have to work such long hours that I don't see them.*

Extension idea Ask students: *Are there any other reasons you would like to add to the list?* Write any extra reasons on the board and ask students how important they are.

BEC Listening part 2   BULATS Listening part 3

2 ① 04 In the exams themselves, the recordings are scripted, whereas here, students listen to extracts from authentic interviews. In the exam, there are two sections of five monologues each.

This part of the Listening Paper tests candidates' ability to identify the topic, function or context of each monologue. This listening exercise concentrates on topic.

As with other parts of the exams, all listening practice is good preparation, but for this part especially, students will benefit from listening to and identifying small snippets of speech, as well as interviews, conversations and discussions where a variety of speakers each intervene briefly.

Play the recording twice. Then ask students to compare their answers in pairs.

Answers

1 d 2 b 3 f 4 e 5 h

Extension idea Ask students to work alone and write their own extract for one of the three options not mentioned, i.e. a, c or g.

They should then work in small groups and take turns to read out their extract. The other students should match what is said with an option.

3 | **Answers**

> **1** work; client **2** freedom; choices **3** fulfilling **4** inspiring **5** what; one **6** exciting

Extension idea When students have finished, ask them to underline words/phrases in the sentences which express what people like (*I love*; *I absolutely thrive on*; *You don't mind*; *That's very inspiring, I think*; *it's exciting (to see)*). They can copy these into their notebooks.

Ask students to suggest other phrases they can use to express what they like.

Speaking

1 Tell students (if necessary) that:

- a good deal of success in working life depends on showing interest in and enthusiasm for what they do, and that this starts from the first job interview
- the questions in this exercise are standard and predictable job-interview questions which they would normally prepare for when going to an interview in real life.

2 *Extension idea* When students have finished, ask them to give each other feedback on ways they could answer each question better.

If you wish, students can change partners and do the exercise again.

Staff training report

Writing

BEC Writing part 2

1 This part of the exam may involve writing a short report based on graphic input and notes. Candidates are expected to cover all the essential elements of the task and be able to interpret information that is presented in graphic form.

After students have done the exercise, go to the Grammar workshop on page 24 and go through the explanation with them. Then ask them to do the exercises which follow on page 25.

Alternative treatment If students are preparing for an exam, tell them that when they write, they should use their own words, not just lift words from the graph/chart. Before they read the extract, ask them to look at the graph and say what it shows in their own words. (**Suggested answer:** It shows how much a company called PDQ has spent on training and developing its employees over the last three years.)

Answers

> **2** took **3** needed **4** fell **5** recruited **6** has signed **7** has set

2 Tell (or remind) students that when they do this type of writing task, they should use their own words as far as possible.

Answers

> employees – staff; budget – spend; agreement – contract; working methods – the way we work

3 Ask students: *What is the function or purpose of the three 'handwritten' notes on the chart?* (**Answer:** to explain why the staff training was necessary, i.e. to give reasons for it.)

Answers

> The main reason for; because; because of this; For that reason

4 Tell students that it is essential to cover all the important information and deal with all the handwritten notes.

Ask them to make their own notes/plan as they discuss.

5 Tell students that they can use the report in Exercise 1 as a model when they write. They should concentrate on covering all the information and handwritten notes, using their own words and using the past simple and present perfect correctly.

Sample answer

> Two years ago, the Bank of Veronezh spent 3,500,000 roubles on language training for staff. The reason for this was that they needed to learn English in order to work with our Polish partners in the Bank of Gdansk. Last year, in contrast, our spending on training rose to 5,250,000 because we needed to teach them how to use the new IT systems which had been installed. Recently, we have introduced new accounting methods which have affected some members of staff, and as a result, this year's staff training budget has been set at 2,300,000 roubles.

Extension idea If you asked students to do this exercise for homework, when they bring their writing to class, ask them to work in pairs and compare their answers.

Give them time to amend and improve their answers if they wish.

They can also compare their answers with the sample answer at the back of the Student's Book before handing in their work.

Getting the right job

Getting started

Go through the Useful language box with students before they start.

Tell students to give reasons for their answers and to add other ideas they may have.

Extension idea Ask students to change groups and take turns to give a mini-presentation (about a minute) on the same subject.

Job satisfaction at Sony Mobile Communications

Reading

1 *Alternative treatment* With books closed, ask students what they know about Sony Mobile Communications, who they are, where they are based, and what they produce. If you have internet access in class, students can look at their website at http://www.sonymobile.com. If you can do this, also ask students: *What impression do you have of the organisation?*

Suggested answers

You can work with people from different countries and cultures, so there is a variety of behaviours and ideas and learning opportunities; opportunities for travel and work abroad; opportunities for promotion based on merit; opportunities may arise to work in other international organisations.

BEC Reading part 1   **BULATS** Reading part 2 section 1

2 This reading task tests students' ability to identify specific information and detail, as well as gist.

By identifying key ideas, students will know what information they need to identify in the extracts.

Paraphrasing the key ideas sensitises students to the need to look for paraphrases when they read. Word spotting (i.e. finding the same words in the text as in the questions) is not a possible strategy for this task.

Tell students they also have to express ideas using their own words when they do Speaking and Writing tasks.

When students have finished, ask them to compare their ideas with another pair of students.

Suggested underlining

2 producing things / people / enjoy 3 improve our ways of working 4 affects the whole company 5 Recent recruits / encouraged / contribute ideas 6 wants / employees / variety of attitudes and opinions 7 To survive / continually / producing new products 8 aware / customers' different ways of thinking

Suggested paraphrases

2 making products people have fun with
3 make our working methods better
4 influences everyone in the organisation
5 new employees are given opportunities to say what they think
6 encourages diversity of points of view
7 To stay in business, you have to always innovate.
8 know about our clients' attitudes

3 Tell students that when they do this type of task, the statements are always printed before the extracts/texts. If they have studied the statements carefully, they should only need to read each extract carefully once to recognise which statement it refers to.

Tell students to work systematically through the extracts.

As they find a statement which is referred to, they should:

- cross the statement off so they do not look at it for other extracts

- underline the words in the extract which gave them the answer. This helps to confirm that there is clear evidence in the text for their choice.

Answers

1 B (*Developing my team and seeing them grow is what makes me happy – seeing them change over time.*)
2 C (*I take real pride in creating applications that are fun and satisfying for our customers to use.*)
3 B (*We work hard, but also we want to do it more intelligently, more efficiently and effectively.*)
4 D (*... our team's thinking and plans shaping and changing all parts of the company from internal culture through to packaging, product design and advertising.*)
5 C (*There's a great culture here where you can really discuss things with all your colleagues, even if you're a newcomer.*)
6 A (*... different views and mindsets are accepted and encouraged.*)
7 A (*There's also fierce competition that's always changing, forcing us to stay on our toes and innovate.*)
8 D (*... it's about understanding the cultural sensitivities of different markets.*)

Vocabulary

Answers

1 mastered 2 crops up 3 to stay on our toes
4 an analytical mindset 5 to challenge the status quo

Extension idea As a homework task, ask students to look up the words/phrases they have found in a good learner's dictionary (e.g. the *Cambridge Learner's Dictionary*). Tell them to copy the words to their notebooks, together with an example from the dictionary.

Speaking

Extension idea Also ask students:

• *Do you know about any companies in your country whose working language is English? Is this a growing trend?*

• *Do you think it's important to be happy with the organisation you work for and to have a job you like? Why? / Why not?*

• *Is it a good thing to encourage everyone to express their ideas and opinions? Why? / Why not?*

A website entry

Writing

1 Tell students that enthusiasm helps people to find jobs and to keep them. These phrases are ways of expressing enthusiasm.

To help focus students' attention on these phrases, ask them *Are they followed by a noun, an infinitive, verb + -ing or something else?* (*Answers: I've always been interested in* + noun; *I think what I contribute most to* + name of company *is* + verb + *-ing; I have a real passion about* + noun; verb + *-ing + is what makes me happy; I take real pride in* + noun / verb + *-ing; It's great* + verb + *-ing* / infinitive; *I also value* + verb + *-ing; I'm lucky* + infinitive; *It's rewarding* + infinitive)

Point out that where a noun is used, often a verb + *-ing* can also be used and vice versa.

Tell students to copy the phrases into their notebooks and to highlight any dependent prepositions.

Extension idea Ask students to work in pairs and use three or four of the phrases to talk about their present studies.

2 This writing task can be given for homework if you wish.

3 *Alternative treatment* If your class has a blog or website, these paragraphs can be posted there. Alternatively, they can be posted round the walls of the classroom for students to circulate and read.

Ask:

Which paragraph sounds the most enthusiastic?

Which is the most persuasive?

Advice on job applications

Listening

Warming up Ask students what advice they would give someone applying for a job. Tell them to give reasons for their advice. If they have experience of applying for jobs, ask them to share the lessons they have learned from it with their partners.

1 *Alternative treatment* Tell students to underline the key ideas in each piece of advice. Ask: *Which three pieces of advice do you think are the best, and why?*

Suggested underlining

a photograph
b send / by email
c not longer than one page
d free-time interests
e someone else / check
f Follow up / phone call
g Tell the truth
h Include / referees

BEC Listening part 2   BULATS Listening part 2

2 (1) 05 You should play the recording twice.

Answers

1 d 2 b 3 g 4 e 5 f

3 Especially if you have a mixed-nationality class, take the opportunity to explore cultural differences in this area with your students. Tell them that the advice on job applications in this unit may be suitable for English-speaking countries but may not have universal validity, and that if they are applying for a job outside their own cultural context, they should find out as much as possible about what is expected before they apply.

A short email and an email of a job application

Writing 1

1 *Warming up* Ask students:
   - *How do people find out about job vacancies and opportunities in your country?*
   - *Do universities have careers information services?*
   - *Are there job centres?*
   - *Would you/ Have you used the Internet to find a job?*

Elicit that *biz* in the job ad is an abbreviation for *business*.

BULATS Reading part 1 section 3 + Reading part 2 section 3

2 This task tests students' grammatical knowledge of verb tenses, modal verbs, prepositions, articles, pronouns, adverbial particles, collocations and conjunctions.

Tell students to read the email first before trying to fill gaps, then to read round each gap, looking at the structure and meaning of the sentence as a whole (and, if the word is at the beginning of a sentence, the previous sentence as well).

Ask students to compare their answers in pairs.

Answers

1 for 2 on 3 it 4 give 5 with 6 If

Extension idea Ask students to look at the structure of the email by asking them:

- *What is the function of each sentence?* (**Answers**: The first mentions the job and where it is advertised; the second says why it is suitable and how it will help Hiroshi; the third says how she can help.)
- *How are the sentences linked together?* (**Answers**: *it* refers to the job mentioned in the previous sentence; *If you apply* refers also by elision to the job.)

BEC Writing part 1   BULATS Writing part 1

3 In the Business Vantage exam, candidates are asked to write between 40 and 50 words. In the BULATS test, between 50 and 60 words.

The task will always be an internal company communication.

Tell students that it is important to:

- communicate all the points in the instructions: if anything is omitted, they will be considered to not have completed the task adequately, and in the exam they will lose marks for this
- complete the task within the word limit. If your students are preparing for an exam, give them one of the word limits above.

Ask them to identify the target reader (a colleague) and decide on a suitable style (less formal).

They can use the email in Exercise 2 as a model, but should supply their own details to complete the task.

Sample answer

Dear Fatma, I saw this job for a technician advertised on my company's intranet and thought it might be right for you because you've studied electronic engineering. I'd be happy to help you with your application if you need it.
Sasha

Extension idea 1 When students have finished writing, ask them to exchange emails and comment on whether they:

- have covered all the points
- introduced anything extra and irrelevant (in which case in the exam they would lose marks)
- communicated clearly and effectively.

Extension idea 2 Ask students to compare their answers with the model in Exercise 2 and with the sample answer at the back of the Student's Book.

They can then make any changes they wish to their answer before handing it in to you for correction.

4 You can point out that some of these things should be included in a CV, but not in the email/letter of application (covering letter).

Elicit the function of the email of application (to tell the prospective employer which job you want to apply for, who you are and why you make an interesting applicant, why you are interested in the job, and as a bridge between the job vacancy and the CV).

Suggested answer

You should include all points except 4 and 10 (10 can be put in your CV).

5 Point out that an email of application should not be too long, perhaps one page maximum, as the recruiter may have to read through large numbers of applications. Students should therefore aim for four or five paragraphs and will have to combine the points on the list in these paragraphs.

6 | **Christa's plan**
paragraph 1: the reason for writing the email, how she heard about the job
paragraph 2: her CV, what she studied, a summary of relevant work experience
paragraph 3: what she studied, relevant work experience in more detail
paragraph 4: why she is interested
paragraph 5: saying she is ready to be interviewed, references from her employers

7 This exercise tests candidates's grasp of sentence structure and their ability to find errors in written work.

Tell students that to do this task they should read the whole text first (which they have already done for Exercise 6), then read it sentence by sentence, not line by line, to identify the extra words.

When they have finished, tell them to read the whole text again to check their answers.

Answers

3 now **4** time **5** *correct* **6** have **7** the **8** and **9** *correct* **10** more **11** However **12** *correct* **13** my **14** an **15** too

Speaking

Extension idea Ask students to copy useful words and phrases from the two emails into their notebooks.

Vocabulary

Tell students that these sentences contain frequent errors made by business English students at this level. They should pay special attention to avoid them in their speaking and writing.

Answers

2 ~~interested~~ interesting **3** ~~interest~~ interested **4** ~~opened~~ open **5** ~~convenience~~ convenient **6** ~~absence~~ absent

Writing 2

Extension idea If you have set this task for homework, give students a deadline to bring their answer to class.

Elicit this checklist for applications from students and write the points on the board:

- Is the application neatly and attractively laid out and presented?
- Does it give a clear, brief picture of the applicant and their background?
- Does it say why the applicant wants the job?
- What impression does the applicant give?

Ask students in small groups to read each other's applications and give each other feedback based on the checklist.

Round up by asking students if there are any important, general points they discussed.

Students can follow up by helping each other to correct any mistakes in the applications before handing them in to you.

Doing interviews

Speaking

1 This task tests candidates' ability to speak at length, structure their speech and speak relevantly.

Remind students that they listened to human resources officers giving advice about applying for jobs earlier in the unit. Students should take a minute or two to make notes, but not to write out what they are going to say.

2 ① 06 Play the recording twice. Tell students they need to tick the correct boxes, but also take notes in the 'reason' column.

Answers

	Adam	Harriet	reason(s)
1	✓		The organisation needs someone like you, you made it to the interview.
2	✓		
3	✓		
4	✓	✓	Gives impression that candidate is interested, they've done their homework, you'll be able to portray yourself better.
5		✓	They know what you're like.
6		✓	You get to know people there, and they know you.

3 Give students some time to review their notes from Exercise 1 and add to them if they wish. Tell them to speak for at least one minute (you can time them).

Making contact

Topic:	first impressions and telephoning
Reading:	a telephone quiz; taking notes; references; replacing gapped sentences in a text
Writing:	short emails to apologise, instruct, suggest, agree and explain
Listening:	note completion
Speaking:	discussing body language; telephone role-plays; a short presentation; a collaborative task
Grammar:	comparatives: talking about large and small differences

Getting started

1 **Warming up** With books closed, ask students:

- *Why is it important to make a good first impression on people you meet in business?*
- *How can you do this?* (Students should suggest some of the ideas which are covered in this section.)

With books open, tell students to give reasons for their answers.

2 ① 07 Play the recording twice.

Alternative treatment Tell students to note down any figures which Chandra quotes while they listen. They can check these afterwards by looking at the transcript at the back of the Student's Book.

Answers

1 much more important than 2 a lot less 3 easier 4 a little more
5 not quite as important as

3 If you teach a mixed-nationality class, students will find it interesting to compare differences in body language across cultures.

Also ask them *What distance should you stand from the person you're speaking to?*

If you teach people of the same nationality, ask them what they know about body language in different cultures, from their experience or what they have read.

Ideas which should come up in the discussion are: the need to prepare for phone calls or video-conferencing, tone of voice, use of polite words such as *please* and *thank you*, some friendly small talk, sounding interested and enthusiastic, dressing well for video-conferences, correct English and good layout for written communications such as email.

Grammar workshop

Talking about large and small differences

Elicit from students some occasions when they might have to make comparisons in business (for example, when comparing products, estimates or quotes, financial performance, job candidates, etc.).

Tell them that these structures add precision to the way they make comparisons.

You should go through the explanation in the Grammar workshop on page 25 with students before they do the exercises.

Answers

2 L 3 S 4 S 5 L 6 L 7 L 8 S

Extension idea Ask students to choose three of the structures and to write three sentences using them.

A phone call to a hotel

Listening

1 Remind students that they will perform better in listening exercises if they know what information they need before they listen.

Answers

1 a person's surname, possibly spelled out 2 the name of a company 3 a type of room in a hotel 4 the reason for needing the room 5 a date 6 something else that a person hiring a room might need

Extension idea If necessary, remind students of the names of English letters before they start.

You can do this by spelling some names and asking students to write them down.

They then dictate the names back to you, and you write the names on the board.

2 ① 08 Play the recording twice, then ask students to compare their answers in pairs.

Remind them that unless they spell their answers correctly, they will be marked as wrong.

Answers

1 Kutsov 2 Top Flight 3 meeting 4 job interviews 5 13th May
6 coffee

Extension idea Write these answers on the board and ask students which are wrong and why:

1 Kutcov (*wrong spelling*) **2** Top Fleet (*wrong company name*) **3** small meeting (*'small' is already on the form*) **4** interviews (*not precise enough*) **5** on the 13th of May (*not in note form*) **6** cofee (*wrong spelling*)

Role-play

Alternative treatment 1 With weaker classes, you can ask students to prepare their roles in pairs. In this case, ask students with the Student A role to work together and students with the Student B role to work together, then ask them to:

– underline the details of what they need to talk about

– decide the language (questions, etc.) they need to use. They should do this by looking at the transcript.

When they are ready, ask them to change partners and do the role-play.

Alternative treatment 2 You can make this role-play (and others involving phoning) more authentic by asking students to do it using their mobile phones. In this case, ask Student As to leave the room and call their partners from outside.

Round up by asking students if they had any difficulties and elicit strategies for overcoming difficulties on the phone.

A telephone quiz

Reading

Before students start, elicit why using correct language and register is more important on the phone than face to face. (**Answer:** Because you cannot see the person you are speaking to or gauge their reactions.)

Alternative treatment Ask students to do this activity in groups of three. One student should look at the answer key at the back of the Student's Book and tell the other two students if their answers are correct or not.

Suggested answers

1 B and C are normal if the call has been routed through a switchboard; D would be appropriate if you are a receptionist, for example; A is just unhelpful because the caller doesn't know if he or she has reached the right person or company.
2 B
3 C
4 A and C are both correct, but B is not.
5 A is quite formal, B is informal and C is neither correct nor polite.
6 C is formal, A is informal and B sounds rude.
7 A and B are both correct, although you would only use A with someone you know well.
8 B and C are both correct, depending on what information you are looking for.
9 B

Speaking

BEC Speaking part 2   BULATS Speaking part 2

1 Remind students that, in the exam, they cannot discuss their ideas before doing their 'long turn'.

Tell them the bullet points are there to help them, but that they can use their own ideas if they wish.

Ask them to make a few notes as they discuss, as they will later have to give a short talk on the subject.

2 Before they start, tell students that it is important to structure their talks so that their listeners can follow their points easily. This includes telling people:

– how many points they are going to make

– when they are introducing a new point

– when they are giving an example

– when they are finishing or making their final point.

Go through the Useful language box with students and tell them they should use these phrases when speaking.

Tell them that when they speak, they should get to the point quickly, as they only have a minute. You can time them and, when the minute is up, say 'thank you' to tell them they have finished.

Enquiring about a job

Listening

1 ① 09 *Alternative treatment* Before they listen, ask students in small groups to say what questions they would ask if they were phoning to enquire about a job; for example, *When does the job start?*

Round up with the whole class by asking them to suggest questions. This is an opportunity to check their ability to ask questions correctly. Write the questions on the board.

When they listen, they can also check whether the woman asks the same questions as theirs.

Answers

Speaking, My name's…

BEC Listening part 1   BULATS Listening part 2

2 ① 09 Before students listen again, elicit that they should identify the type of information they need to complete the notes.

Play the recording twice.

Remind them that they need to spell their answers correctly. You can particularly check that they have spelled words with double letters correctly.

Answers

1 office administrator **2** mornings (only) **3** bookkeeping **4** beginning **5** (by) email

Role-play

1 Remind students that the situation is a phone call with someone they do not know: they should try to sound interested, enthusiastic, friendly and polite.

If they wish, they can look at the transcript at the back of the Student's Book to help them prepare.

Alternative treatment With weaker classes, you can follow the same alternative treatment procedures as with the previous role-play (see page 18).

2 For variety, ask students to change partners to do this task.

Phone-answering tips

Reading

1 To get students started, ask: *Have you ever been annoyed by being asked to hold the line for a long time with music playing while you wait to speak to someone? What other things annoy you?*

BEC Reading part 2

2 Tell students that by noting down the main ideas, they are seeing the structure of the passage and where information is located before they deal with the questions.

Suggested answers

paragraph **2**: how you should answer the phone
paragraph **3**: putting callers on hold
paragraph **4**: taking messages correctly
paragraph **5**: call back soon
paragraph **6**: train other staff

3 Tell students that underlining these words/phrases will help them to relate the sentences to the correct parts of the article.

Alternative treatment If you wish, ask students to do this exercise and Exercise 4 together as part of the same process.

Answers

B For example **C** it **D** these callers **E** However ... this **F** Then ... it **G** This

4 Remind students to read before and after the gaps when they answer the questions.

Answers

2 B 3 D 4 F 5 C 6 A

Extension idea If you wish, go over the process for this type of reading task again:

Read the text carefully, noting the main ideas as you read.

Identify cohesive devices in the gapped sentences (and in the text).

Read before and after each gap and place the sentences.

Read the completed text to check your answers.

5 *Alternative treatment* Do this activity as a whole-class discussion.

If your students are working, ask Which advice would it be useful for your company to follow? Why?

Speaking

BEC Speaking part 3   BULATS Speaking part 3

Give students some time to think and prepare before they speak.

Grammar workshop 1

Countable and uncountable nouns

1 U: advice, equipment, feedback, freight, information, knowledge, parking, recruitment, research, software, spending, teamwork, training, transport, travel
C: budget, car, computer, programme, report, team, training course

2 1 an advertisement 2 equipment 3 research; work 4 amount of information 5 advice 6 little travel; many training courses

Present perfect and past simple

1 1 have worked 2 went; have not gone/been 3 was; left; haven't seen; went 4 have changed; started; finished 5 posted; has been; has got; (has) started 6 wrote; haven't received 7 has grown; have taken on; opened

2 1 expected 2 have done 3 has decided 4 have arranged 5 increased 6 has become 7 decided 8 made

Talking about large and small differences

1 *Suggested answers*
  1 far more / six times more / six times as many
  2 nearly as many (letters) as ten years ago / far fewer (letters) than ten years ago
  3 quite as many (meetings) as now
  4 considerably / far / many / a lot more (phone calls) than now / twice as many (phone calls) as now
  5 slightly fewer (text messages now) than ten years ago / not quite as many (text messages now) as ten years ago

Breaking into the market

Unit objectives

Topic: marketing methods and strategies

Reading: a passage with multiple-choice questions;
              matching statements to extracts

Listening: an interview

Speaking: discussing advantages and disadvantages; a
              collaborative task; brainstorming; a short talk

Grammar: infinitive or verb + *-ing*

Vocabulary: *launch*, *ploy*, etc.

Getting started

1 **Warming up** With books closed, ask students to work in small groups. Tell them that in this unit they are going to work on marketing and promotion.

Ask them to brainstorm as many different ways of promoting a company or product as they can think of. Give them two minutes for this.

To get them started, you can suggest sponsoring a football team so the players carry the company's name on their shirts.

With books open, ask students to do the exercise.

Ask: *How is your list different from this one?*

Answers

1 b 2 d 3 f 4 e 5 c 6 g 7 a

2 If your students are already working, ask them if they have experience of any of these types of promotion.

Suggested answers

2 Free samples or gifts may be expensive to produce and distribute and may require extra staff for this. On the other hand, potential customers have a chance to actually experience the product.

3 Leaflets and brochures need to be well designed, which is also expensive. There are also distribution costs. However, they can explain the product/service in detail and make it sound attractive.

4 Point-of-sale displays are expensive because they need to be placed in a large number of shops which will charge for this. However, customers may make the decision to buy on the spot.

5 Sponsorship can be very expensive, but it links the company's image with a successful and attractive person, team or event.

6 Television and radio advertising is also expensive, but reaches a mass audience and may still be the most cost-effective.

7 The website may be the cheapest of the options listed and can also reach a mass audience if people can be encouraged to visit it.

Extension idea Ask students in pairs to choose one of the promotional activities and prepare a short talk on:

– what type of company/products it is suitable for

– its advantages and disadvantages.

When they are ready, they should work in small groups and take turns to give their talks.

Promoting AXE

Reading

1 Tell students they do not need to confine themselves to the promotional activities listed in this section.

BEC	Reading part 3
BULATS	Reading part 1 section 3
BULATS	Reading part 2 section 5

2 At this level, the questions in the exam test opinion and inference rather than factual information.

Tell students that they should skim the text first to get a general idea of its contents before tackling the questions. Skimming is running your eyes quickly over the text without trying to understand every word or detail.

Give students a maximum of two minutes for this activity and be strict about the time limit.

When they have finished, ask them to compare answers in pairs with their books closed.

Answers

Promotional activities: a slogan, online game, free samples, point-of-sale displays, media advertising, PR, a house party, direct mailing, online publicity, leaflets, advertisements in magazines, website, television show, free CD

3 Tell students they should:

– read each question

– find where it is answered in the text

– read the text carefully to understand what it says

– read the options to choose the correct one.

Tell students that they will find the answers in the text in the same order as the questions, so they will only need to read the text carefully once.

When they have finished, they should compare answers in pairs; if there is disagreement, they should quote from the text to support their answers.

Alternative treatment Ask students to underline the main ideas in the questions before they read the text for the answers. (**Suggested underlining: 1** target audience **2** get an invitation **3** aim of the publicity **4** aim of the promotional campaign **5** unique **6** effect)

Answers

1 B (*… young men's natural interest in pretty girls … appeal to American male youth culture.*)
2 D (*… young men to log on to the Internet to play a video game on the AXE website … If the player reached a certain level, he entered a lottery to win a trip to the party.*)
3 C (*AXE focused on the intrigue and discovery of the party.*)
4 A (*'It was all about getting into the mind of the 20-something guy,' …*)
5 B (*'To our knowledge, nobody has ever taken a consumer promotion and turned it into a television show,' …*)
6 C (*… a 22% increase in general brand awareness among males aged 11 to 24 …*)

Vocabulary

Tell students to quickly locate the words and phrases in the text before choosing the definition.

Answers

2 d **3** c **4** e **5** b **6** a

Extension idea For homework, ask students to look up the words in their dictionaries and note the word and an example from their dictionary in their notebook.

Grammar workshop

Infinitive or verb + *-ing*

Tell students that this is an area of grammar where candidates make a lot of errors.

After they have done the first four questions, ask them to check their answers by looking back at the text.

Answers

1 to make **2** to bring **3** playing **4** doing **5** to dance **6** using
7 not to let **8** Building **9** to launch

Extension idea Tell students that the main area of difficulty is verbs followed by infinitive and verbs followed by verb + *-ing*. Suggest they keep a page of their notebooks for these, note down the ones in the Grammar workshop section, add to them when they find others, and learn them.

Role-play

Tell students that brainstorming a range of ideas or solutions to problems is a useful activity in business and can often lead to the best idea or solution.

Tell students to follow the instructions step by step. They should think particularly about how to make contact with their target customers.

Extension idea When all groups have finished, you can round up with the whole class as follows:

– Ask each group to present their plan.
– Discuss the pros and cons of each plan after it has been presented.
– Discuss a unified plan using the best ideas from all the groups.

Supermarkets' own brands

Listening

1 **Suggested answer**

Supermarkets can package, price and market the brand to suit their particular customers, their own marketing plan and make use of the supermarket's brand image. Own brands can be sold more cheaply because less advertising is required and production can be more easily adjusted to match demand.

Extension idea Ask students to give examples of own brands in their countries.

Ask: *Do you buy own brands? Why? / Why not?*

BEC Listening part 3   BULATS Listening part 4

2 ① 10 Before students listen, ask them to underline the key ideas in each question, but not in the options. Tell them this will help them to focus on the question when they listen. (**Suggested underlining: 1** originally introduce / own brand **2** reason for / own brands **3** can sell / more cheaply / because)

Answers

1 C **2** A **3** B

Extension idea Ask students: *In your country, do you think own brands are better quality than other brands? Why? / Why not?*

Going viral in India and China

Reading

1 Students may have to speak from what they have read or heard rather than direct experience. Points arising may be:
- Consumers in these countries will not pay the same prices as in Levi's traditional markets
- There may be a higher proportion of young people, a new, young, upwardly mobile middle class eager for fashion goods.

BEC Reading part 1   **BULATS** Reading part 2

2 Remind students that they should pay careful attention to the statements and underline the key idea(s) in each before reading the paragraphs. They should then read each paragraph carefully once and choose the statement(s) it refers to.

Alternative treatment 1 Ask students to think of paraphrases for the key ideas in the statements – they will know that the ideas will be expressed in the paragraphs using different words. (**Suggested answers:** 2 negative comments – *criticism* 3 new location for bringing a new product to market – *different place for launching a product* 4 worn at work – *worn in the office* 5 keep customers loyal – *keep clients faithful* 6 change their behaviour – *develop new habits* 7 express their emotions – *show their feelings* 8 competitor's example – *what a rival did*)

Alternative treatment 2 Elicit from students why the example (paragraph D) refers to statement 1 (**Answer:** India, being among the three largest markets for Levi's in Asia, is also a market where denim is the fastest-growing clothing category, producing 35 to 40 million pairs a year.)

Alternative treatment 3 If you want to replicate exam conditions, give students 12 minutes to do this exercise (the time they would have for it in the live exam).

Answers

2 A (... *the video stacked up to 700,000 views on YouTube, even though it was criticised widely in the media.*)
3 C (*The launch of Denizen in China last month was the first time that Levi's has moved outside the United States for the global launch of a brand.*)
4 D (*With work environments becoming more casual, for the younger generation, denim is the clothing of choice.*)
5 C (... *is now keen on expanding the price ladder lower to prevent consumers from crossing over to competitors.*)
6 A (... *campaign to encourage consumers to take risks and move beyond the smart and sensible life* ...)
7 B (*They blog about the brand and how the brand makes them feel.*)
8 A (*Most, if not all, have gone digital, and Levi's now seems to be doing the same.*)

Speaking

Give students two or three minutes to prepare their ideas before they give their talks.

Launching a product

Unit objectives

Topic:	launching products and promotional budgets
Reading:	referencing; replacing gapped sentences in a text; editing a report
Writing:	a marketing report; analysing the task; planning
Listening:	an interview with someone who developed a product
Speaking:	a short talk; role-play planning a marketing campaign
Grammar:	prepositions in phrases describing trends
Vocabulary:	*distribution, commuting,* etc.; promotional methods

Getting started

Warming up With books closed, ask students to brainstorm products that did not exist before, but have appeared in the last ten years. Write these on the board.

With books open, students can use some of the ideas on the board to discuss.

Extension idea Ask: *What risks do companies run when they decide to develop and launch new products?* (**Suggested answers:** Customers don't buy the product, it doesn't meet a market need, it is obsolete before coming to market, competitors produce a similar product at a lower price or better quality, the product doesn't meet safety standards.)

Developing and launching Drink Me Chai

Listening

1 Before students do the exercise, go through the Useful language box with them.

BEC Listening part 3   BULATS Listening part 4

2 ①11 Before students listen again, they should read the questions and underline the key ideas. (**Suggested underlining: 1** *chai* originally **2** start importing **3** decide to develop **4** test / product **5** supermarket buyer's reaction)

Alternative treatment You may already have played the recording twice for students to do Exercise 2. If this is the case, ask them to answer the questions from what they have already understood.

Play the recording one more time for them to check their answers.

Answers

1 A 2 A 3 B 4 B 5 C

3 | **Answers**

She did market research to identify competing products; she tried importing it; she developed the product and tested it with customers at her station bar; she approached supermarkets with samples; she met a supermarket buyer and made a pitch; she branded and packaged the product for the supermarket.

Reading

BEC Reading part 2

1 The technique is as outlined for the second reading passage in Unit 4 on page 19 of this book.

Give students two minutes to skim the article. They can then discuss their answers in pairs without looking back at the article.

Alternative treatment With weaker classes, you can do the vocabulary exercise which follows this section now so as to pre-teach some words/phrases.

Answers

1 When her customers said they would like to drink the product at home
2 At that stage, the product had no packaging or branding.

2 *Alternative treatment* If you wish, you can refer students to the Exam skills section on page 137 (Business Vantage edition only) to read what it says about 'cohesive features'.

Answers

B *However* and *the journey*: *The journey* may refer to the journey to London.
C *it*: *It* may refer to *chai*.
D *But the major problem*: There may have been other problems mentioned earlier.
E *It*: Something which happened
F *Since then*: Refers to an earlier time mentioned in the text.
G *As a result*: This is the result of something mentioned in the text.

3 If you want students to have exam practice, you can ask them to do this task in ten minutes (they have already spent two minutes skimming the passage and would have 12 minutes in total in the live exam).

Answers

2 B 3 C 4 A 5 F 6 E

Extension idea 1 Ask students in pairs or small groups: *From the listening and reading you have done, what impression do you have of Amanda Hamilton? What has made her a successful businesswoman?*

Extension idea 2 Ask students to visit the Drink Me Chai website at http://www.drinkmechai.co.uk/index.php to see the range of promotional activities Amanda is involved in.

Launching and promoting a new product

Listening

1 Students should bring together ideas from work they have already done in this unit. Tell them that they will later have to give a short talk on the subject.

2 ①12 Play the recording twice.

Answer
Amanda mentions doing market research and testing the product on the market.

3 Before students speak, remind them that they should introduce and structure their points, giving examples and reasons where necessary.

You can refer them to the Useful language box in Unit 4 on page 22.

4 Students should remember promotional methods from Unit 5 *Getting started*.

5 ①13 Play the recording twice and ask students to take notes.

Suggested answers

method	reason
write-ups in magazines/ newspapers	raises awareness and increases sales
sampling at shows/fairs/ festivals	people can try unique taste; she doesn't have a big budget, cannot advertise
website	like a shop window; connects with customers and receives orders

A marketing report

Writing

1 Elicit:
- which prepositions are used when describing figures (**answers:** *by* – to say how much something has changed; *from* – to say the starting figure; *to* – to say the end figure)
- why the present perfect is used (**answer:** to give information which combines past and present time).

When students have finished the exercise, go through the explanation in the Grammar workshop on page 42 with them and ask them to do the exercises which follow.

Answers
2 by; from; to 3 ... spending on stands at trade fairs by A$75,000 from A$100,000 to A$25,000. 4 ... has risen by A$200,000 from A$450,000 to A$650,000.

Extension ideas Elicit the difference between *rise* and *raise*. (**Answer:** *Rise* is intransitive and so not followed by an object; *raise* is transitive, so must be followed by an object.)

Ask students to suggest synonyms for *rise*, *raise* and *reduce*. (**Suggested answers:** *rise* – go up, increase; *raise* – increase (note: *increase* is both transitive and intransitive), put up; *reduce* – lower, decrease)

You can also point out that *fall*, *drop* and *go down* are intransitive, i.e. opposites of *rise*, not *raise*.

2 Point out to students that when they do this sort of task, there will be some information given to them, but they will have to invent some of the ideas which need to be expressed to complete the task.

When they have finished, they can compare their ideas with another pair of students.

3 Tell students to relate the content of the report to the handwritten notes on the charts.

Ask *Has the writer dealt with all the handwritten notes?* (**Answer:** yes)

Remind students preparing for an exam that they would lose marks if they did not deal with all the notes.

BEC Reading part 5

4 Remind students to read the report sentence by sentence to find the extra words.

Answers
2 the 3 *correct* 4 due 5 only 6 too 7 *correct* 8 down 9 being 10 *correct* 11 up 12 off 13 *correct*

5 Round up ideas with the whole class.

Ask them to look back to the sample report in Exercise 3 to see what language is used there which could also be used in this report.

Tell students they will find further models and advice in the Writing reference on pages 120–121.

Suggested answers

1 Spending on point-of-sale displays has fallen from £30,000 to £15,000; spending on magazine advertisements has risen from £12,000 to £46,000; spending on leaflets has been raised from £6,000 to £35,000.
2 Point-of-sale displays were not particularly effective because there was strong competition for customers' attention from other brands, but we managed to sell large numbers of chocolates through our magazine advertising because we advertised in slimming magazines. It is clear that our leaflets are reaching our target customers, who are generally people who are concerned about their health and like to keep fit.
3 The total budget rose from £48,000 last year to £98,000 this year. However, it will be reduced to £65,000 next year.
4 We should continue to spend the same amount on leaflets. However, we should stop promoting with point-of-sale displays, reduce our magazine advertising and consider using viral advertising on YouTube.

Extension idea Tell students that reports have titles and often have sections with section headings (as in the sample in Exercise 3). Ask students to decide what title and section headings they should use for this report.

Tell them that by deciding on the sections, they are deciding how to structure their report and making sure they include all the essential information.

BEC Writing part 2

6 This exercise can be done for homework. If your students are preparing for the Business Vantage exam, tell them they should write their answer in 120 to 140 words.

Sample answer

Introduction
The object of this report is to summarise how we have spent our promotional budget on Slimchocs over the last two years, its effectiveness and to make recommendations for next year's budget.

Our promotional activities
We reduced our outlay on point-of-sale displays from £30,000 to £15,000, as these failed to attract customers' attention due to strong competition from other brands. However, we raised our budget for advertising in slimming magazines by £34,000, as this proved an effective way of reaching target customers. We also increased our budget for leaflets by £29,000 because with these, we also managed to reach our target customers, who are primarily people interested in staying healthy and keeping fit.

Recommendations
Our promotional budget will be reduced next year to £65,000. As a result, I recommend that we should continue to spend the same amount on leaflets. However, it would be a good idea to stop promoting with point-of-sale displays, reduce our magazine advertising and consider using viral advertising on YouTube.

Extension idea Give your students a deadline for bringing their answers to class. When they do so, ask them to work in pairs and compare their answers. They should read each other's reports to
– check that all essential points and especially the handwritten notes have been covered
– decide how convincing the explanations and recommendations are.

They should discuss these points with their partners and give feedback.

Students can also compare their answers with the sample answer at the back of the Student's Book.

Give them some time to make changes to their answers before they hand them in to you.

For information about how Business Vantage exam answers are marked, look at the Cambridge English Business Certificates Handbook for Teachers, downloadable at https://www.teachers.cambridgeesol.org/ts/digitalAssets/117698_Cambridge_English_Business_BEC_Handbook.pdf.

An interior design company

Role-play

1 *Alternative treatment* Ask students to work in pairs. Give each pair a role and ask them to read the situation and prepare the role together.

   They should then separate to do the role-play in groups of four.

2 *Alternative treatment* Tell students that in the meeting, each of them will have a minute to present their point of view. Tell them to prepare a short presentation where they present their position, supported by reasons.

3 You can ask the Managing Directors to chair the meetings and make sure that everyone has a chance to present and argue their positions.

4 *Extension idea 1* Discuss with the whole class which group had the best solution.

   Extension idea 2 Ask students to write a brief report:
   – explaining the situation
   – outlining the options
   – making recommendations.

A stand at a trade fair

Unit objectives

Topic:	organising and choosing a stand at a trade fair
Reading:	open clozes; matching statements with extracts; a multiple-choice cloze
Writing:	short memos; emails; planning emails
Listening:	short extracts
Speaking:	deciding which stand
Grammar:	formal requests
Vocabulary:	*find out, know, learn* and *teach*

Getting started

Warming up Ask students in small groups:

– *Which part of your job do you / would you enjoy most: working with colleagues in the same company, or working with customers and suppliers outside your company? Why?*

– *How might your behaviour be different when dealing with colleagues and when dealing with customers and suppliers?*

Whether your students are already working or pre-service, the answers may well depend on the culture they come from. If you teach a mixed-nationality class, this may be an interesting area to explore.

Answers

1 These are trade fairs, where companies hire space and set up stands. Company representatives and salespeople are talking to potential customers who visit their stands. People visit trade fairs to identify possible products and potential suppliers.
2 *Suggested answers*
Potential customers can see and handle the products on display. They can talk to sales staff.
Companies can invite potential customers to visit them at their stand.
A good stand can give a company prestige.
It gives the company an opportunity to promote its products to its competitor's customers.

Extension idea Ask students: *Have you ever visited or worked at a trade fair? What was it like?*

Get them to tell their partners about the experience.

The London Contemporary Design Show

Reading

1 Before they start, you can give your students some background information: The London Contemporary Design Show is an annual interior design show held in London with more than 400 exhibitors. You can visit their website at http://www.100percentdesign.co.uk.

Students can answer the questions in the book in pairs.

Answers

1 A memo is an internal note circulated to people in an office (nowadays usually by email) containing information or instructions, possibly about a new policy or activity.
2 Directly, with the subject of the memo. If you wish, you can finish it with *Many thanks* (or something similar) and your initials or your signature.
3 Start with the name of the addressee and finish with *Thanks, Best wishes* or nothing and the name of the writer.
4 Contact the organisers of a trade fair to find out information about setting up a stand.

2 | **Answers**

2 at **3** in **4** for **5** for **6** for **7** in/with **8** with **9** out

Extension idea Ask students to identify and note in their notebooks prepositions from the memo and email which are:

– part of a phrasal verb (*ask for, carry out, find out*)

– dependent prepositions (*conversations with, preparing for, help with, get in touch with*)

Tell students that they have to learn prepositions with the words they depend on, so it is worth making a list in their notebooks to study.

BEC Writing part 1   **BULATS** Writing part 1
3 Tell students to make sure they cover all parts of the instructions.

When they have finished, they should count their words. If they are outside the limits, ask them to rewrite their email within the limits. (You can tell your students that, in the exam, if they have written less than the limit, it is likely that they have not completed the task, i.e. covered all the points in the instructions. If they have written more, their answers may contain things which are irrelevant. They will not lose marks on the basis of word count, but they will lose marks if they have not completely answered the question or if they have included things which are irrelevant. If necessary, remind them that the Business Vantage word range is 40–50 words, and BULATS is 50–60 words.)

Extension idea 1 If one of your students has written an answer which is too long, with the student's permission, copy it, or project it on the board and ask the class to suggest ways of shortening it to within the limits. This may involve

- finding ways of combining points in one sentence
- identifying and eliminating irrelevance
- generally expressing points with fewer words.

Extension idea 2 Ask students to compare their answers with the sample answer shown below. How is the sample different?

Sample answer

Dear Sir/Madam

We are a Swiss furniture design company. We are interested in exhibiting at the London Contemporary Design Show this year. Can you please tell us

- how much it would cost to exhibit at the show?
- when we would need to make a booking?

Many thanks.

Grammar workshop

Formal requests

1 | **Answers**

2 e 3 a 4 c 5 d

Extension idea Tell students that there is a special event at their school with someone who is going to speak about Business English. Ask them to use the beginnings of the sentences (1–5 in Exercise 1) to write questions to the head of the school to find out about the event, e.g. *Can you please tell us how much it will cost to attend the event?*

2 Ask students to add the answers to question 4 to their list of words with dependent prepositions.

When students have answered the questions, go through the explanation in the Grammar workshop on page 43 with them.

Students should then do the exercises in the workshop either in class or for homework.

Answers

1 1b (It has the form of a question, starting with *Can*.)
2 2, 3, 4 and 5
3 we
4 details of, information about

Vocabulary

1 Tell students that these are frequent errors and that they should pay special attention when using these words/phrases in their speaking or writing.

Answers

1 d 2 a 3 c 4 b

Extension idea Ask students to write one extra example of their own for each definition.

2 | **Answers**

1 learn 2 find out 3 teach 4 found out 5 know; teach 6 learn 7 know 8 find out

Listening

BEC Listening part 1   BULATS Listening part 2

1 | **Suggested answers**

1 something with an area 2 something which costs £115 3 a date 4 something which can be sent by email 5 something which might happen to the space

2 ①14 Play the recording twice. When students have finished, ask them to compare their answers in pairs and particularly to check spelling.

Answers

1 Floor space 2 Insurance 3 13th June 4 bank details 5 guaranteed

3 *Alternative treatment* Ask students to work in pairs and plan how they are going to:

– start the email
– organise the information
– end the email.

You can refer them to the Writing reference on pages 117 and 119 for ideas on beginning and ending emails.

Sample answer

Subject: London Contemporary Design Show

Hello Ulrike,
The organisers have given me the following information:

- Floor space costs between £295 and £340 per square metre plus VAT. We also have to pay £115 insurance and a £300 registration fee. The balance must be paid by 22nd August.
- The deadline for reservations is 13th June.

Best wishes
Marcel

Extension idea Students can compare their answers with the sample answer at the back of the Student's Book.

Preparing an exhibition stand

Writing 1

1 Students should suggest that Marcel needs to say what his company does, why they need a stand and when for.

You can ask them to imagine receiving an email without this information. Would they know how to reply?

Ask them to discuss how they can express this information.

2 Before they write, ask students to look back at the Grammar workshop on Formal requests (page 43).

Tell them to try to use one or two of the patterns they studied in their answer.

When they have finished, ask them to compare their answers with the sample answer at the back of the Student's Book.

Sample answer

Dear Sirs

We are a Swiss furniture company. We are planning to have a stand at the London Contemporary Design Show next September. We would be grateful if you could send us some sample designs and an estimate of costs. Can you also tell us roughly how long it will take to build?

Many thanks
Marcel Schaub

Reading

BEC Reading part 1   BULATS Reading part 2

1 **Suggested underlining**

2 international experience 3 on time 4 promotional activity
5 can afford 6 needn't buy 7 as many people / as possible

2 Remind students to underline words in the publicity which give them the answers: this confirms that there is evidence in the extracts for their choices.

Answers

1 A (*Our prices are keen and competitive due to our huge stocks of ready-made equipment.*)
2 B (*We have delivered customised exhibition solutions worldwide and designed stands for almost every market you can name.*)
3 B (*Our project-management skills ensure deadlines are met ...*)
4 C (*We can provide a complete marketing solution for your project, including pre-event promotions, stand design and show activity.*)
5 B (*... a solution that meets your brief and matches your budget.*)
6 A (*... by supplying custom-built exhibition stands – for hire or for sale.*)
7 C (*... we'll also work with you to maximise your visitor numbers.*)

Extension idea 1 Ask students to underline unfamiliar vocabulary in the extracts.

They should then work in pairs and try to guess the meanings from the context.

When they have finished, ask them to look at the Word list on page 127 to check their ideas.

Extension idea 2 Ask students: *Which stand supplier sounds the most attractive to you? Why?*

BEC Reading part 4   BULATS Reading part 2 section 2

3 Remind students to:

– read the whole email quickly to get a general idea of its contents before completing the gaps

– read before and after each gap and the whole sentence before making a choice.

Answers

1 D 2 B 3 A 4 A 5 B 6 C 7 C 8 D 9 B 10 A 11 A 12 D 13 B
14 B 15 D

Writing 2

1 Before students discuss, remind them that they should choose a design from a business point of view. You can elicit the following criteria: Which

– gives the best image of the company?

– looks the most inviting?

– is the most practical?

2 Students will have to write a slightly longer email in this case with no word limits.

– Tell them to write a plan for it: what information should they put in each paragraph?

– Before they write, go through the Useful language box with them.

Sample answer

Dear Mr Steel

Thank you for your designs. In answer to your questions:
1 We have booked 40 m² of floor space.
2 Our stand is on a corner, and we would prefer it to be open.
3 We would like to be able to accommodate up to 15 people at any one time.
From the designs you sent us, the one we like the most is number 3.
We look forward to receiving your design and quotation.

Best wishes
Marcel Schaub

Extension idea Ask students to compare their answers with a partner's and with the sample answer at the back of the Student's Book. They can then make any changes before handing their answers in to you.

3 Ask students to write this answer in 40–50 words if they are preparing for the Business Vantage exam and 50–60 words if they are preparing for the BULATS test.

Sample answer

To: Sales staff
From: Ulrike Schütz
Subject: Stand at London Contemporary Design Show

I'm pleased to inform you that the stand is being designed at the moment. Could you please let me know what equipment you will need for the stand? Also, I suggest you start preparing the graphics you want to put on the stand.

Many thanks
Ulrike

Being persuasive

Topic:	what makes business people persuasive; negotiating
Reading:	paraphrasing key ideas; matching statements and extracts
Writing:	an email replying to an email summarising an agreement; an email summarising an agreement
Listening:	short extracts on persuasiveness; meeting clients at a trade fair; negotiating an agreement
Speaking:	talking about what makes business people persuasive; role-play: breaking the ice/building a relationship; role-play: negotiating a sale; short talk on what is important when negotiating; negotiating a deal
Grammar:	first and second conditionals; prepositions
Vocabulary:	*sell*, *sales*, *selling*; *proxy*, *vendor*, etc.

Getting started

1 *Extension idea* Ask students: *Are there any other factors you would add to the list? Why?*

2 ①15 Play the recording twice.

Alternative treatment Before listening, ask students to paraphrase each idea. (**Suggested answers:** *be truthful* – don't tell lies; *be persistent* – keep trying, don't give up; *make sure your customers like you* – build a friendly relationship with your customers; *pay attention to what your customers are saying* – listen to clients; *prepare your strategy carefully* – take care with your planning; *know your customers' requirements* – find out what your clients need; *treat customers with respect* – be polite to customers; *have confidence in your product* – believe in what you are selling)

Answers

	K	A	R	D
1				✓
2	✓			
3				✓
4			✓	
5		✓		
6		✓	✓	
7	✓			
8		✓		

3 Tell students that they should think of a work or study context.

Breaking the ice

Speaking

1 Tell students that for many business people, the hardest part of doing business is breaking the ice and making small talk in English to build a relationship. Pre-service students especially may not have considered this aspect of business English and its importance for success.

Breaking the ice is often just a question of offering a series of positive or interested comments and questions which allow the other person to respond equally positively and give openings to more meaningful engagement.

Tell students that the ideas in this exercise are typical things that British or Americans might say to break the ice.

Alternative treatment Ask students:

– *What sort of things do people say and do in your culture to break the ice?*

– *How important are personal relationships when doing business in your culture?*

– *Are there any customs which are usually followed, such as exchanging business cards? How is this / are these usually done?*

– *What things does a business person coming to your country for the first time need to know?*

– *Are there any bad mistakes of behaviour that they can make?*

2 ①16 Play the recording twice. Ask students to note down the phrases the speakers use.

Answers

2 Did you have a good trip?
3 Lovely city, isn't it?
4 Where are you staying?
5 Now, can we show you a few of our products?
6 Busy, isn't it?
7 Would either of you like a cup of coffee or a cup of tea before we get started?

Extension idea 1 Play the recording again, but stop it at each of the answers above. Ask students to imitate the stress and intonation (of someone speaking positively and interestedly).

Extension idea 2 Ask students to work in pairs and think how they would respond to each of these phrases.

They can then listen again and note the speakers' responses.

3 Remind students that expressing positive feelings is part of being persuasive – people are encouraged to respond positively.

Answers

Nice to meet you; That's great; Very smart; thanks for inviting us; we like people to see our stand; Very good; the airport's so convenient; Lovely city, isn't it; Yes, lovely; it's the best hotel in town; Oh, good; Busy, isn't it; Incredibly; This fair is getting more popular every year.

Extension idea Ask students to work in small groups and suggest other positive things they can say when breaking the ice.

Role-play 1

Students should prepare their roles in pairs. If they wish, they can look at the transcript at the back of the Student's Book.

Encourage students to do the exercise without notes and standing up – as if the visitors are just arriving at reception.

Alternative treatment Ask groups to perform the role-play in turns in front of the whole class. The students watching can say afterwards how successful they think each group was in breaking the ice and starting a positive relationship.

Role-play 2

1 *Alternative treatment* With weaker classes, ask students to prepare their roles in pairs before changing partners to do the role-play.

2 *Extension idea* Ask students to discuss how successfully they played each role: what they did well and what they could have done better.

When they have finished, round up ideas from the whole class.

The art of agreeing

Reading

`BEC` Reading part 1   `BULATS` Reading part 2 section 1

1 Before they start, ask students:

– *What things do you have to negotiate?*

– *How do you achieve success in your negotiations?*

Pre-service students may talk about negotiations with fellow students or with teachers, or negotiations with their family and friends – the negotiations may have a very informal framework.

Alternative treatment Ask students to glance at the whole reading section and remind themselves in pairs how to approach this type of reading task (as outlined in the note for Reading Exercise 2 on page 22 of this book).

Suggested answers

2 gain confidence / exchanging information (*They can build trust by telling each other things.*)
3 in control of their feelings (*They should never get angry or upset.*)
4 acquire / information / in advance (*They should find out as much as possible before they start.*)
5 work out ways / other party / flexible (*They should try to think of ways for the other side to change their position.*)
6 not always financial gain (*Their aim is not always to make money.*)
7 non-verbal behaviour / influence (*Their body language will affect the outcome.*)
8 opening proposal / advantage (*The person who starts the negotiation will be in a better position.*)

2 Where possible, ask students to support their ideas with examples from their experience or things they have heard about.

3 If you wish to replicate exam conditions, give students ten minutes to answer the questions (assuming they have 12 minutes for this in the exam, including reading the statements).

Answers

1 C (*You can negotiate well only if you have the ability to walk away from an unfavourable agreement ...*)
2 B (*While you are continuing to receive factual data, with both parties following the give-and-take principle, you are building trust gradually.*)
3 D (*Also remember never to lose your cool or emotions.*)
4 A (*The better prepared you are with factual data before heading into a negotiation, the more effective you will be.*)
5 C (*You should also factor in the fall-back options for the other side.*)
6 A (*... identify the real needs and goals. Though the most obviously stated need is money, it can be a proxy for other physical or more refined needs (shelter, reputation, self-esteem).*)
7 B (*... your body language will have an impact on people and on the outcome of your negotiation.*)
8 D (*Try and be the first to make an offer. It will help anchor the client to your view, and the final agreement is more likely to end closer to your proposal.*)

Vocabulary

Ask students to copy the words and phrases into their notebooks.

Answers

1 proxy **2** vendor **3** impact **4** outcome **5** factor in
6 fall-back/back-up (options) **7** lose your cool

Extension idea For homework, students can look up the words and phrases in their dictionary and copy an example for each into their notebook.

Speaking

BEC Speaking part 2

Give students a minute or so to prepare their notes. Tell them they can use their own ideas and ideas from the Reading text.

Ask students to each talk for a minute.

Alternative treatment Elicit and write this checklist on the board:

Did he/she:

- introduce the talk?

- introduce each point clearly?

- give reasons and examples to support each point?

- keep speaking for a minute?

- look at you more than at their notes?

- round off at the end of the talk with a concluding sentence?

Ask students to complete the checklist while their partner is speaking and to give him/her feedback afterwards.

Round up feedback of interest with the whole class. If they wish, ask them to change partners and do the activity again.

Listening

1 Elicit that the point of grammar here is conditional sentences.

If necessary, elicit basic rules for verb tenses in first and second conditionals.

Answers

Names of actual speakers are given.
1 could (Jack) **2** took (Helga) **3** 'll accept (could be either, but in fact it's Jack) **4** wouldn't make (Susie) **5** buy (Helga) **6** gave (Jack)

2 ①17 When students have finished, go through the explanation in the Grammar workshop on page 43 with them. Then ask them to do the workshop exercises.

Writing

1 *Alternative treatment* Before they complete the email, ask students to listen to the conversation again and check that all the details in the email are correct apart from the 3,000 units (**answer:** the other details are correct).

Answers

2 for **3** with **4** on **5** at **6** for **7** In **8** on **9** with **10** for **11** in **12** in

Extension idea Tell students to copy words and phrases + preposition into the section on prepositions which they have in their notebooks e.g. *do business with, supply with*, etc.

2 Students should also copy these into their notebooks as something to study and learn e.g. *in addition to this*.

3 Go through the Useful language box with students. Students can do this writing task for homework.

When they have finished, they can compare their answers with the sample answer at the back of the Student's Book and make any changes they wish before handing it in to you.

Alternative treatment Ask students to prepare this email in pairs by deciding

- what to say to cover the handwritten notes

- how many paragraphs they need and what they should contain.

Sample answer

Dear Helga

Thanks for this – the pleasure was all mine.
There are just a few details we need to clear up. First, the quantity we were talking about was 2,000 units, not 3,000 on the terms agreed. I hope this isn't a problem for you. Also, after discussions with my colleagues, would it be possible for us to return any units we haven't sold after six months instead of 12 months? We think this would be beneficial for both of us, as things tend to go out of fashion so quickly these days.
Finally, we would be happy to pay in cash on condition that you deliver the goods at your expense.
I hope you can agree to all these points and that we can proceed with the order.

Kind regards
Jack

Speaking and writing

1 Make enough copies of the role cards on page 32 to give one to each student. Cut them out and distribute them, ensuring students are working in Buyer/Seller pairs. Tell students to note down details of the agreement they have reached.

Alternative treatment With weaker classes, let students prepare the role-play in pairs, then do the negotiations as groups of four.

2 Students can do this task for homework.

Extension idea When students have done their homework, they can work with the partner they did the role-play with and compare their letters to answer these questions:

- *Do the letters contain the same terms of the deal?*

- *Which letter is more effective? Why?*

Grammar workshop 2

Infinitives and verb + -ing

1 1 training 2 dealing 3 to get 4 Advertising; to invest
   5 developing; to be 6 leaving; to start 7 (to) develop; lending
   8 Studying; to be
2 1 choosing 2 to hear 3 closing 4 checking 5 to look
   6 hearing

Prepositions in phrases describing trends

1 1 at 2 by; to 3 from; to 4 by
2 *Suggested answers*
   Three years ago, the number of exhibitors stood at 450.
   Two years ago, the number fell by 80 to 370.
   Last year, the number of exhibitors rose from 370 to 515.
   This year, the number has fallen by 125.
3 1 to 2 at 3 by 4 at 5 from; to 6 by

Formal requests

1 2 ~~give~~ could/would give 3 ~~you let~~ you could/would let
   4 ~~can~~ could/would 5 ~~are~~ would be

First and second conditionals

1 1 are 2 decide 3 require 4 advertised 5 contained 6 book
   7 were
2 *Suggested answers*
   1 … our accountant approves.
   2 … the project was more interesting.
   3 … I'd spend far less time travelling.
   4 … you pay the full price in advance.
   5 … there are no interruptions.
   6 … it's really urgent.
   7 … it was a promotion.
   8 I'll be happy to do business with him …

Photocopiable role cards for Unit 8, Speaking and writing, Exercise 1 (SB page 41)

BATTERY PEELER

Buyers

You are really keen to have this product, because you know that at €9.95 recommended retail price, this will sell like hot cakes. The sooner you get it the better, because you suspect that one of your competitors is going to launch a similar product onto the market in a few months' time. However, you would prefer to pay in 90 days when you'll have more cash available.

Quantity: 5,000
Price: €5.00
Discount: 7.5%
Payment terms: 90 days
Delivery date: immediately

BATTERY PEELER

Sellers

You are having real difficulties keeping up with demand for this product and can really only supply 2,000 in the next three weeks. You are unwilling to make any concessions at all.

Quantity: 2,000
Price: €6.00
Discount: 0%
Payment terms: at sight
Delivery date: 3 weeks

Starting a business

Unit objectives

Topic:	starting your own business; buying into a franchise
Reading:	multiple-choice questions; editing a letter
Writing:	a letter of enquiry
Listening:	short extracts – reasons for starting a business
Speaking:	role-play: giving advice
Grammar:	prepositions in time phrases
Vocabulary:	*concept, gross revenue*, etc.; phrases for giving advice; financial terms (*profit, turnover*, etc.); phrases requesting information

Getting started

Warming up With books closed, ask your students:

– *Can you name any successful entrepreneurs from your country?* (Write *entrepreneur* on the board and explain that an entrepreneur is someone who starts new businesses.)

– *What businesses have they started, and why do you think they have been successful?*

Alternative treatment If you think students might look further down the page, ask them to continue with books closed.

Extension idea Ask: *What business would you start? Why?*

Why start your own business?

Listening

1 *Extension idea* Ask students to paraphrase each of the reasons in their own words. (**Suggested answers: a** to improve the way people see you / to rise to a higher social class; **b** to give yourself a job, for example if you are unemployed; **c** to do what you have always wanted to do; **d** to make your own decisions; **e** to make money / become wealthy **f** to launch a new product/service because you have seen a business opportunity which no one is taking advantage of **g** to escape boredom)

BEC Listening part 2   **BULATS** Listening part 3

2 ①18 Play the recording twice.

Answers

1 f 2 b 3 g

Extension idea Ask students: *What were the key words from the recording which gave you the answers?* If necessary, play the recording again. (**Answers: 1** there was nowhere you could buy handmade home-made pasta. So, I thought, here's my opportunity – no competition and a really good product **2** I was made redundant ... Perhaps I'd better take charge of my own future **3** I wanted to be doing something with a bit more excitement)

You can point out that, for example in 2, students will have to connect two things said at different moments to get the answer.

3 Before students start, elicit what a franchise is. If necessary, play the section of the recording featuring Naiara again.

Elicit names of well-known franchises.

Suggested answers

2 Advantages: franchisers supply you with an established business model and brand; they do market research for you prior to opening and perhaps provide finance for the start-up; they will take care of advertising and marketing; they may supply you with the products you sell; they will give advice and help in making the business a success.

Disadvantages: you are not completely free to implement your business ideas (you have to keep to the rules/guidelines established by the franchiser); it can be expensive to buy into a franchise; you have to share part of your profits with the franchiser.

Grammar workshop

Prepositions in time phrases

Elicit when business people might have to use time phrases (e.g. to say when a meeting will be, to fix a deadline or to organise schedules, etc.).

When students have finished the exercise, go through the explanation in the Grammar workshop on page 60 with them and ask them to do the exercises which follow.

Answers

1 in 2 on 3 for; until 4 at 5 for; by

An international franchise

Reading

1 The second and third questions are partly answered in the Reading text which follows.

BEC Reading part 3
BULATS Reading part 1 section 3
BULATS Reading part 2, section 5

2 You can tell students to:

– skim the passage in two minutes

– underline or highlight the answers when they see them.

Be strict about the time limit.

Answers

1 They receive cash immediately, a percentage of revenue, an international presence, they can expand when the economy is weak at home, outlets in places with strong demand, new ideas.

2 It requires resources (especially time and other costs), the brand needs protecting from copying, maintaining control of the brand, distraction from home market.

3 Remind students to underline the main idea in each question before reading the article. (**Suggested underlining: 1** interested / Alghanims' offer **2** western franchises find emerging economies attractive **3** advice / company owners / overseas deals **4** secure trademarks **5** worries / brand identity in the Middle East **6** main concern / outlets in the Middle East)

If you want students to do this exercise under exam conditions, ask them to answer all the questions in ten minutes (they would have 12 in the exam, but they have already spent two skimming the article).

When they finish, ask them to compare their answers in pairs and quote from the article where necessary to support their answers.

Answers

1 B (*… an immediate cash infusion … an immediate international presence.*)

2 C (*As western businesses cope with tight lending markets and a weak economy, many emerging economies have strong consumer demand as well as investors with plenty of capital.*)

3 D (*… look at where it makes sense to go …*)

4 A (*Otherwise, a potential investor could soon turn into a troublesome copycat.*)

5 B (*Adler worries that the fresh, youthful atmosphere of Dlush's southern California locations can't really be duplicated in the Middle East, where the culture is more conservative.*)

6 D (*But Adler's main concern is that the Middle Eastern outlets have taken a lot of his time — and shifted his focus away from building the Dlush brand at home.*)

Vocabulary

Ask students to copy vocabulary from this section into their notebooks in a section on finance.

Answers

1 capital **2** trademark **3** investors **4** outlets **5** concept
6 lucrative **7** retail **8** supply chain **9** gross revenue **10** resources

Extension idea As in previous units, suggest to students that for homework they look these words up in a dictionary and copy an example to go with each of them into their notebooks.

Tell them that they should do this as a regular activity as it helps them to remember the word and how it is used, and acts as a useful reference when they come to study the words or want to use them.

Role-play

1 Divide the class up into equal numbers of As and Bs. If necessary, some students can work in groups of three.

Give them three or four minutes to prepare this role-play.

2 Before they start, go through the Useful language box. Ask students to suggest ways of completing each phrase.

Tell students that Pair B should also discuss the advice Pair A gives them – they should ask for the reasons for the advice and say if they do not agree with it.

Extension idea Round up with the whole class to find out what:

– franchises they are thinking of investing in

– advice they thought was most useful.

Financial terms

Vocabulary

1 If they wish, students can do this exercise using their dictionaries.

Answers

1 b **2** h **3** d **4** a **5** c **6** g **7** f **8** e

2 ### Answers

1 turnover **2** costs **3** profit **4** credit **5** interest rate **6** asset(s)
7 tax **8** liability

Extension idea Write the answers to the exercise on the board.

Ask students to close their books and, in pairs, use the words on the board to discuss what the information and advice they have just read was.

When they have finished, they can check by looking in the book again.

A letter to a franchiser

Reading

1 Tell students they can also use ideas they had from the role-play they did earlier.

BEC Reading part 5

2 Remind students to:

- quickly skim the whole letter before they start to look for extra words

- read the letter sentence by sentence when looking for extra words, as the correct choices depend on understanding the sentence structure.

Answers

1 working 2 was 3 ✓ 4 the 5 ✓ 6 is 7 for 8 more 9 ✓ 10 my
11 to 12 ✓

Extension idea Ask students: *Did Günther ask the same questions as you?*

Writing

Before students write, go through the Useful language box and also refer them back to Grammar workshop 2, Formal requests, on page 43.

Alternative treatment 1 If your students are preparing for the Business Vantage exam, ask them to write 120–140 words. If they are preparing for BULATS, ask them to write 180–200 words.

Alternative treatment 2 Ask students to research a real franchise on the Internet and decide what else they would want to know about it. They can then write the letter to the franchise they have researched.

You can refer them to these two websites to get started:
www.entrepreneur.com/franchise500/index.html
www.franchise.com

Financing a start-up

Topic: how to raise finance to start a business

Reading: matching statements and sections

Listening: note-taking from an authentic interview; multiple-choice questions on the interview

Speaking: role-play giving advice about starting a business; short presentations

Vocabulary: types of finance (*bank loan*, *mortgage*, etc.); verb–noun collocations connected with starting companies; *assets*, *collateral*, etc.; short phrases for starting questions

Getting started

Warming up With books closed, ask students: *What ways are there of obtaining money to start up a business?* Students should work in small groups and brainstorm possibilities.

With books open, they can compare their list with the list in the book. If they did the *Warming up*, they do not need to do question 6.

Suggested answers

1 a bank loan; personal savings
2 personal savings or a loan from family or friends
3 This is very variable, depending on the entrepreneur's individual circumstances, location and type of business
4 cheapest: personal savings, a loan from family or friends, going into partnership, private equity, a government grant
most expensive: a bank loan, a mortgage
5 more control: a bank loan, a mortgage, a government grant, personal savings
less control: venture capital, private equity, going into partnership

Setting up a food consultancy

Listening

1 *Alternative treatment* Ask students if they can predict any of the answers.

Tell them that even if they think they can predict some answers, they will still have to listen carefully to check if they are correct.

Students should also underline key ideas in the notes. (**Suggested underlining:** activities / organising; Before launching / business; tutors / realistic; people / contacted / became; better at attracting new customers; cover overheads / did / job; advice / borrow / afford)

2 ① 19 Play the recording twice. Afterwards, students can compare their answers with a partner, then check by reading the transcript at the back of the Student's Book.

Answers

1 exhibitions 2 start(-)up 3 business plan 4 clients
5 (more) enthusiastic 6 part-time 7 pay back

Note: Since the recording was made, Not Just Food has become a food-and-drink project management consultancy working with major producers both in the UK and overseas.

Extension idea Ask students:

– *What impression do you have of Jane Milton? What qualities does she have which have made her successful in business?*

– *In what ways do you think she is typical of people who start their own business?*

– *Do you agree with her advice at the end? Why? / Why not?*

You can also refer students to Not Just Food's website at http://www.notjustfood.co.uk.

Raising finance

Vocabulary 1

1 *Alternative treatment* Encourage students to use their dictionaries for this activity.

– They can also copy the collocations to their notebooks, along with examples from their dictionaries.

Answers

raise finance / money / a loan
borrow money
carry out market research / a business plan
launch a company
cover overheads
write a business plan
repay a loan / money

2 Students can do this exercise in pairs.

Answers

1 launch a company 2 carry out market research 3 raise finance / money / a loan / borrow money 4 write a business plan 5 repay your/the loan 6 cover (your) overheads

Extension idea To help fix these collocations in students' minds, ask them to cover over this exercise, but not Exercise 1.

Ask them to try to recreate the paragraph in Exercise 2 from memory: they need not use exactly the same words/phrases, but should use the collocations from Exercise 1 to reproduce the same message. They can do this either speaking or writing.

When they have finished, they can uncover Exercise 2 and compare their answers.

Reading

BEC Reading part 1   BULATS Reading part 2 section 1

1 Remind students that with this Reading task, they should study the statements carefully before reading the extracts.

   Alternative treatment Ask students to underline the key ideas in each statement. (**Suggested underlining: 1** cover / debts / not worried / make money **2** Do not accept/ money / formal contract **3** share information **4** lend money / create employment **5** other institutions / afraid **6** pay less interest **7** owners or joint owners **8** property to guarantee the loan)

Answers

a 2, 3
b 1, 4, 5, 6, 7, 8

2 If students are preparing for an exam, give them ten minutes for this exercise (in the exam, they would have 12 minutes, but they have already spent time reading the statements).

   Alternative treatment Ask students to work in pairs. One student should read Extracts A and C, the other Extracts B and D and match statements from Exercise 1 with their extracts. Give them five minutes for this.

   When they have finished, ask them to explain their extracts to their partners, using their own words as far as possible, and say which statements they chose to match, and why.

Answers

1 A (*Banks don't care whether or not your business has great profit potential. They are only interested in the business's ability to cover the principal and interest payments.*)
2 B (*You should prepare a written agreement …*)
3 B (*Don't be embarrassed to show financial statements, tax returns or whatever else they want to see.*)
4 D (*… to facilitate … the generation of jobs …*)
5 C (*Venture capital is intended for higher risks …*)
6 D (*… terms of interest … are less than the market rate.*)
7 C (*… the investing institution acquires a share in the business.*)
8 A (*Banks like to use assets such as premises, motor vehicles or equipment as collateral (or security) against loans.*)

Vocabulary 2

Ask students to copy these words/phrases into their notebooks.

Answers

1 assets **2** collateral/security **3** tax returns **4** ordinary shares **5** preference shares **6** equity finance **7** soft loans **8** market rate

Advice about starting a business

Role-play

Alternative treatment If you have internet access in class, or as homework preparation, you can ask students to look at websites which give advice to small businesses and ask them to note down ideas and advice they find useful.

You can suggest they put 'business start-up advice' into their search engine and look at the pages which appear.

Tell Pair A they can use ideas from the websites they have visited.

Tell Pair B, they can ask about advice they have seen on websites to get an idea of how useful it is in their case.

Extension idea Ask 'advisors' and 'entrepreneurs' to work together and produce a brief business plan in note form. They should have the following headings, which you can write on the board:
– *Business idea*
– *Equipment and premises*
– *Staff*
– *Sales forecast and profits forecast*
– *Finance required.*

When they have finished making their notes, ask them to change groups and take turns to present their plans from their notes.

Carter Bearings

Listening

BEC Listening part 3   BULATS Listening part 4

1 Ask students to look at the photograph. Ask:
   – *What sort of industries need these products/ components?*
   – *If your line manager asked you to source high-quality precision components for your company, how would you start?*

   If your students are preparing for an exam, remind them that they should always read through multiple-choice questions, underlining the key ideas before they start.

   Suggested underlining

   2 succeed against competitors **3** way of finding clients **4** give / discount when **5** written communication / works best **6** advantage of buying from a distributor **7** sort of companies / suppliers **8** key to survival

   Extension idea Ask students to look quickly through the options and check that they know what each of them means.

2 ①20 Play the recording twice. When students have finished, ask them to compare their answers.

   They can then check by listening again and following the transcript at the back of the Student's Book.

Answers

1 B 2 C 3 C 4 B 5 C 6 A 7 B 8 C

Extension idea 1 Ask students to compare how each correct answer is expressed in the transcript with the wording of the option.

Extension idea 2 Write these phrasal verbs and expressions on the board and ask students to find them in the recording script:

*backed off   run with   build up   fit into   call up
show up   come in   top   track back   go through*

Ask students to work in pairs and discuss what each expression means from the context.

Finally, ask students to check their answers by looking at the Word list on page 128.

Speaking

1 This activity serves as a round-up for the unit. Before they start speaking, ask students to look back through the unit and at their notebooks for ideas and vocabulary they can use.

2 **BEC** Speaking part 3

Go through the Useful language box with your students.

Give them a minute to organise and add to any notes they made in Exercise 1.

When they speak, tell them they have a minute each.

Check that they get to the main points they want to make soon after starting to speak (many students talk around the subject without saying too much for about half of the allotted time).

Be quite strict about the timing.

Alternative treatment Write the checklist from Unit 8 Speaking (see page 31 of this book) on the board.

Ask students, while they are listening, to use it to give feedback and comments to their partners.

Expanding into Europe

Unit objectives

Topic:	finding the right location for a technology company
Reading:	multiple-choice cloze; matching information with extracts; open cloze completing a proposal
Writing:	a proposal
Listening:	note completion from a telephone conversation
Speaking:	discussing the requirements for a new location
Grammar:	linking words and phrases
Vocabulary:	*place, space, room*; *opportunity, possibility, option*; phrases highlighting features; phrases making recommendations

Getting started

1 *Warming up* With books closed, ask students in small groups to list reasons why companies from other continents might think of expanding their operations into Europe. (**Answers:** Many of the reasons will be similar to those for expanding anywhere overseas: to get closer to their markets, to get closer to suppliers or raw materials, to make use of investment grants, to break into new markets, to make use of European expertise, to compete on more advantageous terms with other companies in the sector, etc.)

Alternative treatment With books open, ask students to read the email as they might read an email they have printed out, i.e. highlighting or underlining the important points. (**Suggested underlining:** R&D facility / Switzerland / Germany / close to a major international airport)

> **Suggested answers**
>
> how much BioBok is willing to invest
> number of staff
> where the staff will come from

2 *Alternative treatment* Ask one student to present their ideas to the whole class. When they have finished, ask the other students to add any other extra ideas.

A new location in Europe

Listening

BEC Listening part 1   **BULATS** Listening part 2

1 Ask students also to underline key ideas in the notes. (**Suggested underlining:** *Initial investment / Staff … rising to / Staff … recruited from / Recruit … internally / Check for availability of*)

> **Suggested answers**
>
> 1 another type of investment 2 number of staff 3 places where staff can be recruited from 4 something/someone that can be recruited 5 something that they need

2 ①21 Play the recording twice. When students check their answers, tell them to make sure they are spelled correctly.

> **Answers**
>
> 1 equipment 2 60 / sixty 3 divisions 4 manager
> 5 (government) grants

Extension idea Ask students in pairs to summarise Alicia's assignment: what does she have to do for BioBok?

Ask:

– *Would you enjoy an assignment like this as part of your work? Why? / Why not?*

– *How would you go about investigating locations if you were Alicia?*

Reading

BEC Reading part 4   **BULATS** Reading part 2 section 2

1 Before they read, ask students *Why is choosing the correct location so important?* (**Answer:** Because it may affect the performance and success of the venture; because of the amount of money they are going to invest in it.)

Remind students that they should:

– skim the whole text first

– read the text sentence by sentence to choose the best options.

> **Answers**
>
> 1 C 2 B 3 C 4 A 5 A 6 D 7 D 8 C 9 B 10 A 11 D 12 B 13 C 14 B 15 C

Extension idea Ask students: *Imagine you work with Alicia. What are the strengths of Heidelberg as a location?* (**Suggested answers:** It is a science park, associated with a university, many similar companies, a biotech site, supported by services, training, advice, conference centre, in an attractive location, close to a major airport.)

Ask: *What are the advantages of sharing a location with other biotech companies?* (**Suggested answers:** the chance to collaborate, cross-fertilisation of ideas, recruitment opportunities, etc.)

BEC Reading part 1   BULATS Reading part 2 section 1

2 *Alternative treatment* Ask students in pairs to read the nine statements and, without reading either text, to decide from memory which statements refer to Heidelberg (H).

They can then check their answers by:
- looking back at the text in Exercise 1
- reading the text in this exercise.

Answers

2 B 3 H 4 B 5 H 6 H 7 B 8 H 9 B

3 Before students do the exercise, go through the Useful language box with them.

Alternative treatment Tell students that they are going to decide which location to choose in a formal business meeting.

Tell them that they should prepare for the meeting in pairs by making a list of the advantages of each site (and any disadvantages) and matching them with BioBok's requirements, as outlined by Charles earlier in the unit.

Appoint a chair for the meeting. If you have a large class, divide it into several groups, each conducting their own meeting.

Give students five or ten minutes, as you see suitable, to discuss and reach a decision.

If you have divided the class into a number of groups, round up by comparing the decisions they have reached and the reasons for them.

Vocabulary

1 If appropriate (i.e. if your students are west European), tell students that the confusions often arise from similar words in their own languages: this means they should take extra care when using the words.
- Point out that *room* and *space* have some overlap of meaning and sometimes can be used in the same context.

Answers

1 e 2 d 3 a 4 f 5 c 6 b

2 Tell students to refer back to the dictionary entries in Exercise 1 while doing this exercise.

Answers

1 place 2 room 3 space 4 options 5 opportunity 6 possibilities

3 **Answers**

1 room 2 space 3 place 4 opportunity 5 option 6 possibility

Extension idea Ask students to write their own sentences using each of these words.

A proposal

Reading

BULATS Reading part 1 section 4
BULATS Reading part 2 section 3

1 *Alternative treatment* Ask students to skim the proposal, without paying attention to the gaps, and say if they think Alicia has made the correct choice. Why? / Why not?

Before they write words in the gaps, elicit that they should:
- read the whole text quite quickly first to get a general idea of its contents
- read carefully before and after the gap to see what type of word they need (pronoun, preposition, etc.)
- read through the completed answer again when they have finished to check that it makes sense and reads grammatically.

Answers

2 as 3 which 4 own 5 around 6 their 7 both 8 some 9 most 10 This 11 there 12 for

2 **Answers**

I recommend that we …; Our next step should be to …; and I suggest that, at a later stage we …

3 **Suggested answers**

1 I recommend that we find premises which are close to the airport.
2 I suggest we commission an architect to design a building for us.
3 Our next step should be to contact Lausanne University.
4 I recommend that we advertise for staff in international science magazines.

4 Tell students that when they write, it is important to link their ideas clearly so that the reader can follow the development of their arguments without confusion.

In the exam, they will gain marks if they can do this effectively.

When they have answered the questions, go through the explanation in the Grammar workshop on page 60 with them and then ask them to do the exercises which follow.

Answers

1 *although, however* and *on the other hand*
2 *moreover, also*
3 *on balance*

Writing

1 *Alternative treatment* Before they start, ask students in pairs to answer these questions about the proposal on page 54:

- *What do you notice about the layout of the proposal?* (**Answer:** It has a title and is divided into sections with headings, like a report.)

- *Does the proposal concentrate on the existing situation or what should be done next?* (**Answer:** Its focus is on what should be done next.)

- *What are the purposes of the first and the last sections?* (**Answer:** the first to introduce, the last to recommend a course of action)

Refer students to the notes on more formal and less formal styles in the Writing reference on page 116. Ask *Can you see any phrases or expressions which make the proposal sound formal?*

When students look at the task, ask them:

- *Who will read the proposal?*

- *How can you express the ideas in the task using your own words as far as possible?*

Remind them, if they are preparing for an exam, that they will be expected to use their own words where possible, not merely lift from the task.

Ask students to discuss which location they will recommend, and why.

Extension idea Ask students to write a brief plan for their proposal.

2 Remind students to use:

- language for recommendations

- linkers.

Sample answer

Introduction
The aim of this proposal is to evaluate Gdansk and Wroclaw as possible sites for our office in Poland.

Workforce
Both technology parks are attached to large universities where it may be possible to recruit graduate students and teachers as staff.

Other IT companies
Since both parks already host a number of IT companies, customers will be used to coming to these locations. Wroclaw Technology Park contains some of the largest global IT companies, which makes the possibility of co-operating with them easier. On the other hand, the companies in Gdansk are very small, so they are unlikely to be such useful partners.

Location
Although Gdansk is a pleasant city, Wroclaw undoubtedly offers the advantage of being closer to international centres such as Berlin or Prague, where many of our customers are based.

Other facilities
Gdansk offers subsidies or grants to new businesses setting up in the area. This would be an excellent way of reducing the initial investment in premises and equipment. On the other hand, Wroclaw can provide us with business and legal counselling, which will help us to comply with European regulations.

Recommendations
On balance, although Gdansk is a strong contender, I recommend that we should choose Wroclaw because it is closer to our principal markets and it will be easier to attract the right staff to work there.

Extension idea When students bring their answers to class, ask them to work in pairs and exchange their answers with another pair.

Ask them to imagine that they are the Operations Manager and a colleague. They should read the proposals and discuss these points:

- *Does the proposal cover all the points in the task?*

- *What impression does it give you?*

- *Is it persuasive? Are you inclined to implement the recommendations in the proposal? Why? / Why not?*

When students have finished, they should give feedback to the writers, who can then make changes before handing their work in to you.

Presenting your business idea

Topic:	giving full-length business presentations
Reading:	matching statements and sections: advice on presenting
Listening:	completing notes
Speaking:	discussing presentation technique; giving structured presentations; role-play: presenting a business idea
Grammar:	*can* and *could*
Vocabulary:	phrases to structure a presentation

Getting started

1 Ask students to give examples of good and bad presentations they have given or attended.

2 If students are stuck for ideas, ask them to suggest two things which it is important **not** to do.

If it does not arise during the discussion, you can point out that the most important thing of all is missing from the list: preparation.

BEC Speaking part 2

3 Give students some time to think and prepare before they speak.

Alternative treatment Ask students to work in pairs and take turns to talk about either a presentation which went well (and why) or a presentation which went badly (and why).

Structuring a presentation

Speaking

If appropriate, point out that this section works on full-length business presentations, not 'mini-presentations' such as those of Business Vantage Speaking Part 2 or BULATS Speaking Part 2, which last just one minute.

Answers

1 c 2 e 3 d 4 f 5 b 6 g 7 a

Extension idea Ask students in pairs to think of ways of saying c, e, d and a.

Write ideas from the class on the board, correcting where necessary.

Signalling the parts of a presentation

Listening

1 **Answers**

1 b, j 2 h 3 k 4 c, e 5 a, d, i 6 f 7 g

Extension idea Ask students to pick out positive signals in the extracts (*welcome, hoping, happy, it's been a pleasure, patience, interest, feel free, Thank you all very much*). Ask *Why are positive signals important?* (**Answer:** People react positively to them, feel better.)

2 ①22 Play the recording once only.

Point out that these signals are particularly useful for less-experienced presenters because they give a framework around which the presentation can be given.

More experienced presenters may use less obvious signals.

Extension idea 1 Write these words on the board: *positive, negative, businesslike, disorganised, humorous, enthusiastic, bored.*

Ask *What impression does the speaker give you? Why?* (**Suggested answers:** positive, businesslike, enthusiastic – he's well organised, a good serious tone of voice, positive adjectives, well prepared.)

Extension idea 2 Play the recording a second time and ask students to repeat the extracts in Exercise 1 to capture the stress and intonation. You may have to play some extracts several times.

BEC Listening part 1   BULATS Listening part 2

3 ①22 Tell students to write numbers as figures rather than words: this avoids spelling mistakes.

Alternative treatment Ask students in pairs to decide what information they need before listening.

Ask them to complete any gaps they can from what they have just heard.

When they listen, they can check answers they have already written and complete the notes.

Play the listening once or twice as necessary.

Answers

1 advertising 2 drivers 3 traffic conditions 4 main (road)
5 leasing 6 2,000 7 premium rates 8 500,000

Extension idea Select a presentation on a business theme from www.ted.com. If you wish, make a worksheet for it to check comprehension.

Ask students to watch the presentation and comment on:

- body language
- tone of voice
- building rapport with the audience
- using signals to move from one part of the presentation to the next
- positive vocabulary.

Speaking

BULATS Speaking part 2

Give students several minutes to prepare their presentation.

If you wish, also give them an opportunity to rehearse before they change partners.

Alternative treatment If your students are preparing for the BULATS test, give them just one minute to prepare and ask them to speak for one minute only.

Extension idea 1 If your students are preparing for the BULATS test, ask them to choose another of the topics and repeat the process.

Extension idea 2 Invite volunteers to come to the front and give their presentations to the whole class.

In this case, ask students to give feedback using the checklist from the extension idea in the previous activity.

Making the most of presentations

Reading

BEC Reading part 1   BULATS Reading part 2 section 1

1 Remind students that they should study the statements quite carefully.

Alternative treatment Ask students to underline the key ideas in each statement. (**Suggested underlining: 1** course on presentation skills **2** Speak / suitable speed **3** filming yourself **4** look / at your listeners **5** Plan **6** Practise / nervousness **7** Prepare for / questions **8** photocopies / long / complex)

Once students have underlined, ask them to paraphrase each of the key ideas using their own words. (**Suggested answers: 1** Get some training on how to present. **2** Don't speak too fast or too slowly. **3** Record yourself and then play it back. **4** Make eye contact with your audience. **5** Prepare with care. **6** Rehearse to deal with worries or nerves. **7** Think what questions you might be asked and have answers ready. **8** Don't explain things which are too complicated – put them on a handout.)

2 Give students ten minutes to answer the questions.

Alternative treatment Ask students to work in groups of four. Tell each student to read one extract and choose the statement(s) which it refers to.

They should then take turns to explain what the extract says in their own words and the reasons for the statements they have chosen.

Answers

1 A (*... some basic training ...*)
2 D (*Remember to speak slowly and clearly.*)
3 C (*Recording and listening to yourself ...*)
4 D (*... make eye contact with members of the audience as often as possible.*)
5 B (*The first step in making a really effective presentation is to prepare.*)
6 A (*Rehearsing the presentation will greatly reduce anxiety.*)
7 B (*... which things it is worth knowing about in case anybody asks you about it.*)
8 D (*... put any lengthy detail into a handout ...*)

Extension idea Ask students to look at the first sentence of Extract D. Ask:

- *Why is enthusiasm essential?* (This is not explained in the extract.)
- *Do you think enthusiasm is essential in all aspects of work? Why? / Why not?*
- *How can you generate enthusiasm 1) for yourself, 2) in people you work with?*

3 *Extension idea* After students have discussed, ask them to work alone and write a paragraph like the extracts in Exercise 2.

Post the paragraphs round the walls of the classroom for students to read.

Round up by asking which they think is the best advice, and why.

Grammar workshop

Can and *could*

Alternative treatment Do not correct this exercise with students immediately: go through the explanation in the Grammar workshop on page 61 first, then ask students to revise their answers on the basis of what they have read.

Ask them to do the exercises which follow the explanation once you have clarified the answers to this exercise together.

Answers

1 could 2 can 3 can 4 could 5 can 6 can

Presenting your business idea

Role-play

Before students prepare their presentation, ask them to look back through the unit for language they can use and for advice.

Ask students to give their presentations at the front of the class.

Alternative treatment If you have a data projector in class, you can ask students to prepare their presentations with PowerPoint for homework. They can then give their presentations with PowerPoint slides in the following lesson.

Extension idea After each presentation, ask students who are listening to give helpful feedback to the presenters.

Grammar workshop 3

Prepositions in time clauses

1 1 for 2 for 3 on/until 4 in 5 in/during; at 6 since 7 at 8 for; from; to/until 9 until 10 by 11 during/on 12 for
2 1 ~~until~~ by 2 ~~For~~ During/In 3 ~~at~~ on/– 4 ~~since~~ for 5 ~~since~~ from 6 ~~on~~ for

Linking ideas

1 1 although / even though 2 However; On the other hand; on balance 3 Although / Even though 4 However / On the other hand; On balance 5 However 6 However 7 Although / Even though
2 *Suggested answers*
  1 ... I have little time to study.
  2 ... I would like to find a more challenging job.
  3 ... always seem to have too much work on my desk.
  4 ... I wouldn't put it before my family and friends.

Can and *could*

1 1 could 2 could 3 can 4 can 5 could 6 could
2 1 could 2 could 3 could 4 could 5 can

Arranging business travel

Unit objectives

Topic:	business travel: reasons for it / is it still necessary?; social media and travel
Reading:	open cloze; multiple-choice cloze
Writing:	short emails to apologise, instruct, suggest, agree and explain
Listening:	short extracts
Speaking:	structuring and concluding a short presentation; a collaborative task
Grammar:	past modals
Vocabulary:	*travel*, *journey* and *trip*

Getting started

Warming up With books closed, ask students to imagine they work with someone they have never met (they usually liaise with them over the phone or by email). Ask *How do you think meeting the person might change the way you work together?*

Extension idea Tell students that apparently, business travel is on the increase despite new communications technologies. Ask: *Why do you think this is?*

Vocabulary

1 **Answers**

   1 trip **2** journey **3** travel

Extension idea Ask students:

– *Why is the title of the unit 'Arranging business travel'?* (**Answer:** Because it is talking about the general activity.)

– *Which word would you use for someone going on business to San Francisco for three days?* (**Answer:** a business trip)

2 **Answers**

   1 travel **2** trip **3** trip **4** trip **5** trip/journey **6** trips/journeys

Extension idea Ask students to write three sentences of their own as examples.

A company meeting

Speaking

BEC Speaking part 2   BULATS Speaking part 2

1 *Alternative treatment* If your students are studying for the BULATS test, write this alternative task on the board for them to discuss:

Describe a time you travelled on business.

You should say:

– *where you went*

– *why you went*

– *who you met*

and how successful the trip was.

Extension idea If your students work, ask them to give examples from their experience to support their ideas.

2 ①23 Play the recording once for students to answer question 1. Play it again for them to answer questions 2 and 3.

Remind students that success when speaking at length depends partly on using phrases to mark the different points you want to make.

If your students are preparing for an exam, tell them that using phrases like these will improve their marks.

If your students are preparing for the Business Vantage exam, tell them that the examiner will be expecting them to be concluding what they are saying at the end of a minute. Using a phrase like *all in all* or *in conclusion* shows the examiner they are making their final point and completing the task in the time given.

Answers

1 Meeting clients: essential for building relationship, liking you, trust and persuasion
Expanding your business: explore new markets – see them for yourself
Meeting colleagues from different offices: get to know each other, builds team spirit, exchange ideas and communicate values
2 **a** important **b** vital **c** essential
3 All in all (other possible phrases: *to sum up*, *in summary*, *to conclude*, *in conclusion*)

Extension idea To work a little on pronunciation, play the recording again, focusing on the phrases from Exercise 2 a, b and c, and ask students to repeat them with the same stress and intonation.

3 Tell students they should use their notes from Exercise 1. Give them a little time to prepare.

Tell them that if they wish, they can use some of Dimitri's ideas as well.

Give them a minute to speak and be fairly strict about the timing, i.e. they should be concluding at the end of the minute.

4 Tell students their talks should be business-oriented. Pre-service students may have to use their imagination a little to produce ideas. Working students should be encouraged to use some examples from their experience.

Alternative treatment Ask students to work separately to prepare their talks.

5 Again, time the talks to last a minute.

Tell students who are listening that they should pay attention so that they can say if there is something they disagree with and ask a question at the end.

Arranging to travel

Writing

BULATS Reading part 1 section 4   BULATS Part 2 section 3

1 Remind students to read the whole email before filling the gaps.

Answers

1 at 2 who 3 in 4 at 5 while/when

Extension idea Ask students: *Is this a congress you would be interested in going to? Why? / Why not?*

BEC Writing part 1   BULATS Writing part 1

2 Remind students if they are preparing for an exam that in this Writing task, they will have to use a number of functions such as the ones listed.

Ask: *What is the difference between an instruction and a request?* (**Answer:** An instruction is an order, though it may well be framed in the language of a request in order to soften it / make it sound more polite.)

Answers

1 I'm sorry to … 2 I'd like you to … 3 You could …

Extension idea Elicit other ways of apologising and suggesting.

Write these on the board, then refer students to the Functions bank on pages 123–124 of the Writing reference for more examples.

3 Go through the Useful language box before students do Exercises 3 and 4.

Ask students to do this exercise alone – for homework if you wish. Tell them they should spend about 10 to 15 minutes on it.

If your students are preparing for the Business Vantage exam, their answer should be 40–50 words. If they are preparing for BULATS, it should be 50–60 words.

Tell them that

– if necessary, they should rewrite their answers to fit the word limit

– they should think about their reader (Dimitri) and make sure they communicate all the points clearly and without irrelevance.

Sample answer

Hi Dimitri

I'd be happy to go to the Congress. If you agree, I think it would be a good idea to take Paola with me, as she could make some useful contacts while we're there. We'll be at the Congress for the whole week.

Best wishes

Magda

Extension idea When students have finished, or when they bring their answers to class, ask them to exchange them with a partner and compare them with the sample answer at the back of the Student's Book. They can then make any changes they wish before handing it in to you.

4 You can follow any or all of the suggestions in Exercise 3 above.

Sample answer

Pablo – I'm planning to go to the Mobile World Congress in Barcelona this month. Could you please book flights for myself and Paola and rooms at the Hotel Palace, arriving 24th and leaving 31st? Also, can you suggest places where we can entertain clients in Barcelona? Thanks, Magda.

How business travel is changing

Reading

1 *Alternative treatment* If students are stuck for ideas, ask them to look at the title of the article and use that to help them.

BEC Reading part 4   BULATS Reading part 2 section 2

2 Remind students that they should skim the article before dealing with the gaps.

Suggested answer

Hotels becoming more technological, having to do more than just advertise and offer discounts; business people less loyal to particular chains, looking for cheaper hotels, more loyalty programmes; travellers read reviews on websites and can choose rooms, booking while travelling, i.e. just before arriving.

3 Remind students to read the completed text again when they have finished to check it makes sense.

Answers

1 A 2 C 3 B 4 D 5 B 6 A 7 D 8 B 9 A 10 D 11 C 12 D 13 C
14 A 15 C

Speaking

BEC Speaking part 3   BULATS Speaking part 3

Tell students that after the collaborative task, the examiner will ask them a number of more general questions which they can discuss with their partner (if they have one) and with the examiner.

Alternative treatment Make this a class discussion if you wish.

Extension idea Also ask: *How do you think technologies will change business travel in the future?*

Conference problems

Listening

BEC Listening part 2   BULATS Listening part 3

1 *Alternative treatment* Before students answer the questions, and with books closed, ask:

– *Do you ever go / Have you ever been to a conference?*
– *Do you enjoy them?*
– *What things can go wrong at conferences?*
– *Why are they useful for business people?*

2 ①24 Play the recording twice. When students have finished, ask them to compare their answers with a partner.

Answers

1 E 2 D 3 F 4 H 5 B

3 ①29 Play the recording again for students to write their answers.

Answers

1 should have sent 2 should have practised 3 should have hired

Extension idea 1 Ask students:

– *Are these things the people did or didn't do?*
  (**Answer:** didn't do)

– *Are the speakers criticising or complaining?*
  (**Answer:** both)

Extension idea 2 Ask students to look at the transcript at the back of the Student's Book to see how the speakers expressed themselves.

Then ask students to work alone and choose one of the alternatives from Exercise 1 which was not mentioned by the speakers, i.e. either A, C, G or I.

Tell students to write a complaint or criticism about one of them, but without mentioning it by name (like the examples in the transcript).

When they are ready, they should work in small groups and take turns to read out their piece.

The other students should say which thing (A, C, G or I) the person is talking about.

4 *Alternative treatment* Go through the explanation in the Grammar workshop on page 78 and ask students to do the exercise which follows before they do this exercise.

Extension idea Ask students to describe (or imagine, if they are pre-service) a business trip where things went wrong.

They should work in small groups and describe their trips, saying what people should/could have done to avoid the problems.

Planning a business trip

Speaking

BEC Speaking part 3   BULATS Speaking part 3

Before they start, tell students that for the:

– first point, they can give quite general reasons, since the company is a fictional company

– second point, they need not name people, but can think about whether they should be managers or more junior members of staff

– second and third points, they should give reasons to support their suggestions and decisions.

Give students a minute to think before they start.

When they have finished, round up ideas and decisions with the whole class.

Business conferences

Topic: business conferences, their uses, how to get the most from them; networking

Reading: matching statements to sections; skimming

Writing: short emails explaining, requesting and informing

Listening: taking short telephone messages and notes; identifying functions; an interview with an executive from a destination management company

Speaking: deciding who to send to a conference; a networking role-play; giving a short presentation

Getting started

Warming up With books closed, ask students:

– *Why is it sometimes useful for business people to meet business people from other companies and competitors in their industry?*

– *What can they learn from each other?*

(**Suggested answers:** They can meet to talk about industry problems, regulations, share experiences and solutions, occasionally work together, lobby politicians, learn how each others' companies are performing, pass on know-how, learn about jobs, opportunities, working methods and technologies, etc.)

If you do the *Warming up* idea, you can perhaps skip question 1, which is likely to produce many of the same answers.

> **Suggested answers**
>
> 2 networking, conference talks, presentations and seminars, entertainment events for conference-goers

Arranging conference facilities

Listening

BEC Listening part 1   BULATS Listening part 2

1 Remind students, if they are preparing for an exam, that they will hear three conversations with four questions each.

Suggested answers

1 numbers of people who are not delegates
2 other people/things
3 an event where there might be traditional dance
4 something belonging to Air New Zealand
5 a piece of equipment
6 something speakers should bring
7 something about the availability of sound equipment
8 a place where exhibitors might have stands
9 something always available

2 (1) 25–26 Play each recording twice as in the exam.

Ask students to compare their answers in pairs.

> **Answers**
>
> 1 partners 2 guest speakers 3 Opening ceremony 4 logo
> 5 computer 6 pen drives 7 on request 8 reception area
> 9 (Free) refreshments

Extension idea Ask students to check their spelling by looking at the transcripts at the back of the Student's Book.

3 **Answer**

> instructions: phone National Auditorium, tell them where to put projector
> reason: an urgent meeting

Extension idea 1 Ask students to note that the reason can come before the instruction – in this case, it is more natural; when writing to a colleague, they can give instructions quite directly using *Can …?* and/or an imperative.

Point out the informal beginning and ending of the message to a colleague.

Extension idea 2 Ask students in pairs to role-play the phone conversation between Safia and SPTO.

Before they start, refer them back to the telephone language they studied in Unit 4 (page 21).

4 Before students write:

– go through the Useful language box with them

– tell them they can use the message in Exercise 3 as a model, but they should supply their own ideas and details.

Note: there is a sample answer at the back of the Student's Book.

Sample answer

Katya

Unfortunately, I've had to take my wife urgently to the doctor, which means I haven't booked the teleconferencing facilities for Dr Lung. Remember, her talk is scheduled after the plenary in the main conference hall at 10 a.m., so could you please notify the organisers and book it for then?

Thanks, Piotr

Extension idea Ask students in pairs to read and check each others' emails.

When they have finished, they should exchange one of their emails with another pair of students.

They should read the email they receive together and role-play a telephone conversation where they have to make the booking.

5 *Extension idea* You can also ask:

– *What do you think it involves?*
– *What qualities do you think someone needs for this sort of job?*

If you have someone in class who has done this sort of job or something similar, ask them to talk about it to the rest of the class.

Making the most of business conferences

Reading

1 Round up this activity by asking students *What impression do you get from reading this advice of how to make business conferences useful? Is it the same or different to the ideas you had in Getting started question 1?*

Alternative treatment Ask students to underline the key ideas in each statement as they read them. (**Suggested underlining: 1** needn't attend each session **2** Be flexible **3** one useful idea **4** Highlight / points / act on later **5** Organise meetings before **6** Think / things / relate to your work **7** meet people / valued by your colleagues)

2 Tell students that by focusing on the main idea or purpose of each section, they may be able to decide which statements it refers to more quickly.

Suggested answers

A Put a star by the Action Steps.
B Think about what you learned from each session.
C Don't think you should go to every session.
D Make sure you meet people between sessions.

3 Give students a maximum of ten minutes for this. Ask them to underline the words in the extracts which gave them the answers.

Answers

1 C (*Don't assume you should go to every event.*)
2 C (*The greatest benefits of a conference are often circumstantial ... a chance conversation ... don't feel pressured by the structure.*)
3 B (*... distill each presentation down to a central point.*)
4 A (*... the Action Steps ... dealt with after the conference. I had recorded these Action Steps with a star ...*)
5 D (*Reach out to your contacts in advance and suggest grabbing an early breakfast together, lunch, or dinner during the conference.*)
6 B (*Perhaps there was a specific tip that you could adapt when you get back to your office ...*)
7 D (*Encourage each person to invite one or two people that they deeply respect ...*)

Extension idea Ask students to underline any vocabulary from the extracts that they would like to have explained.

Ask them to work in pairs and try to guess the meanings from the context.

Refer them to the Word list on pages 129–130 for definitions.

4 This exercise can also be done as a class activity.

Speaking

BEC Speaking part 3   BULATS Speaking part 3

Give students a minute to read and think about the task before they start, then three or four minutes to discuss it.

Tell them to make sure they deal with both parts of the task adequately.

Round up by asking each group what decisions it has reached.

Alternative treatment Especially with pre-service students, elicit possible follow-up after the conference.

You can start by asking *What follow-up was mentioned in the Reading extracts?* (**Answer:** Action Steps to be dealt with after the conference; tips or advice for when you return to the office or real life).

Suggest some more formal follow-up, e.g. meetings to discuss and feed back on conference sessions; cascading (when someone passes on what they have learned at the conference to people who were not there); a written report or summaries in the company newsletter.

Extension idea Ask these follow-up discussion questions to the whole class:

– *Apart from going to conferences how can people keep up to date with developments and new ideas in their industry?*
– *How can networking help people to develop their careers?*
– *Why are many conferences held in unusual or exotic locations?*

Networking at a conference

Listening

BEC Listening part 2   BULATS Listening part 3

1 If your students are preparing for an exam, tell them that quite often one of the matching tasks requires them to identify functions, i.e. what people are actually doing with the language they are using.

In this case, they need to listen to the gist of what each speaker says.

Tell students that in real life, it is clearly important to recognise the functions someone you are speaking to is expressing, so that you can respond appropriately.

Alternative treatment Before students look at the exercise and with books closed, write the eight functions a–h on the board.

Ask students to work in pairs and decide what they might say in each case.

Round up with ideas from the whole class.

Finally, with books open, they compare their ideas with 1–8.

Answers

1 g 2 a 3 b 4 c 5 e 6 d 7 h 8 f

2 ① 27 Before they listen, tell students that each speaker will say more than the short phrases in Exercise 1 and will use different words. Students should listen for the gist (the general idea) in each case.

Play the recordings twice, then ask students to compare their answers in pairs.

Answers

1 f 2 d 3 e 4 b 5 a

3 Ask students to compare these phrases with the phrases in Exercise 1 and copy all of them into their notebooks.

Role-play

Tell students to try to make the conversation sound as natural as possible.

Alternative treatment Especially with weaker classes, ask students to prepare their roles in pairs. They then change partners to do the role-play itself.

Extension idea Ask students in pairs to discuss how well they did the role-play.

If they wish, they can change partners and do the role-play again.

A destination management company (DMC)

Listening

1 | **Suggested answer**

A specialist company will know destinations, have contacts, and possibly be able to obtain discounts for facilities where events will be held. They will know event organisers. Also, by outsourcing this to a specialist company, your organisation does not need to devote time and resources to organising things themselves.

BEC Listening part 3   BULATS Listening part 4

2 ① 28 Give students 40–60 seconds to read the questions before you play the recording.

Check that they underline key ideas while they are doing this.

Play the recording twice.

Alternative treatment If you want to give your students practice in this, ask them to close their books while they listen and take notes.

Students should then compare notes with a partner.

Ask them to open their books and answer the multiple-choice questions on the basis of what they have noted down and understood.

If necessary, play the recording one more time for them to check their answers.

Answers

1 C 2 B 3 A 4 B 5 C 6 A

Extension idea Ask students to look at the transcript at the back of the Student's Book and underline the phrases which express each answer.

Speaking

1 When students have finished, either round up ideas with the whole class, or ask students to take turns to present their ideas in small groups.

BEC Speaking part 3   BULATS Speaking part 3

2 This exercise is slightly longer than an authentic exam task might be, so give students about 30 seconds to read and prepare, then five minutes or so to discuss.

When they have finished, round up ideas with the whole class.

Business meetings

Getting started

1 *Warming up* With books closed, ask students in small groups to brainstorm as many reasons as possible for holding business meetings, e.g. to pass on information. Give them two minutes for this.

When they have finished, round up with the whole class.

With books open and when students have done the exercise, ask them which reasons on the list they mentioned.

Point out to students that the correct combinations are collocations.

Ask them to copy them to their notebooks.

Answers

1 e 2 d 3 h 4 g 5 f 6 c 7 a 8 b

2 If your students are pre-service, tell them that they also may attend some of these types of meetings in their school, college or as part of other activities, so they can still answer the questions.

3 Encourage students to give reasons for their answers.

Extension idea 1 If your students are preparing for the Business Vantage exam, ask them to work alone and give them a minute to prepare a one-minute talk on 'What is important when holding a business meeting?'

Tell them they should use ideas and vocabulary from *Getting started*. (In the live exam, they would have two prompts with the question.)

When they are ready, they should work in pairs and take turns to give their talks.

Extension idea 2 If your students are preparing for BULATS, write this Speaking task on the board:

Describe a business meeting you attended recently.

You should say

– *what the meeting was for*

– *who attended it*

– *what the outcomes were.*

What were the most useful aspects?

Ask students to prepare in the same way as for Business Vantage above.

Talking about meetings

Listening

1 Point out to students that these combinations also form collocations, as do the definitions.

Answers

1 e 2 c 3 a 4 f 5 g 6 d 7 b

Extension idea Tell students to work alone and think about a time they did one of the things in this exercise.

In groups, they should then tell each other about the occasion, but without using any of the phrases 1–7.

The other students should say which action 1–7 each student is talking about.

BEC Listening part 2   **BULATS** Listening part 3

2 ①29 Play the recording twice, then ask students to compare their answers in pairs.

Answers

1 Martyna: 3 2 Sasha: 6 3 Mei Lin: 2 4 Paul: 1

Extension idea Ask students:

– *Which speaker do you feel most sympathy towards? Why?*

– *Have you ever had similar experiences? Tell us about them.*

A survey of meetings

Speaking

1 Before students start, go through the Useful language box with them. Tell them to
- think how they can relate the useful language with the information contained in the charts
- decide what each chart shows, and the principal information it contains
- discuss how business is changing.

2 *Alternative treatment* Ask students in groups of three to each present the information from one of the charts.

Extension idea Ask students to write a short report which summarises the main points from the three charts.

Reading

BEC Reading part 3
BULATS Reading part 1 section 3
BULATS Part 2 section 5

1 Give students two minutes to skim the article. When they have finished, ask them to compare their ideas in pairs.

Suggested answer

You get facial expressions, hand gestures more easily; they develop transparency and trust; people feel more comfortable with each other; deadlines become more important; people become friends they respect on a personal level; tailored solutions for business-to-business meetings; opening the relationship; closing the decision: presenting critical information; moving forward on a project; getting a dialogue started.

2 Tell students that understanding referencing is essential for understanding texts, and at their level, they may have to understand ideas which are expressed over several sentences linked by reference devices.

If they are preparing for an exam, remind them that effective use of referencing gives their writing cohesion and will gain marks in the exam.

Answers

the two (line 6): video conferencing and meetings held offsite
none of them (lines 20–21): conference calls, etc.
them (line 27): team members
its (line 34): a leading New York-based organisation
the majority (line 36): the majority of the organisation's customers
one (line 37): a hybrid meeting
ones (line 40): meetings
Both ... each other (lines 40–41): face-to-face meetings and virtual ones
This emerging practice (line 42): hybrid meetings
their (line 47): Sprint-Nextel's
them (line 49): face-to-face meetings
they (line 51): the company
the rest (line 52): the other members of the team
this (line 60): the mixture of face-to-face and virtual meetings
it (line 64): the dialogue with customers

Extension idea Go through the explanation in the Grammar workshop with students and ask them to do the exercises which follow.

BEC Reading part 3

3 Remind students that this part of the exam tests inference and opinion.

Point out that questions may cover several sentences, hence the importance of understanding referencing within and across sentences.

Give students ten to 12 minutes to answer these questions and remind them to:
- read the question and find where it is dealt with in the text
- read the text carefully to understand what it says in answer to the question
- read the options and choose the one which matches the meaning of the text
- underline words/phrases in the text which give the answer to confirm that there is evidence for their choice.

Answers

1 C (*Instead of looking at video conferencing as an alternative to meetings held offsite, many companies are now combining the two, as well as using social networking tools as a powerful follow-up to face-to-face connections.*)
2 A (*It's harder to follow cues such as expressions on people's faces in two dimensions ...*)
3 D (*... her deadlines now take on greater importance for her, because the project is ... a friend and colleague who is now real to her... people think twice before firing a colleague or friend that they respect on a personal level.*)
4 B (*More and more, companies don't see a black-and-white divide between face-to-face meetings and virtual ones. Both are complementing each other.*)
5 C (*As a result, Sprint trims meeting costs ...*)
6 D (*Social networking is important, because companies can keep the dialogue going with their customers ... But getting it started depends on being face-to-face.*)

4 If your students are pre-service, elicit types of remote meetings technologies they may use, e.g. Skype, instant messaging, video calls, etc.

Extension idea Ask:
- *Do you think people should be giving meetings their full attention, or is it all right to multi-task during meetings? Why? / Why not?*
- *What is appropriate body language in a work or business meeting?*
- *How important for you are the social aspects of meetings? Why?*

Vocabulary

Tell students to find and highlight the vocabulary in the article first.

They should then guess the meaning from the context before finally matching the words/phrases with their definitions.

Answers

1 e 2 d 3 b 4 c 5 a

Extension idea Tell students, for homework, to look up these words in their dictionaries and copy them into their notebooks with an example from the dictionary.

Looking for solutions

Listening

1 Point out that in meetings, perhaps especially amongst native speakers, people will use less formal language on many occasions to express their opinions. This means you may have to listen quite carefully to make out what the speaker thinks.

Answers

a: 4, 7, 9
b: 3, 10
c: 1, 8
d: 2, 5, 6

2 ①30 **Answers**

The phrases are heard in this order:
What do you think?; Well, I think …; Yes, and …; I'm not sure; Personally, I feel that …; … don't you think?, Yes, but …; Frankly, I think that …; That's right; That's true

Extension idea Ask students to listen a second time and note down what the people in the meeting decide to do. (**Answer:** have some market research done by a specialist firm; visit the country to get a feel for it)

Ask students to look at the transcript at the back of the Student's Book and to underline other useful phrases.

Writing

BEC Writing part 1   BULATS Writing part 1

If your students are preparing for the Business Vantage exam, ask them to write 40–50 words.

If they are preparing for BULATS, they should write 50–60 words.

Alternative treatment Ask students to look at the Writing reference on short emails before they write. Tell them to look for words and phrases they can use.

Sample answer

Hello Barry,

I would be happy to visit China during the first two weeks of June. I shall need to take about 100 leaflets, brochures and catalogues. I will also need a case containing samples of all our main products.

Could you please let me know what expenses the company will pay for my trip?

Many thanks,
Sandra

A meeting at a medical equipment company

Role-play

Ask students to read the background. Ask *What sort of meeting are you going to hold?* (They can look at the list of meetings in *Getting started*.) (**Answer:** a meeting to solve a problem)

Give students a few minutes to prepare what they want to say and how to say it.

Appoint one student in each group as the chair. Tell this student that they are responsible for giving everyone an opportunity to express their views.

If you wish, tell students that each of them should present their viewpoint in turns before they discuss.

Tell students that when they hold the meeting, they should maintain eye contact with the other people in the meeting (if appropriate in their culture) and not look too often at their notes. They should express the ideas using their own words where possible.

When they have finished, round up by asking each chair to present to the class any conclusions they have reached from their discussions.

Spending the sales budget

Unit objectives

Topic:	thinking about sales, sales techniques and costs
Reading:	dealing with an open cloze; report reading
Writing:	writing a report based on graphic input and handwritten notes; writing the introduction; making recommendations
Listening:	note-taking from an authentic source; listening to short extracts
Speaking:	giving opinions; discussing sales and travel
Grammar:	giving reasons and explaining methods; using the passive to express opinions and ideas

Getting started

Warming up With books closed, tell students to work in small groups and say *Tell each other about a particularly good sales person you know: what makes them so good at their job?*

Before students answer the questions in the book, go through the Useful language box with them. Elicit other ways of expressing opinions and write them on the board.

If your students are pre-service, you can ask them *If you had something to sell (e.g. T-shirts to raise money for a college trip), who would you approach first: people who have bought things from you before, or people who have never bought anything from you? Why?*

Spanish sales

Listening

1 **Suggested answers**

1 something which produces successful sales
2 a number
3 a place or time
4 something related to customers and centres
5 something reps know about
6 something related to customers
7/8 numbers
9 something other than numbers that gives the team an ability to compete

2 ②01 Play the recording twice. Then ask students to compare their answers in pairs.

Answers

1 planning 2 80/eighty 3 December 4 list 5 products
6 relationship 7 5/five 8 6/six 9 quality

3 ②01 *Alternative treatment* It may not be necessary to play the recording again for students to answer the question. However, if you wish, you can play the recording while students follow the transcript at the back of the Student's Book.

Suggested answer

Existing customers – his team builds up a relationship with customers and visits them five or six times a year.

DF Software

Reading

1 *Alternative treatment 1* Before they look at the questions, ask students in pairs to discuss what each chart shows and what conclusions they would draw from them.

Alternative treatment 2 Ask students to write their answers to the questions. Particularly check that they use the correct tenses to refer to the data.

Suggested answers

1 National sales have risen slightly; international sales have fallen a lot.
2 Total sales have fallen.
3 Their in-country budget has risen by **50**%; their international budget has fallen by **50**%.
4 There is a correlation between rising and falling sales and rising and falling budgets.
5 While visits to potential customers have remained the same, visits to existing customers have fallen.

BULATS Reading part 1 section 4
BULATS Reading part 2 section 3

2 Remind students to:

– read the whole report quickly first

– read before and after the gaps

– decide what type of word they need for each gap.

When they have finished, ask them to check some of their answers by looking at *Prepositions in phrases describing trends* in Grammar workshop 2 (page 42).

Ask students to compare their answers in pairs.

If your students are preparing for an exam, remind them that they are not penalised for wrong answers (i.e. a mark is not subtracted), so it is always a good idea to make an intelligent guess when they do not know the answer. By identifying the type of word, students can narrow down the possibilities to guess from. It is important not to leave any question without an answer.

Remind them that verbs need to be in the correct form or tense; they need to decide if nouns should be singular or plural. They should read the complete text again with their answers to check these things.

Answers

2 past/last 3 make 4 As 5 However 6 period 7 by 8 with 9 this 10 more 11 to 12 same 13 spent 14 them

3 *Extension idea* Ask students if they would organise the information and recommendations differently if they were writing the report, and if so, why.

4 Ask students to copy the phrases they identify into their notebooks.

Tell them they should aim to use some of these phrases when they themselves write reports, and that in exams, it will help them to achieve a higher mark.

Answers

1 a It is thought to be equally effective.
  b It was expected to be a more lucrative market.
  c They paid less attention to existing customers.
  d Customers prefer to meet sales staff face to face.
  e So that they don't lose them.
2 a as b on the basis that c can be put down to the fact that
  d since e so that
3 by using video conferencing
4 by reducing the budget for the annual sales conference
5 by means of, by

5 Go through the Useful language box with students. Point out that:

– the collocation is *make a suggestion/recommendation*

– they can use *should* with *suggest* or *recommend* or they can use the base form of the verb in the dependent clause. Using the base form is slightly more formal

– *propose* is generally not used to make recommendations or suggestions except in very formal circumstances, e.g. to propose a candidate or a toast or to propose marriage.

Suggested answers

1 I recommend using low-cost airlines for business travel when/if/where/whenever possible.
2 I strongly suggest that we spend more time meeting customers instead of writing reports.
3 I strongly recommend that we incentivise sales staff by awarding prizes when they exceed their targets.
4 I would suggest that we offer our staff a training course to enhance their product knowledge.
5 I recommend that we should hire local staff in international markets, on the basis that this will save us money.

6 Ask students to refer to the Useful language box in Exercise 5 when doing this exercise.

Answers

1 make 2 suggest 3 make 4 suggest 5 use

Extension idea Ask students to work in pairs and write some recommendations of their own for the school or college where they are studying.

Grammar workshop

Using the passive to express opinions and ideas

1 Students can suggest answers in pairs.

Alternative treatment If necessary, quickly revise what the passive is and how it is formed (with the verb *to be* and the past participle).

Ask students to underline the verbs in the passive (*was decided; should be reduced; were encouraged; was thought; was given; was expected*).

Elicit that the infinitive is used after *was thought* and *was expected.*

Suggested answer

Using the passive avoids saying who made the decisions; it is more formal.

2 Tell students that there may be several ways of expressing these sentences using the passive.

Ask students to check their answers by reading the explanation in the Grammar workshop on page 79. They should follow up by doing the exercises in the workshop.

Suggested answers

1 At a recent board meeting, it was decided to increase the number of sales staff / that the number of sales staff would/should be increased.
2 Front-office staff are being encouraged to write emails to customers instead of phoning, as this is thought to save money / as it is thought that this will save money.
3 An incentive scheme has been implemented, as this is expected to encourage staff / as staff are expected to be encouraged by this / as it is expected that staff will be encouraged by this.

A report on the use of private company jets

Listening

1 *Extension idea* Ask: *Are there any disadvantages?* (**Suggested answer:** Clearly cost is the major disadvantage, but environmental impact is another issue.)

2 *Alternative treatment* Ask students which of the points (A–G) they think are the best arguments in favour of using company jets.

3 (2)02 Play the recordings twice.

Answers

1 G 2 B 3 D

Extension idea Ask students to imagine they also work for Florentino International.

Ask them to work alone and choose another of the reasons, i.e. A, C, E or F, and write a short explanation of why they use the company jet, expressing the reason using other words.

They then read out their reason to their group, who say which reason (A, C, E or F) is being given.

Writing

BEC Writing part 2   BULATS Writing part 2

1 Remind students that:
- they should use their own words as far as possible
- their report should have a clear structure
- they should deal with all the handwritten notes.

Suggested answer

1 Chart 1 shows the number of flights taken by top managers over the last two years and the number forecast for next year. Chart 2 shows what the flights were used for.

Extension idea Ask students to write a brief plan for their report.

When they have finished, they should compare it with two or three other students and make any changes they want.

2 Elicit that the report should be written using more formal language and that the handwritten notes are quite informal.

Go through the Useful language box with students and encourage them to use one or two of the phrases in their introduction.

If your students are preparing for the Business Vantage exam, they should write this report in 120–140 words, taking about 30 minutes for the task.

If your students are preparing for BULATS, they should write the report in 180–200 words, taking about 30 minutes for the task.

Sample answer

Report on the use of company aircraft by senior managers
Introduction
The reason for writing this report is to summarise and recommend changes in the use of the company aircraft by senior managers at Florentino International.
Number and purpose of flights
The number of flights per year has risen from 56 last year to 63 this year, with 80 expected next year.
Last year, the aircraft was mainly used to meet with clients (56%). Although this year the majority of flights have been for internal meetings, this is expected to change next year, when the plane will be used to meet customers on 60% of occasions.
Recommendations
We need to use the plane less, since the travel budget has been reduced. I therefore recommend that the plane should be used exclusively for meetings with key clients, as this boosts the company image. Furthermore, managers should switch to using scheduled airlines to go to internal meetings.

Grammar workshop 4

Modal verbs: perfect forms

1 could/should have asked 2 could/should have stayed 3 could have rested 4 might/may/could have been 5 might/may/could have made 6 might/may/could have just dialled 7 could/should have told

Referencing

Suggested answers

1 … especially ones / those / the ones …
2 … to use it. That is why …
3 … and this will lead …
4 … and this has meant that they …
5 … ask them what training they need.
6 … with a client, we usually email each other to summarise …

Passives

1 1 … has been sent to head office.
  2 … will be opened by the Minister for Industry.
  3 … must be submitted by 19 March.
  4 … have been taken by the Board of Directors this morning.
  5 … are being interviewed for the job at the moment. / … for the job are being interviewed at the moment.
  6 … of finished articles are rejected as substandard.
  7 … was opened by mistake.
  8 … must always be kept in a locked safe.
2 1 … to fall next year due to increased competition.
  2 … are expected to rise by 50% in the next six months.
  3 … been announced that profits have reached record levels.
  4 … reported to be losing money.
  5 … by most people to be an excellent human resources manager.
  6 … to meet its deadlines.
  7 … to be bringing out a new smartphone.
  8 … items in our product range should be replaced.

Social media and business

Unit objectives

Topic:	the uses of social media in business
Reading:	a short email, thinking of synonyms; matching statements and sections; editing an email
Writing:	a short email explaining, informing and asking for a suggestion; planning a longer email; writing a longer email asking for information
Listening:	note completion; predicting information
Speaking:	discussing how to use social media
Grammar:	use and non-use of definite article
Vocabulary:	verb–noun collocations; phrases to talk about steps; more formal and less formal vocabulary

Getting started

Warming up With books closed, ask students in small groups to discuss: *How are new technologies changing the way companies operate and people work together?*

While students are discussing this and the questions in the book, ask them to note the main points.

Extension idea Ask one student to present their group's ideas to the whole class. Other groups should follow up by mentioning other ideas that they had.

Social media and customers

Listening

1 | **Suggested answers**

  1 an adjective which describes how websites are to use
  2 people who can be reached by websites
  3 something which is communicated
  4 a link or relationship between companies and customers
  5 a type of employee
  6 a number
  7 something new

2 ②03

Answers

1 cheap 2 younger consumers 3 brand message 4 conversation
5 (unemployed) actors 6 25 million 7 special offer

BEC Speaking part 3   BULATS Speaking part 3

3 ***Extension idea*** Ask:

– *How do you feel about commercial organisations making use of social spaces on the Internet?*

– *Are you 'friends' with any companies or organisations? Tell us about it. How do you benefit from this?*

– *How good is Françoise Blaye's advice? What other advice would you give to a company wanting to use social media?*

Vocabulary

1 If your students are preparing for an exam, remind them that if they use collocations correctly, they will score higher marks, so they are worth learning and using.

When students have finished, play the recording again (CD 2 Track 3) for them to check their answers. They can also look at the transcript at the back of the Student's Book.

Tell them to copy the collocations into their notebooks.

Answers

1 miss 2 make 3 make 4 make 5 conducted

Extension idea Ask students to write their own sentences using these collocations.

Alternatively, they can work in pairs and say sentences using them.

2 Tell students that candidates in the exam find they often want or need to use collocations (which is good), but occasionally make mistakes with them.

It is worth keeping a section of their notebooks for collocations. When they have the opportunity, they should try to use them in Writing or Speaking tasks and study them for the exam.

Answers

1 run 2 hold 3 place 4 made 5 conducted 6 make 7 making

3 | **Answers**

  2 d 3 b, c 4 b, d 5 b 6 d 7 c 8 c 9 a 10 a, d 11 c, d 12 a

Extension idea Ask students to brainstorm as many verb–noun collocations as they can with *meeting*, e.g. *hold a meeting*.

When they have finished, ask them to remind themselves by looking back at Unit 15 (page 70).

4 | Answers

1 make **2** do / carry out / conduct **3** arrange/hold/schedule
4 carry out / implement **5** set/meet **6** arrange/schedule/set
7 attend

Extension idea 1 Ask students to underline the time phrases in the email (**answers**: *Last month*, *now*, *later this week*).

Ask *How do the time phrases link the paragraphs together?* (**Answer:** They show a process with what happened previously, what has just happened and the next stage in the process.)

Extension idea 2 Ask students to write a similar email to this one, where they talk about something which happened last month, something which happened recently and the next stage in the process.

BEC Writing part 1   **BULATS** Writing part 1

5 If your students are preparing for the Business Vantage exam, ask them to write their answer in 40–50 words.

If they are preparing for BULATS, they should write their answer in 50–60 words.

In any case, they should summarise the reason for the meeting, not explain at the same length as Petra.

Suggested answer

Dear Igor, Martyna and Tatania

Petra has asked me to organise a meeting in her office to discuss Felicity Bannerman's research into how we can use social media. Can you please let me know a day and a time which would suit all of you?

Thanks
Sasha

Extension idea 1 When students have finished, ask them to work in pairs and compare their answers.

They should then make any changes or improvements they wish.

Extension idea 2 Ask students to pass their email to another student.

The other student should write a reply (you can write these instructions on the board):

– *Apologise for being unable to attend this week.*

– *Explain why you cannot attend.*

– *Suggest alternative time and place.*

(**Sample answer:** Dear Sasha

I'm afraid I can't make the meeting later this week as I'm away visiting customers in St Petersburg. However, I don't want to miss the meeting, so could you possibly reschedule it for Monday of next week so we can implement changes without delay? Thanks)

Some ways of using social media

Reading

1 Ask why it is good to think of synonyms for the statements while they read them (**answer:** because the statements contain paraphrases of ideas expressed in the article).

Suggested answers

1 mistakes **2** employees/workers; aims/goals/objectives **3** Internet
4 customers; ends/aims/objectives **5** teaching/development/
education **6** external; business/organisation **7** listen to **8** using

2 Give students ten minutes to do this task (they would have 12 minutes in the exam, including the time taken to read and think about the statements).

Answers

1 C (*... acknowledge your mistakes ...*)
2 B (*... how they use social media within their global organisation to align all their employees to their overall business objectives.*)
3 D (*Research published by Proctor and Gamble stated that an influencer's story spreads up to one million times within their social network on the Internet within one year.*)
4 A (*Your strategy can then be to marry your business objectives with your insights into your customers.*)
5 C (*... you can help them by providing everything from hands-on classroom work to virtual instruction, from written guides to recorded video and webinar-style sessions.*)
6 D (*... making use of external influencers in the marketplace. These people have three characteristics: they like to try new things because they are new, they are intrinsically motivated, and they share stories with friends.*)
7 A (*Your social strategy should include an element of listening to what is already being said in the space.*)
8 B (*... use of social tools across all business functions, from PR to marketing to customer service.*)

3 Ask students if the synonyms they thought of in Exercise 1 were different from the ones in the extracts.

Answers

1 mistakes **2** people who work for you / employees; objectives
3 Internet **4** customers; objectives **5** instruction **6** external;
organisation **7** listen to **8** use

BEC Speaking part 3   **BULATS** Speaking part 3

4 If you wish, you can make this a whole-class discussion.

Grammar workshop

When to use *the*

When students have finished the exercise, do not correct it; go through the explanation in the Grammar workshop on page 96 with them, then ask them to check their answers to this exercise.

Students should then do the exercises which follow the explanation.

Answers

3 the **4** the **5** the **6** the **7** – **8** – **9** – **10** the

An email enquiry

Speaking

BEC Speaking part 3   BULATS Speaking part 3

Before students start, go through the Useful language box with them.

Tell them they should make sure they deal with all the points in the task and make sure everyone in the group participates in the discussion.

Give them 30 seconds to read the instructions and think before they speak.

Although in the Business Vantage exam, the collaborative task is normally done in pairs and takes three minutes, this one is slightly longer and is being done with small groups, so give students five minutes to complete it.

Writing

BEC Writing part 2   BULATS Writing part 2

1 Remind students that when they write a business email:

- they should plan it in the same way as they would plan a letter
- it should have a fairly formal style, with correct English and good layout especially when written to someone they do not know.

Ask students:

- *Who will read this email?* (**Answer:** Moira Lang, a consultant)
- *Does Katrin know the person?* (**Answer:** no)
- *What does Katrin want to achieve by writing it?* (**Answer:** She wants to find out if Moira is available to give advice on how to use social media, and how much it will cost.)
- *Does Katrin just have to use the handwritten notes, or are there other things she must deal with in the task?* (**Answer:** She must also deal with the final instruction from Bill.)

Answer

1 *Suggested underlining*
introduce our company / say why we want to use social media / find out if she can help / how much she charges

BEC Reading part 5

2 If your students are preparing for the exam, point out that Katrin's email contains about 140 words, so is a similar length to a Business Vantage Writing Part 2 answer.

Answers

2 1 that 2 *correct* 3 open 4 to 5 with 6 the 7 make 8 a
9 employing 10 *correct* 11 about 12 making

3 Point out to students that they are expected to use their own words as far as possible when doing Writing tasks, and that the task itself will often require this, e.g. the task is worded in a less formal way, but requires the answer to be written in a more formal way requiring more formal vocabulary and structures.

Answers

1 told me this firm was good / consultancy has been recommended to us
help /assist
how much she charges / what your fees would be
2 Bill's email is informal; Katrin's is more formal.

Extension idea 1 If you have not already done so, refer your students to the Writing reference, page 116 (Levels of formality) and page 120 (A letter of enquiry).

Extension idea 2 Ask students to look more closely at Katrin's email.

Ask them to find a passive verb in the email (**Answer:** It has been suggested) and ask *Why has the passive been used?* (**Answer:** So as not to say who has suggested this (Moira will not know the person anyway) and because it is more formal.)

Ask *What two ways of making a request are used?* (**Answer:** *We would be grateful if you could …, Could you please let us know if …?*)

Students at this level are expected to write fairly complex sentences. Ask:

- *How is different information joined together in the first sentence?* (**Answer:** using participles: *specialising, including*)
- *How is information joined in the third sentence?* (**Answer:** using relative clauses: *in which; who*)
- *Why does Katrin finish the letter 'Yours sincerely'?* (**Answer:** She started with the addressee's name.)
- *What other polite phrases can you think of which are similar to 'Thanking you in advance'?* (**Suggested answers:** We look forward to hearing from you, I look forward to an early reply)

4 Tell students they can use their own plans if they wish, or use the answer in Exercise 2 as a model.

Tell them that it is normal in a letter of enquiry to introduce the company and its activities first.

If your students are preparing for the Business Vantage exam, they should write their answer in 120–140 words and 30 minutes.

If they are preparing for BULATS, they should use 180–200 words and 30 minutes.

Sample answer

The sample is Katrin's email in the unit.

Business and the environment

Unit objectives

Topic: making businesses more environmentally friendly

Reading: skimming; replacing gapped sentences in a text; reading about making offices more environmentally friendly; note-taking; using references to recognise cohesion within a text

Writing: a short memo; internal emails explaining, asking for suggestions, suggesting and offering

Listening: authentic interview with an environmental consultant; note-taking; multiple-choice questions

Speaking: talking about offices and the environment; companies and social responsibility; giving short presentations

Grammar: expressing causes

Vocabulary: *issues*, *impact*, etc.; *method* or *way*; phrases to talk about future possibilities

Getting started

1 *Warming up* With books closed and students in small groups, write these questions on the board for students to discuss:

- *To what extent do you think business and industry is responsible for the world's environmental problems?*
- *How can businesses and industry do less damage to the environment?*
- *Is it possible to be environmentally friendly and remain competitive?*

2 Round up ideas with the whole class.

Ask: *Do you think if our class or school was more environmentally friendly, we would be less productive? Why? / Why not?*

The green office

Reading

1 *Alternative treatment* Ask students to work in groups of three. Ask each student in the group to work on one of the statements (you should make sure they each work on a different statement). Give them a minute or two to work alone and

- decide whether or not they agree with the statement
- prepare a short talk explaining their point of view and the reasons for it.

They should then take turns to present their ideas. The other students should listen and when the speaker has finished, discuss to what extent they agree with what the speaker said.

BEC Reading part 2

2 Tell students they should skim the passage in about two minutes. Be strict about the time limit.

Answers

a F b F c T

3 Point out that in all types of writing, paragraphs should have a clear topic which is different to the paragraphs around it.

Suggested answers

Paragraph 2: saving electricity by switching off your computer
Paragraph 3: using standby mode
Paragraph 4: printers still with us
Paragraph 5: ways of saving printing costs
Paragraph 6: sharing computers

4 *Alternative treatment 1* Ask students to do the task in this exercise and Exercise 5 at the same time.

Tell them that if they have noted the topic of each paragraph, they should quite quickly recognise where each sentence goes, so underlining references and placing the paragraphs should take them a maximum of ten minutes.

Alternative treatment 2 Make enough photocopies of the text for each student to have one, and enough photocopies of the missing sentences for each pair of students.

Cut up the list of missing sentences into strips, with one sentence per strip.

Ask students in pairs to close their books and work from the photocopy.

Hand out sentence A and ask students to place it.

Get feedback from the class about where it should go and why.

Do the same with sentence B and so on till they have placed all sentences. Point out that if they have read the passage quite carefully first, the sentences can be placed quite quickly and easily and there is not usually any confusion about where each should go.

Students should quite quickly identify when they read sentence D that it is a distractor and does not fit anywhere.

Suggested underlining

B Once you have finished with the documents
C to set this up
D these measures
E Clearly this is not the case
F An obvious solution would be / power it down
G In addition

5 See the alternative treatments in Exercise 4.

Answers

2 F 3 C 4 E 5 B 6 A

Vocabulary

Answers

2 b 3 e 4 g 5 a 6 f 7 d 8 c

Extension idea Ask students to identify what type of word each is. (**Answers: 1** noun **2** verb **3** adjective **4** verb **5** adjective **6** adjective **7** verb **8** adverb)

Ask them to look the words up in their dictionaries and copy them, together with an example, into their notebooks.

Speaking

BEC Speaking part 2   BULATS Speaking part 2

1 *Alternative treatment* Ask students to prepare their talks alone.

2 Give students time to think and consider their ideas before they speak.

Alternative treatment Use these questions and the list of points for a discussion with the whole class.

Grammar workshop

Expressing causes

1 Ask students to check their answers by looking back at the text.

Elicit that *due to* is followed by a noun phrase and *due to the fact that* is followed by a clause.

Answers

1 Due to 2 due to the fact that

2 **Answers**

1 b 2 a 3 a 4 b

3 **Answers**

1 Due to / Owing to / Because of
2 due to / owing to / because of
3 because / due to the fact that / owing to the fact that
4 because / due to the fact that / owing to the fact that
5 Due to / Owing to / Because of

4 **Answers**

1 The reason why; is 2 cause 3 result in 4 The reason why; was 5 was caused 6 result in

Extension idea Ask students to write five of their own sentences expressing causes using phrases and patterns from this workshop.

When they have finished, ask them to compare their sentences in small groups.

Round up by asking students to read out sentences they are not sure about, which you can then correct with them.

Reducing waste

Vocabulary

1 **Answers**

1 way 2 method

Extension idea Ask students to cover over Exercise 2. Ask *Which word would you use for something quite complex?* (**Answer:** method)

2 Tell students that Business English students often make mistakes with these words, so they should pay special attention when using them themselves.

Answers

1 methods 2 way 3 way 4 method(s) 5 way 6 method 7 way

Writing

1 Encourage students to use their dictionaries to do this exercise.

Answers

1 Because of 2 amount 3 grateful 4 ways 5 give

Extension idea Ask students:

– *How effective do you think Isabel's email is?*

– *Would you suggest ideas if you received this email? Why? / Why not?*

2 *Extension idea* Ask:

– *Is reducing costs the only reason for reducing electricity consumption?*

– *Could there be any disadvantages to reducing electricity consumption in the office?*

3 Tell students they should think of ways of expressing the ideas using their own words as far as possible. You can elicit *cut down* as a synonym for *reduce* as an example.

They may not easily find a synonym for *waste*, in which case they should use *waste*.

4 Tell students to use the email in Exercise 1 as a model.

Remind them that they are writing to their colleagues, so a less formal style may be more suitable.

Sample answer

Dear colleagues

Due to rising costs, we need to cut down on the amount we waste in this office. Can you tell us how to make the office more efficient? The prize for the best idea will be two cinema tickets.
Looking forward to your suggestions!
Rajiv

5 | **Sample answer**

Hi Rajiv
I think staff generally need to keep their desks tidier. If they do this, they will find papers and other documents more quickly and it will make the working environment more pleasant for all staff.
Hassan

Extension idea Ask students to look at the sample answer at the back of the Student's Book. Ask them what reference devices the writer uses to make the email cohesive. (**Answers:** If they do this; it will make)

An environmental consultant

Listening

1 *Extension idea* If your students are working, ask *Do you have an environmental consultant working for your company? If so, what does she/he do?*

2 ②04 Tell students not to look at Exercise 3 for the moment.

Play the listening once, then ask students to compare the answers they gave in Exercise 1.

Answers

1 planning new buildings and the impact of the new buildings on the environment
2 a science degree and a Master's in environmental science

BEC Listening part 3   **BULATS** Listening part 4

3 ②04 Play the recording once or twice more as necessary – this is an authentic interview, so may be somewhat more difficult than students preparing for an exam might expect.

Alternative treatment Ask students to look at the transcript at the back of the Student's Book to check their answers. You may wish to play the recording at the same time.

Ask students to underline the words/phrases which provided them with the answers as they read.

Answers

1 C 2 A 3 A 4 B 5 C 6 B

4 Go through the Useful language box with students before they answer the questions.

Extension idea Ask students to write predictions around the subjects of the questions using the phrases from the Useful language box.

When they are ready, ask them to take turns to read them out to the whole class (or to work in groups and read them out).

The other students should say to what extent they agree with each sentence which is read out, and why.

A staff survey

Unit objectives

Topic:	changes in the way people work
Reading:	analysing a report on a survey; multiple-choice cloze
Writing:	a survey report
Listening:	five short extracts; completing notes on phone calls
Speaking:	talking about benefits and consequences of changes; discussing working conditions and staff social programmes
Grammar:	reporting verbs and reported speech
Vocabulary:	phrases to talk about benefits and consequences; *higher productivity, better work–life balance*, etc.; expressing numbers

Getting started

Warming up Ask students to work in pairs with books closed.

If your students are working, ask *What changes to your working conditions would you like to see? How would they make your life better?*

If your students are pre-service, ask *What for you would be the ideal working conditions when you start your first job? You can talk about working hours, location, training or time off for study, etc.*

Before students do the exercise in the book, go through the Useful language box with them.

Point out that *to* in *lead to* is a preposition and part of a phrasal verb. Therefore it will be followed by a noun or a verb + *-ing*. Similarly, *result in*.

Ask students to try to use the phrases when answering the questions.

Answers

1 **a** optional part-time working **b** career breaks **c** flexible working hours
2 *Suggested answers*
   Benefits of the changes
   For the company:
   Staff may be less stressed by outside factors, and therefore more efficient/effective.
   Possibly less sick leave and other absences.
   May be easier to retain staff, who, due to external circumstances, might otherwise leave.
   Easier to recruit staff.
   Generally, lower costs
   For staff:
   Less stress.
   Better work–life balance.
   Ability to combine working life with family commitments.

Extension idea 1 Ask students to look at the percentages in the table. Ask: *Are there any results of this survey which surprise you?*

Extension idea 2 Ask students to conduct a similar survey of the class to find out their attitudes to the points in this survey.

When they have finished, they can record the results as percentages and compare the percentages for the class with the percentages on the table in the book.

Staff reactions

Listening

BEC Listening Part 2   BULATS Listening Part 3

1 If necessary, ask students to use a good learner's dictionary or the *Cambridge Business Dictionary* online at http://dictionary.cambridge.org.
2 (2) 05 Play the recording twice.
   Students should then compare their answers in pairs.

Answers

1 F 2 H 3 B 4 C 5 E

Extension idea 1 Ask students to check their answers by reading the transcript at the back of the Student's Book and underline the words or phrases which gave them the answers.

Extension idea 2 Ask: *Which speaker do you agree with most? Why?*

Reading a report

Reading

BEC Reading part 4   BULATS Reading part 2 section 2

1 Remind students to skim the passage quickly before tackling the questions. Give them a minute for this.

   Alternative treatment 1 Either ask students to cover over this page or, with books closed, give them a photocopy of *Getting started*.

   Ask them in pairs to look at the information in *Getting started*.

   Tell them they have been asked to write a report on the survey. What sections would they put in their report?

   When they have finished, ask them to compare their ideas with the report on this page.

Alternative treatment 2 Allow students to do this task with the help of their dictionaries.

Answers

1 A 2 C 3 B 4 D 5 A 6 C 7 C 8 D 9 B 10 B 11 D 12 B 13 C 14 C 15 A

2 Answers

1 to summarise staff's reactions to changes
2 No, these are summarised. Normally a report would be accompanied by tables with the figures.
3 Yes
4 The company should go ahead with the changes (under *Recommendations*).
5 Yes, also in *Recommendations*.

Vocabulary

1 Tell students that many of the phrases contain adjective–noun collocations, and that these and the ones in Exercise 2 are frequently used in business and when writing reports.

Suggest that they copy the collocations to the corresponding section of their notebooks and refer to them when they have to summarise figures or percentages.

Answers

1 c 2 a 3 b

2 Answers

1 g 2 f 3 e 4 c 5 a 6 b 7 d

Extension idea If you did Extension idea 2 in Getting started, ask students to look back at the figures they gathered and to write three or four sentences about them, using phrases from this section. They will need to use *students* instead of *staff* in their sentences.

Ask them to compare their sentences in small groups.

Grammar workshop

Reporting verbs and reported speech

1 Point out to students that, at this level, a particular problem is using different reporting verbs, each of which may be followed by a different grammatical pattern or preposition.

Tell students they need to learn these patterns and prepositions along with the verbs.

When they have finished, ask them to read the explanation which follows this exercise.

Answers

1 for 2 about 3 with 4 me 5 to

2 If your students are preparing for an exam, tell them that business English students often need to use reporting verbs because exam tasks require this, and that they sometimes make mistakes.

Tell students to consult the list of reporting verbs in the book to correct the sentences in the exercise.

If you wish, students can do this exercise in pairs.

When students have finished, go through the section in the Grammar workshop on pages 96–97 on *Tense changes in reported speech* to remind students. Then ask them to do the exercises which follow.

Answers

1 ~~complaint~~ complained 2 ~~ask you more~~ ask you for more 3 ~~tell that~~ tell you that / say that 4 ~~staff for a meeting~~ staff to a meeting 5 ~~tell about~~ tell you about 6 ~~agree to my~~ agree with my 7 ~~agree with the~~ agree to the

Extension idea Ask students to look at the key to the exercise and discuss why each mistake may have been made, e.g. 1 *complaint* may sound very similar to *complained*, so the student may not have realised that they were using a noun, not a verb.

Calls to HR

Listening

1 **Suggested answers**

1 the name of the department
2 a complaint about something which is too slow
3 something he needs to do
4 something to change
5 a place for lunch
6 reason for meeting
7 a type of manager
8 something to calculate
9 something in the staff survey
10 something to be a member of
11 something or someone from each department
12 a type of website

BEC Listening part 1   BULATS Listening part 2

2 ② 06–08 Remind students that they need to spell their answers correctly.

Answers

1 logistics 2 internet connection 3 track goods 4 service provider 5 staff canteen 6 working conditions 7 assistant sales 8 expenses 9 proposals 10 working party 11 one/1 representative 12 social media

3 Tell students also to refer back to the Grammar workshop explanation in this unit to check the pattern or preposition they may need to use.

Suggested answers

2 they have/had to (be able to) track orders in real time.
3 changing our service provider.
4 to lunch (in the staff canteen).
5 the meeting was being held was to discuss working conditions.
6 changing the way expenses are calculated.
7 with most of the proposals in the staff survey.
8 to be/form part of the working party.
9 each department sending/that each department send one representative.

Extension idea Ask students to imagine that they work for the same company and that they are going to do a role-play.

Tell them to work in pairs.

One student should take the role of Katrin Reiner in HR, or her assistant. The other should take the role of a member of staff ringing up to say something about working conditions or the staff survey.

Give students a short time to think about what they are going to say.

If necessary, ask them to look back at the telephone language they studied in Unit 4 (page 21).

When they are ready, they should role-play the conversation, which can be quite short.

Finally, they should change partners and report the conversations they had, using reporting verbs from the Grammar workshop.

Working conditions and social activities

Speaking

BEC Speaking part 3   BULATS Speaking part 3

1 Make sure an equal number of students are doing each task.

If your students are preparing for an exam, give them 30 seconds to read and think about the task. Then give them three minutes to do the task itself.

Remind students that they should make this a discussion/conversation with regular turn-taking, i.e. they should

– ask each other's opinions and ideas and react to them

– not monopolise the discussion

– listen carefully to what their partner is saying, not just prepare their next intervention

– cover both parts of their task and try to divide their time fairly equally on both parts.

2 Give each student a minute to present their ideas.

A survey report

Writing

BEC Writing part 2   BULATS Writing part 2

1 Tell students it is important to spend some time studying the input (charts, graphs, etc.) before they plan their writing.

Suggested answer

Chart 1 shows where staff feel the offices should be located;
Chart 2 shows staff opinion about office design or layout;
Chart 3 shows staff opinion about artificial light.

2 When students have finished, ask them to compare their sentences in small groups.

Round up by asking students to read out sentences they are not sure about and discussing these with the whole class.

3 *Extension idea* Ask students to write a brief plan for their report which includes:

– section headings

– ideas or content for each section.

When they have finished, they can compare their plans with another pair and make any changes they think are necessary.

4 If you did the Extension idea in Exercise 3, ask students to write their reports following their plans.

If your students are preparing for the Business Vantage exam, they should write 120–140 words in 30 minutes.

For BULATS, they should write 180–200 words in 30 minutes.

Sample answer

Report on staff survey
Introduction
The purpose of this report is to summarise the results of our staff survey into the company's offices and make recommendations.

Staff preferences
Just under half of staff (46%) said they preferred new offices in this district. Although more than half of employees asked for open-plan offices, managers told me they needed to have their own offices in order to have privacy and quietness. The vast majority of workers also stated that their productivity would increase if their desks were placed near windows.

Recommendations
On consideration, I would recommend first that we renovate our current premises. Despite the disruption, the costs will be considerably lower than the alternatives. We should also accommodate managers in their own offices, while making the office for the rest of the staff open plan. Unfortunately, the shape of the building will not permit everyone to work with natural light.

Extension idea When students have finished / brought their work to class, ask them to compare their answers with the sample answer at the back of the Student's Book. Give them some time to make any changes they wish to before handing their answers in to you.

Offshoring and outsourcing

Unit objectives

Topic:	moving business activities to other companies or locations
Reading:	scanning, skimming and multiple-choice questions
Writing:	a proposal
Listening:	listening to an authentic interview; multiple-choice questions
Speaking:	discussing outsourcing and offshoring; making a short presentation; role-play: discussing the pros and cons of outsourcing
Grammar:	third conditionals
Vocabulary:	phrases for starting and concluding a talk

Getting started

Warming up Ask students:

– *Do you know of any foreign companies which have opened offices or factories in your country?*

– *Why have they done so?*

– *What advantages has it brought them?*

When they do the exercise, tell students they can use the same examples again if they wish.

Suggested answers

1 Advantages
- The company may:
  reduce costs (e.g. labour, land, premises)
  benefit from more flexible working practices
  achieve higher productivity
  be able to produce higher-quality products
  have access to more advantageous labour laws
  be closer to markets
  pay less tax.
- The receiving country may achieve:
  increased employment
  higher tax revenue
  generation of wealth.

2 Disadvantages
- The company may:
  be more vulnerable to political changes
  find offshore operations more difficult to manage/control
  attract negative criticism, e.g. employing people at lower rates of pay abroad
  have higher transport costs due to its operations being more widespread
  have difficulty guarding company secrets/security.

- The receiving country may be vulnerable to:
  changes in company policies
  external market factors
  tax avoidance by multinationals.

When should we outsource?

Reading

BEC Reading part 3   BULATS Reading part 1 section 3
BULATS Reading part 2 section 5

1 Tell students to skim the article in a maximum of two minutes. Be strict about the time limit.

When students have finished, they can compare their answers in pairs.

Suggested answers

reduced costs, chance to focus on what you are good at

2 Remind students that the answers to multiple-choice questions come in the same order in the text as the questions. However, scanning the text to find names mentioned in the questions will speed up finding the answers.

Tell students that sometimes the name may occur more than once – they should underline all instances.

When they come to answer the questions, they should read carefully both direct quotes and the writer's summary of what each person says.

3 Give students ten minutes to answer these questions.

Answers

1 A (*… to let them focus on the functions they specialize in.*)
2 D (*… bring the actual cost of a full-time employee to nearly double their base salary.*)
3 D (*… outsourcing your legal might mean a bi-weekly teleconference with an attorney you couldn't possibly afford to hire full-time.*)
4 B (*… entrepreneurs often come to his firm when they find they can't answer banks' questions about issues such as cashflow projections.*)
5 B (*"Your potential cost savings are totally tied to the type of industry you're in and the complexity of what you're trying to do."*)
6 C (*… offshore contractors may require more time to manage thanks to differences in time zones, language and culture.*)

Speaking

BEC Speaking part 2

1 Give students two or three minutes to do this.

You can suggest that useful notes for this activity may consist of relevant vocabulary which will gain them a higher score in the exam and help guide them through the points they want to make.

Alternative treatment If your students are preparing for the Business Vantage exam, give them one minute to work alone to prepare.

2 Before students start, go through the Useful language box with them. Tell them they should structure their talk and, if they are going to do the Business Vantage exam, the examiner will expect them to be rounding off or concluding at the end of the minute.

Alternative treatment Ask students, when they are listening to their partners, to use this checklist (which you can write on the board) to give feedback when their partners have finished speaking. You can go through the checklist with them, pointing out why each point is important, before they speak:

Did your partner:

– *use vocabulary which was relevant to the topic?*
– *use a variety of suitable grammatical structures?*
– *get to important points in the topic quickly?*
– *structure the talk by introducing points, examples and reasons?*
– *speak for the full minute?*
– *round off or conclude at the end of the minute?*

When students have finished and their partners have given feedback, round up feedback from the whole class and discuss how they can improve their performance in talks.

If students wish, ask them to change partners and give their talks again, putting the feedback they have given and received into practice.

It may be worth your students copying the checklist above into their notebooks as a reference for when they do further practice of this task and to look at before the Speaking test itself.

Outsourcing IT

Listening

1 *Alternative treatment* If you find that there are a number of students in the class who do not have answers to these questions, do them as a whole-class activity using students who do have some information to give answers.

Tell students that, for questions 2 and 3, they can use their own suppositions.

2 (2) 09 Play the recording once only, then ask students to compare their notes.

Play the recording a second time for students to complete their notes.

Alternative treatment If you wish to give your students more genuine exam practice, you can omit this exercise and Exercise 3.

Suggested answers

1 more need for good people, growing, becoming more complex, coding of systems has been offshored, cloud-based IT, no need for companies to have their own data centre and servers
2 computer science, but not necessarily
3 understanding of technology, business understanding and ability to communicate with people

BEC Listening part 3   BULATS Listening part 4

3 Ask students if they can remember the actual words Duncan uses which give them the answers.

4 (2) 09 Play the recording once only.

Alternative treatment 1 If you didn't do Exercises 2 and 3, play the recording twice.

Alternative treatment 2 If you omitted Exercises 2 and 3, ask students to underline the key ideas in the questions. (**Suggested underlining: 1** reasons / needing more people in IT **2** tasks / offshored **3** reason / company to outsource IT **4** need to get to the top **5** which / activities)

Answers

1 B 2 A 3 C 4 C 5 A

Extension idea If you did the alternative treatment in Exercise 3, ask students to read the transcript at the back of the Student's Book and match the key ideas in the questions and the correct option with the words Duncan actually used in the interview.

5 *Extension idea* If your students are working, ask: *What is it best to study to do the job or profession you do?*

If your students are still studying, ask: *What careers are open to people who study the subject(s) you study?*

Outsourcing and offshoring – the pros and cons

Speaking

BEC Speaking part 3   BULATS Speaking part 3

As this activity is a little more complex than an authentic exam task, give students a minute or two to read and think before they speak.

Tell them to make some notes, including relevant vocabulary, while they are preparing.

Alternative treatment Give students five minutes or more to discuss all the points.

Tell them, when they have finished, to note down what they decided for each of the three points.

Especially if they are preparing for BULATS, ask them to write a report for the Board of Directors based on their notes. They should take half an hour and write 180–200 words. They can do this for homework.

A proposal for outsourcing

Writing

BEC Writing part 2

1 Tell students to discuss the pros and cons of each contractor using their own words. They can also suggest their own ideas to complete the notes.

Refer them to the proposal in Unit 11 (page 54) and also to the Writing reference (page 122) to remind them about things they can include in their answers.

Extension idea Ask students to write a brief plan for their answer based on the sections and headings they have decided on.

2 Elicit from students that they should use a formal style for proposals. Refer them to the section of the Writing reference on levels of formality (page 116).

Ask them to point out style features, e.g. contractions, choice of vocabulary, use of phrasal verbs, abbreviations.

Answers

1 b (more formal, less colloquial and therefore more suited to a formal proposal)

2 b (same reason as in 1)

3 Elicit, using the questions, that the third conditional refers to things which did not happen in the past.

When students have finished, go through the explanation in the Grammar workshop (page 97) with them. Then ask them to do the exercises which follow.

Answers

1 past
2 a

4 **Answers**

1 would have saved **2** had not been infected **3** had not broken down; would have completed **4** would have delivered; had been

5 Remind students preparing for the exam that, when doing Writing tasks, they should use their own words as far as possible.

Tell them that sometimes it may be impossible to paraphrase all the words in the task, but they should avoid lifting entire phrases from the task and copying them into their answers.

Suggested answers

If a round-the-clock emergency hotline had been available last year, we would have had an instant solution to our problems.
If staff had received IT support and training last year, they would have worked more efficiently.
If we'd used IT Remote's website hosting service, it would still have been necessary to design the website itself.

6 If your students are preparing for the Business Vantage exam, tell them they should write their proposals in 120–140 words and 30 minutes. They can do this task for homework.

Sample answer

Proposal for outsourcing IT
Introduction
The purpose of this proposal is to recommend an external IT service provider from the two we have investigated.

DataDo
Although DataDo's charges are comparatively high, they include all our requirements for running our website in their fee. If we chose them, this would produce cost savings, since we would not have to staff resources to this job. They also provide systems protection and emergency services, and if we had had these last year, they would have prevented the disastrous virus infection.

IT Remote
This outfit is a low-cost alternative. Among the services they offer is staff training. This would have been useful last year, but since our staff are now fully trained, this is no longer of interest. Although they provide web hosting, they do not do web design. If they did, their services would be more interesting.

Recommendations
I recommend we employ DataDo, as their services are more tailored to our requirements.

Grammar workshop 5

The definite article

1 3 – 4 the **5** the **6** – **7** – **8** – **9** – **10** – **11** the **12** the **13** the **14** – **15** the **16** the **17** the **18** the **19** the **20** the

2 2 to your letter to the letter **3** of a marketing of the marketing **4** all documents all the documents **5** that our new that the new **6** A fall The fall **7** *correct* **8** on a same on the same

Tense changes in reported speech

1 1 he/she found travelling to work at peak times stressful and time-consuming.
2 the new scheme was introduced, he/she hoped he/she would be able to take a career break.
3 had always wanted to travel round the world.
4 we/they could provide on-site nursery care for pre-school children.
5 in his/her last job, they (had) used flexitime, and it was / had been very successful.
6 I/we/they introduced the changes, he/she might decide to work part time.

2 1 arrives/arrived **2** would sell **3** wants **4** would install **5** wouldn't/couldn't go; finished / had finished **6** had sent / would send **7** would be

Third conditional

1 1 would have rearranged **2** had given **3** would have signed; had been **4** had raised; would have stayed **5** had offered; would have bought **6** would not have broken down; had followed

2 *Suggested answers*
1 … we wouldn't have had a cashflow problem.
2 … we had installed a good anti-virus program.
3 … we had had sufficient sales budget.
4 … we wouldn't have fallen behind with production.

Customer satisfaction and loyalty

Unit objectives

Topic:	achieving customer satisfaction and loyalty
Reading:	skimming; multiple-choice questions focusing on opinions and ideas; completing a memo
Writing:	an email apologising
Listening:	note-taking: encouraging customer loyalty
Speaking:	talking about dissatisfied customers; employees and customer satisfaction; short talks in a staff meeting
Grammar:	relative pronouns and relative clauses
Vocabulary:	*revenue, outcome, bottom line,* etc.; verb–adjective–noun collocations

Getting started

1 *Warming up* With books closed and students in small groups, ask them to tell each other about a time when they were a dissatisfied customer.

Ask:

– *What caused the problem, and how was it put right?*

– *What should the company have done?*

– *Can you identify any general causes of customer dissatisfaction?*

Answers

1 25 **2** 8 to 16 **3** thousands **4** 91% **5** about 85% **6** 4 to 100 **7** 68%

2 Go through the Useful language box with students before they do this exercise.

Alternative treatment Ask students to do this activity in small groups, but one student should look at the answers on page 100 and tell the others if they are correct. This will give students practice in reading out and listening to figures.

Extension idea Ask: *Are you surprised by any of the statistics?*

3 If you did *Warming up,* you can omit this exercise.

From satisfaction to loyalty

Reading

BEC Reading part 3
BULATS Reading part 1 section 3
BULATS Reading part 2 section 5

1 *Extension idea* Ask students: *What brands and companies are you loyal to? Why?* (These can be particular shops, products or services.)

2 *Alternative treatment* Ask students to skim the article in two minutes and then, in pairs, brainstorm all the ways which are mentioned of making customers loyal to a company.

Answers

ideas mentioned in the article which make customers loyal to a company:
good relationships between your employees and your customers
the value of the product they are buying
ease of doing business
your staff's responsiveness, integrity, trust and professionalism
having staff who are highly motivated, highly engaged
staff have necessary customer-service skills

3 Remind students to underline words and phrases in the passage which give them the answers.

Alternative treatment Ask students to underline the key ideas in the questions before answering them. (**Suggested underlining: 1** produces customer loyalty / Simco / paragraph 2 **2** Simco / paragraph 3 / key factor / company better than its rivals **3** paragraph 4 / main benefit / loyal customers **4** Hay Group / main factor / changes / satisfaction to / loyalty **5** Royal / difficult for companies to be different from their competitors **6** Royal / essential characteristic of a good employee)

Answers

1 C (*... when your customers have a strong bond with you ...*)
2 B (*... people are your key competitive advantage.*)
3 B (*... the impact that customer loyalty can have on your bottom line ...*)
4 D (*The top factor is value: 'Is this company's product or service having a positive impact on my business? Do I have a strong return on investment?'*)
5 A (*... it's hard to be different from your rivals because best practices spread across an industry very rapidly ...*)
6 D (*... empowerment, which means that organisations need to empower employees to make decisions and take risks ...*)

Extension idea Ask students to discuss these questions as a whole-class activity:

– *Why is staff attitude so important in producing customer loyalty?*
– *Can you think of occasions where bad attitude from employees has caused you dissatisfaction?*
– *What sort of behaviour is good behaviour for staff who deal with customers?*
– *Can you train staff to behave in this way, or is it part of a person's character that can't be changed?*

Vocabulary

Ask students to scan the article to underline the words from this exercise in their context.

Tell them they should read the context before matching each word/phrase with its definition.

Follow this up by going through the Useful language box with them.

Answers

1 f **2** h **3** d **4** c **5** g **6** b **7** a **8** e

Extension idea 1 Ask students to write sentences using four of the words/phrases (with a collocation where possible).

When they have finished, they should read out their sentences to the class.

For homework, ask students to check the words/phrases in their dictionaries and copy them with an example into their notebooks.

Extension idea 2 Ask students to work in small groups and discuss these questions, which you can write on the board:

– *When have you done something which had an unexpected/ satisfactory outcome?*
– *Can you recommend something which will give a good return on investment?*

Grammar workshop

Relative clauses

Tell students that relative clauses are an essential part of being able to combine information in longer, more complex sentences, and that they should aim to include these in their writing.

Alternative treatment Elicit that no relative pronoun is necessary for question 1 because it is the object of the relative clause.

If students have difficulty with this, go through the explanation in the Grammar workshop on page 114 before they do this exercise.

Students should follow up by doing the other exercises in the Grammar workshop.

Answers

1 which/that/– **2** which/that/– **3** which/that; which **4** who
5 which/that/– **6** which/that **7** where **8** which/that; who/that

Speaking

BEC Speaking part 3   **BULATS** Speaking part 3

Before students discuss, go through the Useful language box with them. Point out that there are many times when people don't agree/disagree absolutely, and this language helps them to express the extent to which they agree/disagree.

Ask students to read the questions and think how they can use the phrases from the Useful language box in their answers.

If your students are preparing for an exam, tell them that using phrases like these in the Speaking test will help to improve their score.

Encouraging customer loyalty

Listening

1 (2) 10 Before students listen, elicit that they should read the incomplete notes and

– underline key ideas in the notes
– think what information they need to complete them.

Alternative treatment With their books closed and without having read the notes previously, tell students to take notes as they listen.

Play the recording twice, then ask students to compare their notes in pairs.

Ask students to open their books and complete the notes in this exercise from their notes and from memory.

Finally, if necessary, play the recording again.

Answers

1 service desk **2** comment card **3** loyalty card **4** (local) schools
5 rural areas **6** computer equipment **7** sample shop
8 shopping experience

2 *Alternative treatment* If your students work or have worked, ask them:

– *How does your organisation go about building customer relationships.*
– *How successful is it at doing so, and how could its performance be improved?*

A staff meeting

Writing and speaking

BULATS Reading part 1 section 4
BULATS Reading part 2 section 3

1 Remind students to:

- read the whole memo before they start

- read before and after the gap

- think what type of word they need before writing a word in the gap

- read the whole memo again when they have finished to check it makes sense and is grammatical.

Answers

1 out 2 the 3 which 4 which/that 5 where 6 who/that

Extension idea Ask students:

- *Would you be encouraged to give ideas by the prize which is being offered?*

- *Do you think this is a reasonable prize to offer employees?*

BEC Writing part 1   BULATS Writing part 1

2 Go through the Useful language box with students before they write.

You can also refer them to the Writing reference and its Functions bank on pages 123–124 to help them.

If your students are preparing for the Business Vantage exam, ask them to write 40–50 words.

If they are preparing for BULATS, they should write 50–60 words.

Sample answer

Dear Simone,

I'm afraid I shall be unable make it on time for the meeting on Friday as I have a meeting with a client on the other side of town at one o'clock. However, I should be able to get there by 2.30.

My apologies.

Karl

Extension idea Ask students to compare their answers in pairs and decide if their partners have:

- covered all the points clearly

- not included anything which is irrelevant

- used suitable linking words and phrases

- used relative pronouns.

(You can write these points on the board as a checklist.)

Finally, students can compare their answers with the sample answer at the back of the Student's Book and make any changes they wish before handing their work in.

BEC Speaking part 2   BULATS Speaking part 2

3 *Alternative treatment 1* If your class is large, divide the class into groups of between, say, five and eight students to do this activity.

Alternative treatment 2 While the meeting is in progress, ask students who are listening to take notes on what the speakers say, as they would in an authentic business meeting. Tell them this will help them with the discussion at the end.

Communication with customers

Unit objectives

Topic:	quality and methods of communicating with customers
Reading:	multiple matching – customer care courses; dealing with complaints
Listening:	multiple choice – Not Just Food
Speaking:	collaborative task – why companies lose customers
Grammar:	which pronoun: *it*, *this* or *that*?
Vocabulary:	adjective–noun collocations

Getting started

Warming up With books closed, have students work in small groups.

- If your students are working, ask: *What methods does your company have of communicating with its customers?*

- If your students are pre-service, ask: *As a customer, how do companies whose products or services you buy communicate with you?*

With books open, ask: *Which of the methods in the box did you mention?*

When students do the task in the book, remind them that they should deal with both existing and potential customers.

Training in customer communication skills

Reading

1 *Alternative treatment* With books closed, tell students they have decided their colleagues in the company mentioned in Getting started need to go on a customer-care course.

Tell them they are going to look for courses, but first they have to decide some criteria for choosing one; for example, will it improve people's telephone skills? (You can write this first question on the board.)

Ask students to make a list of other criteria.

2 Suggested underlining is in the Student's Book key.

Extension idea Ask students:

Which of these did you think of when you were doing Exercise 1?

Which do you think are more important and which are less important when doing a customer-care course?

3 If your students are preparing for an exam, remind them that they should take time to understand the statements before they read. If they know what the statements are about, they should be able to read each extract just once only to identify which statements it refers to. Give them ten minutes to do this task.

Answers

1 C (*To address your customers' needs, you must be able to see things from their point of view ...*)
2 C (*Word of mouth is the cheapest and most effective way of marketing your business and extending your customer base.*)
3 A (*... how email can be used for effective communication with your customers.*)
4 B (*... practise customer-handling skills ... enabling a confident return to the workplace.*)
5 A (*... how non-verbal communication is interpreted by customers.*)
6 C (*... learn how to handle awkward customers appropriately.*)
7 B (*... an understanding of customer expectations and the skills to exceed that expectation.*)
8 D (*Call centres and internet sales are the fastest-growing operational departments for many organisations.*)

Extension idea Ask students in pairs to decide which of the four courses they would choose for their company (if they are working) or for themselves (if they are not).

Vocabulary

1 Tell students that using collocations correctly will make their English sound more natural and therefore enable them to communicate more effectively and persuasively.

Point out that collocations can seem to lack logic; for example, we can say *highly reputed*, but we say *a good reputation*. Confident knowledge of collocations comes with extensive reading and exposure to the language.

Answers

1 good 2 large 3 wide

2 Remind students that collocations are not fixed units of language and that more than one combination of adjective and noun is possible.

Tell them that students often make mistakes by using an adjective with these nouns which is not a collocation. They should pay special attention when using them.

Ask them to copy the correct collocations into their notebooks (the incorrect ones are given below).

Answers

2 most significant 3 big 4 important 5 big 6 high 7 big
8 important 9 big

Extension idea 1 Ask students to choose four collocations and write their own sentences using them. They should then read out their sentences in small groups.

Extension idea 2 Ask students to close their books. You then read out nouns from the exercise, e.g. *reputation*. Students then write down or call out collocations e.g. *excellent reputation, good reputation.*

Speaking

BEC Speaking part 3   BULATS Speaking part 3

If you wish to give your students exam practice, give them 30 seconds to read and think before they start speaking.

Since the task is slightly longer than a normal Speaking task, give them five minutes to discuss it.

Students should make sure they deal adequately with all parts of the task.

Extension idea As Part 3 discussion questions, ask:

– *What can companies do to make sure their products and service meet customers' needs?*

– *Some companies believe in continuous innovation. How important is it for companies to innovate?*

– *To what extent are customers becoming more intelligent and informed about companies and their products? How is this affecting the way businesses treat customers?*

Customer communication at Not Just Food

Listening

BEC Listening part 3   BULATS Listening part 4

1 If your students are preparing for an exam, give them 30 seconds for this.

Suggested underlining

2 original purpose / website **3** demonstrates / commitment to clients **4** take trouble / small clients **5** avoided / dissatisfied customers

2 ② 11 Play the recording twice. Students can then compare their answers in pairs and check by listening again and/or reading the transcript at the back of the Student's Book.

Answers

1 B 2 B 3 C 4 A 5 B

3 **Answers**

   1 By giving a discount when it costs less to do the work than they originally quoted, and by swallowing the additional cost when it costs more.
   2 By being fair (see answer to previous question) and by helping small clients who initially made them little money, but who then grew.

Extension idea Ask students: *Why does it make sense for companies to want a long-term relationship with clients?*

Turning complaints to your advantage

Reading

BEC Speaking part 3   BULATS Speaking part 3

1 ***Extension idea*** Ask students in groups:

   – *How do you personally react to complaints or criticism of your work?*

   – *How do you think you **should** react to them?*

2 ***Alternative treatment*** Ask students in pairs to look at the question and the section heading (*Turning complaints to your advantage*) and predict what the article will say before they read.

   After they have read, they should say whether the article reflects their predictions or not.

Answers

It gives an opportunity to build a stronger relationship with customers, increasing loyalty and business, improving reputation, improving services.

Extension idea Ask: *Does the company you work for do something like this? / Do you know companies which do this*?

3 Rather than correct the answers with students when they have finished, go through the explanation in the Grammar workshop on page 115 with them. Then ask them to check their answers in pairs.

   They should then do the exercises which follow the explanation in the Grammar workshop.

Answers

(with reasons based on Grammar workshop 6 explanations)
1 it (not emphatic and no distinction needed between two things already mentioned)
2 This (referring to the last thing mentioned – the opportunity for a stronger, more profitable relationship)
3 it (not emphatic)
4 This (to refer to something we're going to say)
5 that (emphatic)
6 this (to refer to something you are going to say)
7 This (to refer to the second of two things – in this case, how they can be rewarded)
8 this (emphatic)

Speaking

BEC Speaking part 2   BULATS Speaking part 2

1 Before students speak, go through the Useful language box with them and give them some extra time to think about how they can use it in their presentations.

2 ***Alternative treatment*** Ask students who are listening to say at the end to what extent they agree/disagree with what they have heard.

Corresponding with customers

Unit objectives

Topic:	writing to customers and suppliers
Reading:	a letter – multiple-choice cloze; editing skills
Writing:	planning and writing a letter about a new service; a letter of complaint
Listening:	completing notes from a telephone conversation
Speaking:	discussing how to keep customers happy
Grammar:	expressing results
Vocabulary:	*last* or *latest*?

Getting started

1 **Warming up** With books closed, ask students *When a company decides to launch a new product, service or activity, how can they communicate this to their customers?*

Extension idea Ask students: *What generally are the dangers of starting new services or moving into new areas of business?* (**Suggested answers:** lack of expertise, loss of brand identity, mistaken market research, less concentration on core business, increased costs with uncertain profits)

BEC Speaking part 3   BULATS Speaking part 3

2 This activity can also be done in pairs or as a whole-class discussion.

Vocabulary

1 To further clarify, ask *Is the company likely to produce more products and services in the future?*

Answer

most recent

2 Remind students that when they have doubts about which word to use, a good learner's dictionary can often help.

Answers

1 latest 2 latest 3 last 4 latest 5 last 6 last

3 Tell students that sometimes either word can be used, but the meaning will be different. If students suggest both are possible, elicit the difference. For example, *the last job I had* and *the latest job I had*: the former talks

about the most recent before the present one; the latter suggests that there will be more jobs in the future.

Suggested answers

1 the latest 2 the last 3 the last 4 the latest 5 the last 6 the last

4 Round up by asking students to tell stories about each of them to the whole class.

A letter about a new service

Reading

BEC Reading part 4   BULATS Reading part 2 section 2

1 Remind students to skim the letter quite quickly before dealing with the questions.

Elicit the need to:

– read before and after each gap

– look for dependent prepositions and collocations, as well as at the meaning of the options

– answer all the questions

– read through the completed answer at the end.

Answers

1 B 2 C 3 D 4 C 5 B 6 D 7 B 8 A 9 A 10 D

2 **Answers**

1 The letter has a heading after *Dear Mr Müller*. Note: in the US, the heading normally comes before *Dear Mr Müller*; in Britain, a comma (,) or no punctuation is used after the name, while in the US a colon (:) is used; in the US, titles like *Mr.* and *Mrs.* are written with a full stop.

2 valued

3 we shall be offering the same level of service

4 trouble-free

5 contact me personally

Extension idea 1 Ask students to write a plan for the letter with the main contents of each paragraph (**suggested answer:** paragraph 1: new document delivery service; range, speed and prices; paragraph 2: invite further contact).

Extension idea 2 Ask students to read the letter again, highlight any words and phrases they think would be useful in their writing, and copy these into their notebooks.

Ask them to compare what they have highlighted with a partner.

Writing

BEC Writing part 2 **BULATS** Writing part 2

1 If you did Extension idea 1 in the previous exercise, ask students to decide if the same number of paragraphs and general content is suitable for this plan.

Remind students that their letters have to have a clear structure and a logical development. If they are preparing for an exam, the examiner will be looking for this, and it is immediately apparent when writing has not been planned.

Extension idea Remind students that they should write using their own words, not lifting entire phrases from the task.

Ask them to work in pairs and discuss how they could phrase the content and information they need to include in their answer.

2 Students can do this task for homework.

If your students are preparing for the Business Vantage exam, tell them they should write 120–140 words in 30 minutes.

If they are preparing for BULATS, they should write 180–200 words in 30 minutes.

Sample answer

Dear Mr Rodriguez,

New Services from TopTen Leasing

As a valued long-standing client of TopTen, I am sure you will be interested to know that we are extending our leasing services to the whole of Europe. This means we guarantee to deliver the equipment you require anywhere in Europe within 24 hours of you placing the order. Also, for each seven-day lease, we will give you one free day. I enclose a leaflet detailing our service.

As you already know, we make sure that all the equipment we supply is in perfect condition, so you can be certain to start using it as soon as it is delivered. Also, as a premium customer, you are not required to pay a deposit on the equipment you hire.

If you would like to know more about this service, or if you would like to take advantage of it, please do not hesitate to contact me personally.

Yours sincerely,

3 Students can also compare their answers with the sample answer at the back of the Student's Book and make any changes to their answers that they wish before handing them in.

An email from a dissatisfied customer

Reading

BULATS Reading part 2 section 6

1 Remind students that they should skim the whole email first, then read it sentence by sentence, not line by line, to identify and correct the mistakes: there may be more than one mistake per sentence, but the basic grammatical unit is the sentence, not the line.

When they have finished, students should compare their answers in pairs. They should also read through the corrected email to make sure it now makes sense and is grammatically correct.

Answers

2 ~~of~~ with 3 ~~Past~~ Last 4 ~~who~~ which 5 ~~of~~ to 6 ~~an~~ the 7 ~~Although~~ However 8 ✓ 9 ~~last~~ latest 10 ~~they~~ which 11 ~~it~~ this/that 12 ✓ 13 ~~more~~ extra 14 ✓ 15 ~~in~~ over 16 ~~another~~ other 17 ✓ 18 ~~it~~ which

Extension idea Ask: *Do you ever use voice recognition software? How useful do you find it? What problems does it give?*

2 *Alternative treatment* Ask students to do this task while looking at the sample complaint in the email in Exercise 1.

Answers

1 Yes: when, where and the exact nature of the problem
2 Yes: especially if it caused injury, cost money or lost customers
3 Yes: this is essential, otherwise there's no point in writing the letter.
4 No: not unless it is related to the problem which occurred
5 Perhaps: but you should be careful about not angering people by threatening too much, and you should not make absurd threats which you will never carry out.
6 Yes: if this is true.
7 No: not necessary.

Extension idea Ask: *Have you ever written a letter or email to complain about something? What was the complaint about, and how successful was your letter/email? Why?*

3 **Answers**
1 (paragraph 2); 2 (paragraph 3); 5, 6 (paragraph 4)

Extension idea Ask students to write a brief plan for Roberto's email based on their answers to Exercise 2.

Grammar workshop

Expressing results

Ask: *Why is it important to express results or consequences in letters or emails of complaint?* (**Suggested answer:** You have to explain what happened as a result of the person's mistake or negligence, e.g. why it cost you money, wasted your time or lost you business.)

Students can compare their ideas in pairs and with the suggested answers at the back of the Student's Book.

Round up by asking students to read out some of their sentences.

Go through the explanation in the Grammar workshop on page 115, then ask students to do the exercise which follows.

Suggested answers

1 You delivered the wrong model. As a consequence (of this), we had to send it back.
2 Some of the goods were damaged. As a consequence (of this), we lost an important order.
3 You were late sending the information. This meant that we missed an important deadline.
4 There were several mistakes in the invoice. As a result, we had to spend a day sorting it out.
5 You sent the components to the wrong factory. This meant that we had to stop the production line for an hour.
6 Two of the pieces were broken. Consequently, we had to return the entire consignment.

Preparing a letter or email of complaint

Listening

BEC Listening part 1   BULATS Listening part 2

(2) 12 The letter on which the handwritten notes are made is the same as on page 107.

Remind students to read through the notes and check what information they need before they listen.

Play the recording twice.

Answers

1 Remind them 2 five/5 days 3 the results 4 problem-free

Writing

BEC Writing part 2   BULATS Writing part 2

1 Students should also use their answers to Exercises 2 and 3 from *An email from a dissatisfied customer, Reading*.

Tell them their plans should be brief with just the main ideas for each paragraph in their answer.

2 Tell students to write their answers in 30 minutes. They can do this for homework.

If they are preparing for the Business Vantage exam, they should write 120–140 words.

If they are preparing for BULATS, they should write 180–200 words.

Sample answer

Dear Mr Sarawi,

Late delivery of documents

I am writing to you to express my dissatisfaction with your document-delivery service.
Last Monday, we asked you to deliver some important legal documents to our clients in Katowice in time for a meeting with our lawyers on Monday morning. The documents did not, in fact, reach them until four o'clock on Friday afternoon, with the result that we had to cancel the meeting and reschedule it for this week. This nearly resulted in us losing an important contract.
I would like to remind you that we are a long-standing client of yours and that we rely on you to provide us with a trouble-free service. I must emphasise that we will only continue to use your service if deliveries continue to be problem-free in the future.

Yours sincerely,

Extension idea When students bring their answers to class, ask them to exchange them with a partner.

Write this checklist on the board and ask students to read their partner's answer while completing it:

Does the email …

– *cover all the handwritten notes?*
– *use a reasonable and business-like style?*
– *have a logical development?*
– *contain anything which is unnecessary or irrelevant?*
– *use linking words and references?*
– *create a positive impression on the reader?*

When they have finished, students should give each other feedback and suggestions for improvements.

Students then make any changes they wish before handing their work in.

It may be worth students copying the checklist above into their notebooks to keep as a reference for exam Writing tasks.

Business across cultures

Unit objectives

Topic:	how to manage your business career in different cultures
Reading:	who is best suited to working abroad; note-taking; missing sentences; cohesive devices; editing skills
Writing:	a memo/email announcing and explaining
Listening:	an interview about working in China and Europe; multiple-choice questions
Speaking:	typical business behaviour in different cultures; expatriate workers / working abroad; structuring short presentations; discussing a foreign posting
Grammar:	phrases followed by verb + -ing
Vocabulary:	adverb–adjective collocations with phrases followed by verb + -ing

Getting started

As a warmer With books closed and in small groups, tell students to make two lists: one of the attractions of working in a foreign country; the other of the difficulties of working in a foreign country.

Give them about three minutes to do this, then round up by asking the class to pool their ideas.

With books open, avoid students just saying *yes/no* to the listed points: ask them to describe what is typical in each case, e.g. *How do you get to know your customers? Is it important to get to know them? What are your working hours?* etc.

For question 2, students should mention any other points which have not arisen in question 1. This can be quite brief.

Working in another culture

Reading

1 *Extension idea* Ask the class:

Do you know any international or expatriate workers? What motivates them to work abroad?

BEC Reading part 2

2 If students are preparing for the Business Vantage exam, ask them to glance at the task here and in Exercise 4. Elicit that they should:

– first read the article to see its structure

– read before and after the first gap and underline anything which might refer to something in the missing sentences

– read the sentences, underlining anything that might refer to something in the article and looking to see which matches the topic of the paragraph containing the first gap

– work methodically through the article, matching sentences to gaps and crossing them off the list as they match them

– read through their completed answer if they have time.

– By writing a note in the margin, students are seeing the structure of the article and how it develops.

Suggested answers

Paragraph 2: How to find out if you're suited for international work
Paragraph 3: The difficulties of getting an international posting
Paragraph 4: International workers' difficulties
Paragraph 5: Advice for working in a new culture
Paragraph 6: Adapting to new conditions

3 *Alternative treatment* Especially if your students are preparing for the Business Vantage exam, ask them to do Exercises 3 and 4 at the same time. Give them ten minutes to complete the tasks.

Suggested underlining

1 assessments / conducting business
2 problems / Thus, the choice / not be taken lightly
3 to even pass this first hurdle
4 the rigors of a foreign assignment and foreign culture
5 inter-culturally sensitive way / What we may assume / constructs
6 will not be business as usual / Added to the complexity

4 **Suggested underlining**

A they
B Instead, most difficulties
C However / refuse to see things this way
D It will instead contain
E Only then will they be allowed
F This
G –

5 When students have finished, remind them to read through the completed article to check it reads clearly and logically.

Then ask them to work in pairs and compare their answers.

Answers

2 B 3 E 4 A 5 F 6 D

6 If you feel that this area has already been sufficiently covered in previous discussion, you can omit this exercise.

Extension idea Ask students: *Why do companies sometimes prefer to employ expatriate workers rather than employing local workers?* (**Suggested answers:** Costs may be lower; they may want to employ someone with specific skills which are not available locally; they may employ people they trust to work well or keep confidential information; as a bridge between the company's home country and the overseas operation; as a way of developing an employee, etc.)

Speaking

BEC Speaking part 2   **BULATS** Speaking part 2

1 Give students a couple of minutes to go through the article, but one minute to make notes for their presentation.

Alternative treatment Discuss with students what sort of notes they make for these short presentations: you can suggest that, given the short time available, the best notes may be short vocabulary prompts for the two or three points they want to make.

Remind students that the examiners will be listening for, amongst other things, the range of appropriate business vocabulary they use, so it is useful to note words/phrases down before they start.

2 ②13 You can play the recording once or twice as necessary. Students should then reconstruct Grazyna's talk in pairs, using the questions as prompts.

Answers

1 need to be culturally sensitive, learn the language, fit into the new context
2 First point: you'll irritate people, won't work effectively; second point: if not, you'll have problems, people will misunderstand, get impatient; third point: understand things from local point of view
3 Russia: managers more autocratic vs USA: consulting and discussing

3 Ask: *Why is it good to rephrase the question using your own words?* (**Answer:** The examiners expect you to use your own words where possible: this shows you can paraphrase and generate language, not merely repeat.)

Point out that Grazyna's conclusion is one shortish sentence. Students should also aim to be saying their concluding sentence as the minute is expiring.

Answers

1 I think there are three things which are essential when taking up employment abroad.
2 a Firstly, Secondly, Finally
  b because, If you don't, You see
  c To take a personal example
  d If you bear those things in mind

Extension idea Ask students to underline or copy into their notebooks any vocabulary Grazyna uses that they think would be useful in their own talks.

4 Ask students who are listening to note how their partners cover points a–d in Exercise 3 question 2 when they speak.

Extension idea Ask students to tell each other:
– what they did well
– anything they could do better, and how.

Grammar workshop

Phrases followed by a verb + -*ing*

1 ②13 Tell students that the phrases focused on in this exercise are very common. Ask them to copy them into their notebooks.

If necessary, ask students to check their meanings in their dictionaries.

Answers

1 good 2 use 3 worth 4 problems 5 point 6 difficulty

2 Point out the collocations in the Useful language box before students do the exercise. Ask them to note which collocations are used in the exercise itself.

Suggested answers

1 asking / applying to / going to
2 applying / going / trying / interviewing
3 attending / going to / holding
4 giving / showing
5 buying / ordering / installing
6 finding / succeeding in / making a success of

Extension idea 1 When students have finished, ask them to work in small groups and take turns to read out their sentences.

If their partners are from the same country, they can say to what extent they agree with each sentence.

If their partners are from a different country, they can say if the same advice is true for their country or not.

Extension idea 2 Ask students to look back to Speaking Exercise 1 and prepare a short talk on the topic they did not choose earlier.

Tell them they should incorporate phrases from the Grammar workshop into their talks.

Give them a minute to prepare, then ask them to work in pairs and take turns to give their talks.

If students are preparing for the exam, you can invite two or three volunteers to give their talks to the whole class, who can then give feedback on what the speakers are doing well and what they could improve.

Working in China and working in Europe

Listening

BEC Listening part 3   BULATS Listening part 4

1 If you have students who have experience of working both in China and in Europe, or if they know people who have done so, use them as a resource to talk about their experience.

2 ②14 Give students 30 or 40 seconds to read through the questions and underline the key ideas before they listen (**suggested underlining: 1** Rob's job involve **2** attracted / present job **3** comparison / Chinese jobseekers / Western jobseekers **4** advises Westerners / China **5** European companies / business in China **6** Chinese / job interviews in other countries / advises)

Play the recording twice, then ask students to compare their answers in pairs.

Alternative treatment If you want students to develop global listening skills without being distracted by questions and options, ask them to listen and take notes with books closed.

Play the recording twice.

With books open, ask students to use their notes and their memories to answer the questions as a way of checking the accuracy of what they have understood.

Answers

1 C 2 C 3 A 4 B 5 A 6 B

3 Ask students to think before they speak and to see if they can use phrases from the Grammar workshop when they answer.

Alternative treatment If your students are pre-service and struggle with this question, ask *What advice would you give foreign students coming to study in your country?*

Speaking

BEC Speaking part 3

Alternative treatment If you wish to give your students exam practice:

– ask them to do the activity in pairs

– give them 30 seconds to read and think before they start

– give them five minutes to complete it (since the task is longer than a Business Vantage exam task).

Extension idea Ask these follow-up questions:

– *Which do you think are most useful for developing younger members of staff: giving them more experience or further training? Why?*

– *How important is it to speak the language of the country where you are working or doing business?*

– *What are the best ways to encourage younger staff to take foreign postings?*

Writing

BULATS Reading part 2 section 6

1 Remind students to deal with this task sentence by sentence, not line by line. In other words, they may find more than one mistake in each sentence.

When they have finished, ask them to compare answers.

Answers

2 ~~win~~ get/gain 3 ~~know~~ learn 4 ✓ 5 ~~interesting~~ interested 6 ~~last~~ latest 7 ✓

BEC Writing part 1   BULATS Writing part 1

2 Give students a maximum of 15 minutes.

If they are preparing for the Business Vantage exam, they should write 40–50 words. If they are preparing for BULATS, they should write 50–60 words.

Sample answer

Dear colleagues, This is to say that we are looking for three members of staff to work in our Guangzhou office for six months to gain experience of Chinese working methods and to integrate our operations more closely. Those interested should apply to me by email by the end of this month. Thanks

Grammar workshop 6

Relative clauses

1 2 which 3 factory, where 4 which/that/ø 5 which 6 whose 7 which/that 8 January, when … force, and 9 which/that 10 which that 11 Klein, which 12 manager, who is very accommodating, is 13 whose 14 proposal, which 15 What 16 when/that

2 2 ~~programme that~~ programme, which 3 ~~what~~ which 4 ~~that~~ which 5 ~~recruitment that~~ recruitment, which 6 ~~which~~ who/that 7 ~~scheme what~~ scheme, which 8 ~~employees which~~ employees, who / employees who

Which pronoun: *it, this* or *that*?

1 This/That (*emphatic*) 2 this (*referring to the second thing mentioned in the previous sentence – being late, not the computer problem*) 3 that (*conditional*) 4 It (*not emphatic*) 5 this/that (*emphatic*) 6 This (*something more to say*) 7 that (*conditional*) 8 It (*not emphatic*)

Expressing results

1 meant / resulted in 2 means 3 As a result / As a consequence of this / Consequently 4 mean / result in 5 mean / result in 6 As a result / As a consequence of this / Consequently

Writing reference key

Levels of formality

1   2 *show*   3 *satisfactory*   4 *pay back*   5 *with reference to*
    6 *agree with*   7 *I look forward*   8 *asap*
    9 *Meeting's Fri*   10 dashes
2   Email 1 is more formal: uses *Dear ...*, no contractions,
    formal phrases such as *pleased to inform*, complete
    sentences.
    Email 2 is less formal: uses *Hi ...*, incomplete sentences,
    informal phrases (*mix-up*, not *confusion*).
3   2 less formal   3 more formal   4 more formal
    5 more formal   6 more formal
4   2 less formal   3 more formal   4 less formal
    5 more formal   6 more formal
5   1 good   2 bad   3 good

Short emails

1   1   A   to find out when he'll get the information he
            needs
        B   to change the time of a meeting
    2   A   He needs to give a schedule to their Chinese
            suppliers.
        B   A client's visit has been rescheduled.
    3   The information which she will send.
    4   Because he is writing to several colleagues or his
        team.
    5   He wants his colleagues to confirm that Friday
        afternoon is OK for the meeting.
    6   Because he is causing his colleagues inconvenience.
2   1 *Hi*   2 *Dear*   3 first name   4 appropriate   5 team
    6 *Cheers*   7 *Kind regards*   8 closely
3   1 A   2 D   3 F   4 C   5 B   6 E
4   1 as   2 to   3 it   4 as   5 by then   6 However
    7 because   8 but   9 this   10 it   11 and   12 Then
    13 that's
5   A less formal   B less formal   C less formal
    D more formal   E more formal   F less formal
6   1   No problem (F)
    2   I hope you are well (D)
    3   as we have an urgent job to finish (A); I'm meeting
        with the customer in two days and need to have an
        answer for them by then (C); as their end-of-year
        accounts are due (C); because we are hoping to take
        on more staff (D); The reason for this is that it will
        give them flexibility (E)
    4   I have been asked by the organisers if you could (E)
    5   Let's check our diaries (A)
    6   If you like, I would be happy to (E); I'll give our
        client a quote this afternoon (F); I'll get the job done
        tomorrow if that's all right (F)

7   Thanks for the emails yesterday (B); discussed in
    the emails below (C)
8   When will you send me ...? (B); Have we managed
    to backdate the accounts ...? (C); Please advise
    ASAP (C); I would certainly appreciate any
    information that you might have (D)

Memos

1   C (and possibly B, E and F)
2   *Suggested answers*
    A   Visit from Japanese delegation
    B   New training directives
3   1 to   2 so   3 them   4 order   5 therefore   6 this
    7 this

A letter of invitation

1   addressing the addressee by title and surname; no
    contractions; long words (e.g. *academic qualifications,
    combined*); less common words (e.g. *unique*); no
    abbreviations; complete sentences; formal phrases (e.g.
    I would be very grateful if ...)
2   1 c   2 d   3 a   4 b
3   1 f   2 g   3 e   4 h   5 i   6 c   7 b   8 a   9 d

A letter applying for a job/grant, etc.

1   *Suggested answers:* 1, 2, 3, 5, 6, 8 and 10
2   1 d   2 e   3 a   4 c   5 b   6 f
3   Paragraph 1: 1, 2, 3
    Paragraph 2: 5, 6
    Paragraph 3: 8
    Paragraph 4: 10

A letter of enquiry

Suggested answers
1   Paragraph 1: to introduce the company, its activities
    and importance
    Paragraph 2: to explain why he is writing – the product
    he needs
    Paragraph 3: to enquire about prices, installation,
    discounts and training
2   Because he is speaking for the company, not as an
    individual.
3   Indirect questions – they're more formal and polite.
4   Because he is talking about an imaginary or
    hypothetical situation in which they might place an
    order.

A report on a survey

1 1 e 2 c 3 d 4 b 5 a
2 A and B how C which D which E while
   F after G which H whose I so that J even though
3 1 more formal
   2 She uses an impersonal style until the last section
      when she says *I would also recommend.* An
      impersonal style is more formal and serious. The
      personal recommendation shows that she supports
      it.
   3 the number of visits, the sales, enquiries and
      number of respondents to the questionnaire
      The first figures show how important the website
      is, and the number of respondents gives a
      comparison with the number of visitors and shows
      how representative their answers might be; in
      the third section, the figures give an idea of how
      representative certain comments were.
   4 a Introduction b Our website: the figures
      c Our website: the figures d Findings
      e Conclusions and recommendations

A personal report

1 1 On the whole 2 Moreover 3 However/Unfortunately
   4 There was also a tendency 5 Although
   6 Unfortunately/However 7 For example 8 However
2 1 I found the store to be tidy, clean and attractive; the
      staff … were welcoming and helpful; visiting the
      store was a pleasant and satisfying experience; The
      store offers a generally excellent level of service
   2 directions and other written information … should
      be made clearer, and steps should be taken to make
      the music less intrusive.
   3 are issued; should be made; should be taken

Proposals

1 a solution to a problem
2 1 Introduction
   2 Customer complaints
   3 Possible solutions
   4 Employing extra staff; Outsourcing customer care
   5 Conclusion
   6 Conclusion
3 2 concerning 3 irritation 4 monitor 5 adopted
   6 attended to 7 a significant cost 8 outlines
   9 arise 10 resources 11 require 12 issues
   13 generate 14 concern

A short proposal

1 1 Due to 2 before 3 so that 4 until 5 also
   6 who 7 This 8 this
2 1 a 2 d 3 c 4 e 5 b
3 He is using *could* and *would* (the second conditional)
   for a hypothetical solution to a problem.

Exam skills and Exam practice keys

Cambridge English: Business Vantage

Reading Paper Part 1: Exam skills

1 2 Your sales can continue their <u>upward trend</u> even in a <u>difficult market</u>.

   3 You can read about how <u>companies with falling sales became successful again</u>.

   4 <u>Unlike other books</u> on this subject, this one makes <u>enjoyable reading</u>.

   5 You will learn how to <u>exploit resources</u> in your company which you were <u>not aware of</u>.

2 *Suggested answers*

   2 Your sales will continue to rise, even when it is difficult to sell.

   3 You can read about how businesses which were doing badly were rescued.

   4 Other books on this subject are boring. This one will give you pleasure.

   5 You will learn how to use positive aspects of your company which you did not know existed.

3 1 A 2 B 3 B 4 A 5 B

Reading Paper Part 1: Exam practice

1 C 2 D 3 B 4 C 5 A 6 B 7 A

Reading Paper Part 2: Exam skills

2 B <u>For this reason</u>, there is some evidence that franchises are less likely to fail than other business start-ups.

   C <u>Her</u> advice is you should set clear limits as to how much you are prepared to risk when you set up in business and how much you are ready to work.

   D <u>In other words</u>, unless you have a strong concept, your business is likely to fail, and you are likely to be left out of pocket.

   E Some franchises might <u>also</u> charge towards the costs of their advertising.

3 2 B 3 D 4 A 5 C

4 1 D 2 B 3 A 4 E

Reading Paper Part 2: Exam practice

8 C 9 F 10 A 11 B 12 E

Reading Paper Part 3: Exam skills

1 2

2 2 prompted Tim / start / own business

   3 Professor Keep say about apprenticeships

   4 Adecco, young people / taught the ability

   5 point / Tim / final paragraph

3 1 B (*Tim had always known he wanted to do something 'hands-on' …*)

   2 A (*His newly gained finance and management skills, coupled with his craft skills, gave him the confidence to go it alone.*)

   3 D (*… the most successful education systems in Europe combine apprenticeship and higher-education career paths …*)

   4 A (*… called for financial acumen … to form a core part of curricula from an early age.*)

   5 B (*He believes that had there been more awareness of the so-called 'real world' during school, learning the business-savvy skills needed to make it beyond getting a degree, he would have had the confidence to go it alone far sooner. And so might many of his classmates.*)

Reading Paper Part 3: Exam practice

13 C 14 D 15 B 16 A 17 C 18 B

Reading Paper Part 4: Exam skills

1 1 D 2 B 3 C

2 1 C 2 A 3 B

3 1 B 2 A 3 B

Reading Paper Part 4: Exam practice

19 A 20 B 21 D 22 D 23 B 24 A 25 A 26 B

27 C 28 B 29 D 30 A 31 C 32 D 33 B

Reading Paper Part 5: Exam skills

1 1 the 2 being 3 still 4 your 5 for (1st) 6 yet

   7 to (2nd) 8 for

2 1 the 2 it 3 up 4 for (1st) 5 *correct* 6 more 7 it

   8 the 9 of 10 *correct*

Reading Paper Part 5: Exam practice

34 BY 35 WHEN 36 THAT 37 CORRECT 38 IF

39 ARE 40 CORRECT 41 AS 42 ALSO 43 WITH

44 SINCE 45 EXACTLY

Writing Paper Part 1: Exam skills

1 a You have to go to a meeting with suppliers next Monday.

   Write <u>an email</u> to an assistant you know well:

   • explaining <u>why you will be absent</u> from the office

   • saying <u>when</u> and <u>how long you will be away</u>

   • requesting her to <u>deal with customers</u> while you are away.

   Write <u>40–50</u> words.

   b Quite informal – it's a colleague.

2 1 A 2 A 3 B 4 B 5 A

3 1 The first answer is more suitable.

   2 Less formal: contractions; less formal vocabulary such

as *out of*, *a couple*, etc.; phrasal verbs such as *deal with*
More formal: no contractions; longer, more formal
words such as *approximately*, *attend to*, etc.; fewer
phrasal verbs

3 so, while I'm out, in order to, As a result, in my absence

4 **a** You are the Human Resources Manager of a company
and you have decided to <u>change some working
practices</u>. You want to <u>hold a meeting with staff</u>.
Write a **memo** to staff:
- telling them the <u>reason for the meeting</u>
- saying <u>who should attend</u>
- informing them <u>when and where the meeting will be
held</u>.

b 1 We shall   2 holding   3 inform   4 proposed
5 working practices   6 All staff   7 attend
8 take place

Writing Paper Part 1: Exam practice

Sample answer
Unfortunately, due to exceptional costs at the Amsterdam
Trade Fair which we had not budgeted for, we are 1,730€
over budget. Could you please therefore make every effort
to reduce expenditure by phoning clients instead of visiting
them in person whenever possible until further notice.
Many thanks

Writing Paper Part 2: Exam skills

1 1 has   2 to   3 cannot/(can't)   4 on   5 that   6 would
7 that/it   8 to/for   9 sincerely/(truly)
2 1 c, f   2 h, m   3 a   4 i, n   5 j   6 b   7 k, l   8 g   9 e   10 d
3 **a** 1 with reference to   2 and would be interested to have
3 and at present   4 Firstly   5 for example   6 I would
also like to know   7 and whether   8 Finally   9 so that

Writing Paper Part 2: Exam practice

Sample answer
Report on customer communication problems
Introduction
The purpose of this report is to summarise our recent
customer communication difficulties and to suggest a
solution.

Customer complaints
Our customers have given us feedback on a number of areas
of discontent. Firstly, they complain that we flood them
with direct mail, most of which is thrown away unread
and is therefore ineffective. Also, our helpdesk is too slow
answering calls, causing them to ring off. Finally, several
customers mentioned our assistants' generally unhelpful
attitude, which causes irritation.
All this has led to a number of our former customers telling
us they no longer shop with us, resulting in a 20% drop in
sales over the last year.

Recommendation
To remedy these problems, I would strongly recommend that
we implement a customer-care training programme for all
customer-service staff.

Listening Paper Part 1: Exam skills

1 **d** 1 Fareham International   2 (an) invoice
3 never/not ordered   4 mobile (phone)
2 1 plus/+ commission(s)   2 exhibition space
3 business events   4 new clients

Listening Paper Part 1: Exam practice

1 warehouse
2 factory
3 research/Research
4 discount
5 team(-)building
6 feedback forms
7 motivation
8 presentation skills
9 testing/test(s)
10 delay (the) production
11 increase output
12 stock level(s)/stock(s)

Listening Paper Part 2: Exam skills

1 A campaign, copy, target audience
B container, delivery, warehouse
C bonus, deductions, payslip
D application, program, systems
E application, candidates, post, vacancy
2 1 C   2 B   3 A
3 1 e   2 b   3 a   4 d   5 f   6 g   7 c
4 **b** 1 A   2 E   3 C

Listening Paper Part 2: Exam practice

13 D   14 F   15 H   16 A   17 E
18 F   19 H   20 D   21 E   22 A

Listening Paper Part 3: Exam skills

1 **b** 1 B   2 C   3 A

Listening Paper Part 3: Exam practice

23 C   24 C   25 B   26 A   27 A   28 C   29 B   30 B

Speaking Paper Part 2: Exam skills

2 **a** 1 Firstly   2 For example   3 Another important thing is
4 So   5 I mean   6 A further point   7 This way
8 But, to conclude
3 1 Well, I'm going to talk about when …
2 Firstly, …; Another important thing is …; A further
point is
that …
3 For example, …

4 I mean, …
5 But, to conclude, …
6 employees, management experience, knowledge of the product, knowledge of the market, competitors, target customers, working knowledge of finance, sales forecast, estimate your costs, make a cashflow prediction, loan or overdraft, customers

Speaking Paper Part 3: Exam skills

3 a A: Do you agree?; What do you think?
       B: I like that idea; I think that's a good idea because …; Yes, and …
       C: I'm not sure; Well, maybe; Yes, but …

BULATS

Listening Test Part 4: Exam skills

1 b 1 B 2 C 3 A

Listening Test Part 4: Exam practice

33 A 34 C 35 A 36 B 37 B 38 A
39 C 40 A 41 C 42 B 43 A 44 B
45 A 46 B 47 B 48 A 49 C 50 A

Reading Test Part 2 (Section 2): Exam skills

1 1 D 2 B 3 C
2 1 C 2 A 3 B
3 1 B 2 A 3 B

Reading Test Part 2 (Section 2): Exam practice

1 D 2 B 3 C 4 A 5 B

Reading Test Part 2 (Section 3): Exam skills

1

Article	Pronoun	Relative pronoun	Auxiliary/ modal verb	Preposition	Other
an the	it they	what who	are be being can have	to with	although forward much so than

2 b 1 the 2 forward/together 3 had 4 one 5 with
       6 much/far 7 than 8 been 9 who 10 What
3 1 have 2 be 3 the 4 to 5 what 6 are 7 with /to
4 1 they 2 there 3 who 4 would 5 it 6 also
   7 Both 8 In 9 was 10 to

Reading Test Part 2 (Section 3): Exam practice

6 at 7 than 8 with 9 the 10 so

Reading Test Part 2 (Section 4): Exam skills

1 1 B 2 C 3 A
2 1 D (necessity/requirement/need for)
   2 A (spend on, expend, pay for)
   3 C (none of the others take a preposition)
3 1 B 2 A 3 C

Reading Test Part 2 (Section 4): Exam practice

11 C 12 A 13 C 14 B 15 D 16 B

Reading Test Part 2 (Section 5): Exam skills

1 2
2 2 prompted Tim / start / own business
   3 Professor Keep say about apprenticeships
   4 Adecco, young people / taught the ability
   5 point / Tim / final paragraph
3 1 B (Tim had always known he wanted to do something 'hands-on' …)
   2 A (His newly gained finance and management skills, coupled with his craft skills, gave him the confidence to go it alone.)
   3 D (… the most successful education systems in Europe combine apprenticeship and higher-education career paths …)
   4 A (… called for financial acumen … to form a core part of curricula from an early age.)
   5 B (He believes that had there been more awareness of the so-called 'real world' during school, learning the business-savvy skills needed to make it beyond getting a degree, he would have had the confidence to go it alone far sooner. And so might many of his classmates.)

Reading Test Part 2 (Section 5): Exam practice

17 D 18 B 19 D 20 A 21 C 22 B

Reading Test Part 2 (Section 6): Exam skills

1 3 start starts 4 ✓ 5 may can 6 have has 7 being be 8 showing shown
2 3 by in 4 on in 5 ✓ 6 from with 7 to for
3 2 extreme extremely 3 interesting interested 4 expansion expanding 5 brief briefly 6 discussion discuss 7 ✓ 8 possible possibility 9 fill full 10 ✓

Reading Test Part 2 (Section 6): Exam practice

23 affected affecting 24 owners ownership 25 up over 26 ✓ 27 another other 28 competitor competitors 29 too very

Writing Test Part 2: Exam skills

1 a A number of staff have recently told you that they are unhappy about the times when they start and finish work in your company. You have been asked to write a report for the managing director about this.
Write your report. Write about:

- why staff are unhappy with the times
- why it is important to keep staff happy
- what solutions your company should adopt for the problem
- any other points you think are important.

Write 180–200 words.

b 1 You must include the underlined points (see above).
2 Why staff are unhappy, why it's important to keep staff happy, solutions to the problem
3 statistics
4 the managing director, so a formal style.
5 a title and sections with section headings

d 2 It has a title, is divided into sections with section headings and it uses bullet points.
3 yes
4 The first section introduces the purpose of the report. The last section recommends solutions to the problem.
5 Phrases which express results: *means, as a result, as a consequence of*
6 Yes. Nothing has been forgotten.

Writing Test Part 2: Exam practice

Task A

Sample answer

Dear Mr Jaworski,

I am writing on behalf of my CEO, Mr Jaune, to give you a little background to problem areas within our company which we would like you to look at and, if possible, suggest improvements or solutions.

Our greatest area of concern is that we are not giving a sufficiently high level of service to our clients. In particular, we are late in completing orders, and on a number of occasions in the past year, clients have been invoiced incorrectly, leading to irritation and loss of trust.

Another connected problem has been that, on occasion, our production line has become disorganised, leading to delays in output and hence our unpunctuality in completing some orders. We hope you will be able to suggest ways in which we can organise our workforce more efficiently.

Finally, there has recently been more absenteeism both on the factory floor and in the offices. This is usually justified as sick leave, but we suspect that staff morale is low, and we would be grateful if you could look into this and suggest ways in which we can work as a happier and more cohesive team.

We look forward to your visit and your recommendations.
Yours sincerely,

Task B

Sample answer

Report on our company website

Introduction

The purpose of this report is to compare our website with GK Transport's website and to suggest modifications to make ours more competitive.

Our website and GK Transport's website

Our website shows details of our fleet of lorries, the loads they can carry, our rates and our major routes and our contact details. While GK Transport's site also contains this information, it has an interactive page as well, which allows visitors to calculate how much a load would cost for a journey.

Their site also permits customers to track their loads in real time and see exactly where they are in the international transport system.

Our website has some advantages over GK Transport's because it offers straightforward, clear navigation and responds quickly with any bandwidth, making it much easier to use. It also has the option of a quick link to a 24-hour helpdesk.

Recommendations

I would suggest offering a similar tracking system and an automated system for calculating costs, but with a direct link to our very successful helpdesk feature, so that customers using the system are automatically contacted with news of discounts and other special offers.

Notes and keys for activities and case studies

UNIT 1 Activity: The training budget

Objectives

- To develop general business vocabulary in the context of training
- To practise giving reasons and opinions and persuading
- To give exam-style practice in writing a proposal

Time: 40–50 minutes

When?: Early in the unit to avoid a clash with the role-play at the end, or as a follow-up to the unit, perhaps in the next class

Preparation: Make one copy of the activities on pages 100–101 for each student.

This activity looks at training more from the perspective of budgets and need, and gives students the chance to think about how companies might prioritise training needs balanced against the costs involved. Pre-service students should still be able to discuss the issues, as some of them, e.g. computer hacking, are of general interest as well.

As this is early in the book, the Writing task should be done carefully and time allocated in class to preparing students for it.

Go through the task to:

- check that everyone is clear on the language, the aim, the required content, the target reader, the style (neutral/formal)
- elicit likely content for each part and, if necessary, feed in useful language for each section as well.

Briefly discuss the differences between a report and a proposal in exam Writing tasks. (Proposals usually involve one or more of these functions – describing, summarising, recommending or persuading – and are often concerned with future situations. Reports are more focused on describing or summarising, and are more often written about something that has happened or is in progress.)

Answers

Vocabulary

1 c 2 e 3 a 4 b 5 d 6 g 7 h 8 f

Writing

Sample answer

Proposal for training

Introduction

The purpose of this proposal is to recommend which training course will be most suitable for our company, considering the training needs of each department and the cost of the training courses available. The total budget for training is $150,000.

Which training courses?

I suggest the company should spend money on the following training courses:

Course 1: 250-hour online training course in 3D programming (cost $130,000)

Course 2: one-day social media marketing training course (cost $5,200)

Reasons for choosing training courses

I recommend these training courses for the following reasons:

Course 1: Training in 3D programming is vital for our company, as the 3D market is expanding rapidly. If we do not invest in such training, we will be left behind in the market, and none of the other training will be needed anyway.

Course 2: This course will help staff in the Marketing Department to sell the new 3D games to our target market: 18–25-year-old gamers. This group is becoming less easy to reach through traditional marketing.

Benefits of the training courses for the company

The main benefits to the company will be improved sales to the company's target market and a better reputation for cutting-edge games products.

UNIT 2 Activity: Responsibilities and relationships at work

Objectives

- To develop language for describing company structure
- To increase awareness of collocations in vocabulary building
- To practise paraphrasing
- To give exam-style practice in writing a report

Time: 20 minutes

When?: As a review/extension activity before the Human Resources Manager listening, or before the Writing tasks at the end of the unit

Preparation: Make one copy of the activities on page 102 for each student. Make and cut out one set of the role cards on page 103.

Students practise exchanging information within a team while attempting to construct a company organigram. Students with little work experience may need some close support while doing some of the activities, as some of the terminology may be unfamiliar to them. It is suggested that business English dictionaries are available.

For the Reading and discussion activities, you will need to copy and cut up the 14 job descriptions (a–n) in advance. Do an example with the whole class to demonstrate the Reading and discussion activity. Show students how to give hints and clues, but make sure they know not to just read out the title at the bottom of the card before their partners have had a chance to identify the job being described.

When students have completed the Writing task, have a class discussion to decide which group had the best ideas.

Answers

Vocabulary

1 for; of; –; to **2** with; of **3** after; to; to **4** with

Reading and discussion

1 a **2** j **3** m **4** d **5** e **6** l **7** g **8** b **9** i **10** h **11** c **12** f **13** k **14** n

UNIT 3 Activity: Management culture

Objectives

- To develop language for describing working cultures
- To practise comparing and contrasting

Time: 30 minutes

When?: After the Sony Mobile Communications reading, as it changes the focus away from other people's experiences and more towards the students' own views

Preparation: Make one copy of the activities on page 104 for each student.

This activity gives students the opportunity to talk about their management style (if in-service) or their views on how managers should manage (if pre-service). It is a simplified version of the McGregor XY management theory, which is widely covered online, with plenty more information for teachers or students who wish to discover more.

If both pre- and in-service students are present, it might be interesting to pair them up to see how well theory and practice measure up.

Management theory is very culturally influenced, and it could also be fruitful to talk about how this theory might work when applied to different countries or cultures.

UNIT 4 Activity: Body language in interviews

Objective

- To generate discussion on and awareness of body language which can be used in the Unit 4 Case study *Hello Holidays*

Time: 20 minutes

When?: Either as a warmer to the unit (following on from Unit 3) or as preparation for the Unit 4 Case study *Hello Holidays*

Preparation: Make one copy of the activities on pages 105–106 for each student.

The content could be developed by discussion of body language and gesture in the students' own countries. It is certainly important to explore the way certain gestures (such as the ones in this activity) may have different meanings in different cultures.

Answers

Getting started

1 *Suggested answer*
When a candidate walks into the room for a job interview, the first impression is made in between three and seven seconds. Research indicates first impressions are based on 7% spoken language, 38% tone of voice and 55% body language.

Reading

2 **1** j **2** c **3** e **4** i **5** d **6** b **7** g **8** a **9** h **10** f

UNIT 4 Case study: Hello Holidays

Objectives

- To give speaking practice in job interviews and on the telephone
- To practise using question forms
- To practise letter writing

Time: 90–120 minutes

When?: This is a stand-alone activity and can be done after Unit 4.

Preparation: Make a copy of page 105 for the whole class, pages 108–109 for half the class, and page 110 for the other half.

Given the number of stages in the activity, consider running over the timetable for the different stages on the board. If possible, separate the two groups into different rooms so that they can prepare for their roles in private.

To set up the activity, look at the opening advertisement, checking the meaning, and discuss whether such a job would appeal to anyone in the class (anyone saying *yes* should go into Group 2 for the activity). Talk briefly about what such a company would be looking for and what type of person would make a suitable candidate. When dividing the group in two, it would be best if the interviewers were in-service students (but this is not essential) and the applicants were pre-service or those with an interest in practising their interview skills as candidates.

The interviews need to be carefully organised so that every interviewer speaks to every candidate, although interviews could be done with two interviewers to each candidate to save time. Make sure the class realises that they have time limits for the interviews. If necessary, ring a bell to signal that it is time to change to the next candidate. Interviewers need to check with each candidate at the beginning of each interview which job they are applying for.

If you have done it with this class, remember to refer to the Unit 4 photocopiable activity on body language in interviews on pages 104–105 of this book.

Answers

2 *Sample answer (Group 1)*

Dear Mr Roberts,
I am writing to invite you to an interview for the post of Office Manager on Monday 14 October at 11.30 a.m. The interviews will be held at our head office at 22 St James Street, London W1, and will take approximately one hour. Your travel expenses for attending the interview will be reimbursed.
If you are unable to attend at this time, please phone me as soon as possible so that we can try to find an alternative day. Also, please phone me if you decide not to continue with your application. We look forward to meeting you. Yours sincerely,

3 1 h 2 g 3 e 4 b 5 l 6 d 7 c 8 a 9 i 10 j 11 f 12 k

UNIT 5 Activity: Cool hunters

Objectives

- To develop vocabulary for describing types of markets
- To give exam-style practice in an open cloze reading

Time: 20 minutes

When?: At any point in the unit, although just after the AXE reading might be a good point, as the reading covers a similar age group to the 'cool hunters' idea

Preparation: Make one copy of the activities on pages 111–112 for each student.

Pairing mixed-age students (if possible) may prove a fruitful source of discussion.

Answers

Reading and vocabulary 1

1 1 b 2 d 3 a 4 c
3 1 innovators 2 trendsetters 3 innovators 4 early adopters 5 mainstream 6 trendsetters 7 mainstream

Reading and vocabulary 2

3 2 f 3 g 4 a 5 b 6 d 7 e

4 *Suggested answers*
  1 Because they have a lot of disposable income and there are about 32 million of them (in the US alone).
  2 Teens tend to be stubborn, i.e. difficult to persuade through normal advertising, and they only have one thing in common (for advertisers to target): the idea of being 'cool'.
  3 Cool hunters do a lot of research into teens which they then sell to companies, or use when they act as consultants to those companies.
  4 The writer thinks cool hunting sounds 'interesting' and that, in future, it may be a skill that people could put on their résumés/CVs if they want to work in marketing or public relations.

UNIT 6 Activity: Publicity stunts

Objectives

- To develop discussion skills in general and practise speculating
- To give reasons to justify answers and opinions

Time: 30–40 minutes

When?: Best used after the Drink Me Chai listening, as it develops the theme of promotional activities

Preparation: Make one copy of the activities on pages 113–114 for each student. Cut off the results section on page 114 to distribute at the appropriate time.

This activity looks at real-life examples of successful and unsuccessful publicity stunts; students are asked to think about what makes a publicity stunt successful, and how disaster might be avoided.

In the Getting started section, note examples of students' use of language for speculating (*may/might/could have*, etc.), as this will be useful in the Speaking activity.

There is a short role-play in which students are asked to come up with ideas for a publicity stunt. If the class contains both pre-service and in-service students, the former might benefit from being paired with those with more work experience. Emphasise that the aim is to produce ideas for discussion, not a fully rounded marketing campaign.

Answers

Getting started

2 A: Sony's plan was a disaster.

Speaking

2 *Suggested answers*
  KFC should have printed the vouchers in magazines or newspapers so they had more control over the number of meals people could claim.
  Honda should not have tried to deceive its customers by having managers write comments. It was too obvious. They should have accepted the negative feedback, acted on it and apologised immediately. This could have been an opportunity for Honda to work with their customers to make a better product.

UNIT 6 Case study: MyOfficeChef

Objectives

- To practise discussion skills
- To develop vocabulary range
- To improve reading and speaking skills for the exam
- To give reasons to justify ideas and opinions

Time: 90 minutes

When?: Best done after the Student's Book unit, in a separate class

Preparation: Make a copy of the activities on pages 115–117 for each student.

Some parts of this activity, such as the background reading, could be set for homework if time is limited.

Answers

Reading

2 1 F (Paolo Nugnes is a chef. Michel Dubois is a former financial analyst.)
 2 F (Other companies were already active in this field.)
 3 T
 4 F (They became successful due to word-of-mouth recommendations from customers.)
 5 F (Their turnover is £2.5m and they supply more than 1,000 lunches per day.)
 6 T (They plan to open similar businesses in Paris and Milan.)
 7 F (They want advice from a marketing consultant.)
4 1 C 2 A 3 B 4 A 5 B 6 D

Vocabulary

1 a 2 d 3 b 4 f 5 c 6 e

Speaking

2 1 B 2 A 3 A 4 C 5 C

UNIT 7 Activity: Location, location, location: which stand is best?

Objectives

- To extend the topic of trade fairs
- To practise presenting information
- To practise discussing and interpreting information in order to solve a problem
- To give exam-style email writing practice

Time: 40 minutes

When?: Any time after James Steel's email (Reading Exercise 3), as it adds an extra dimension to the design aspect of a stand

Preparation: Make a copy of the activities on page 118 and the floor plan on page 119 for each student.

This activity is intended to be a fun look at the problem of choosing the correct stand in a trade fair. Students have to co-operate to decide which location would be best; at first using their own ideas, then 'professional' advice is fed in bit by bit by the student with the information sheet (make sure you choose someone with confidence to perform this role, as it requires paraphrasing skills).

Depending on their first choice, the students will have to reassess their ideas as they go through the activity. Point out that this exercise also revises making suggestions and agreeing and disagreeing from Unit 1 in the Student's Book.

There is a Writing task at the end to bring all the advice and ideas together.

Answers

Speaking

4 Stands 17 or 11 are probably the best choices, although stand 11 is near the entrance, and this might mean people walk past it before they start to really pay attention to what's going on. Stand 17 has two sides, it is not too near the café, eating areas, toilets or exit, so visitors will not be in a hurry when they walk past. Also, it is in an area of related products or services – lighting, flooring and interior design – but no direct competitors like stands 14, 20 and 22.

UNIT 8 Activity: Quiz: Are you a good negotiator?

Objectives

- To extend and personalise the topic of negotiations
- To practise reading and interpreting information

Time: 30 minutes

When?: Either before the role-play (Negotiating) or as a follow-up activity in a later class

Preparation: Make one copy of the quiz on page 120 and the score sheet on page 121 for each pair of students.

This quiz focuses on the qualities of a good negotiator.

Don't give out the score sheet until all students have finished the quiz.

It is useful to remind students about the quiz results when they are preparing for the role-play or in feedback afterwards (when it may be possible to discuss any differences between how the quiz questions were answered and how they acted in negotiation conditions).

Answers

Vocabulary

1 leaves the table **2** get down to business **3** set my sights high
4 compromise **5** break off **6** demands **7** play it by ear
8 scrupulously **9** get straight down to work **10** your bottom line
11 run rings around you **12** outright

UNIT 9 Activity: A letter to a franchiser

Objectives

- To extend the topic of franchising from the Student's Book
- To introduce new vocabulary
- To develop gist-reading skills
- To give exam-style writing practice

Time: 40 minutes

When?: Best used at the end of the Student's Book unit, as it would pre-empt the material in the Reading *A letter to a franchiser* if done earlier

Preparation: Make one copy of the activities on page 122 for each student.

This activity extends the scope of the franchise letter from the Student's Book by looking at a concrete example of a franchise offer. It also gives students practice in preparing for and writing a Business Vantage-style letter.

The initial stages could be done in class time, with the actual Writing task set for homework.

Answers

Vocabulary

1 f 2 b 3 d 4 a 5 c 6 e

Reading

1 F (The franchiser has created the Petpals Plan for Business Success).
2 T
3 F (Their pet will be exercised and loved in their own environment.)
4 T

Writing

Sample answer

Dear Sir or Madam,

I am interested in the possibility of taking out a Petpals franchise because I have noticed the number of pets in my city and believe there is a buoyant market for the service your franchise provides. There are, however, a number of questions I would like to ask.

1 Could you tell me how much I would have to invest initially, and what turnover and profits I could expect in the first year?
2 What times do Petpals franchisees have to work at, and how many hours a week does it normally involve?
3 I would also like to know what training you offer to franchisees. Does it involve pet care or training in running a business?

I look forward to hearing from you and thank you in advance for the information.

Yours faithfully,

UNIT 10 Activity: Business start-up game

Objectives

- To practise presenting and explaining vocabulary
- To review language from previous units of the Student's Book

Time: 40–60 minutes

When?: Although this activity could be used at any time during the Student's Book unit, as the language covered is not exclusive to Unit 10, it might make a suitable break for some speaking between the Listening and Reading sections

Preparation: Make one copy of the rules and the game on pages 123–124 for each group of four or five students. Ensure that each group has a die and that each student has a counter.

You may have to act as 'dictionary' and referee in this game.

As the aim of the activity is to give students practice in talking about vocabulary and describing meaning, it might be a good idea to run through some useful language for

this beforehand. Ask the class to look at square 1 (*market research*) and elicit ways of explaining its meaning. For example: *This expression means 'finding information about things that people buy or might buy and their feelings about things that they have bought'; It is a kind of survey; Another word/expression for this is …*

UNIT 11 Activity: Location bingo

Objectives

- To provide more work on the topic of locations for companies
- To introduce new vocabulary for describing location
- To practise presenting information and justifying answers
- To practise intensive listening skills

Time: 30 minutes

When?: This activity would probably work best before the final Writing section in Unit 11, but could also fit in well before the Reading section in *A proposal* on page 54.

Preparation: Make one copy of the activities on page 125 for each student. Make and cut out enough copies of the role cards on pages 126–127 so that each student has a role card.

This activity looks at what needs to be considered when choosing a suitable business park for your company. It covers some of the typical vocabulary for describing places and gives students practice in presenting and listening comprehension, as they have to correctly interpret a set of requirements.

Answers

Vocabulary

1 d 2 g 3 j 4 a 5 c 6 i 7 e 8 f 9 h 10 b

UNIT 11 Case study: Finding a new office

Objectives

- To practise language for meetings and negotiations
- To practise writing letters
- To give exam practice of a multiple-choice cloze
- To practise language for comparing and contrasting

Time: 90 minutes

When?: This should be done as a stand-alone activity.

Preparation: Make a copy of the activities on pages 128–130 for each student. Make and cut out one copy of the role cards on pages 131–132. Make and cut out enough copies of the Additional information on page 132 to give one to each group.

Before students begin the case study, prepare a timetable showing the various interactions involved, as this can get complicated. Make sure everyone is clear on the different parties involved. Begin by asking students to summarise Intercomm's situation and aims.

For the second Speaking activity, hand out the additional information sheet to help students answer the question.

Reading 2 sets up the main activity, so go through the information on the two sites, do the summarising activity and discuss students' first impressions. If necessary, ask some comprehension questions to check their understanding.

Divide students into three groups for the role-play and give them their role cards. They will need at least 10 minutes to prepare. Before the first meeting, stress that this is just an information exchange and no negotiation should take place yet. Preparation for the final negotiations will take place during the post-meeting discussions.

After the negotiations, students should work in small groups made up of one person from each team to complete the Writing task. It is very important that the Intercomm representative does NOT reveal the winning site until after the Writing task is completed and checked, so gaps 1 and 4 must be left blank until then. When every group has finished the writing task, the winner can be revealed.

Answers

Speaking

2 *Suggested answer*
On this basis, Intercomm Solutions should lease the building. This is their first step in their expansion, so if it doesn't succeed, they won't have lost so much. Also, commercial property prices are depressed, so a profit on capital growth is unlikely and rents are also low, so a lease will be cheap. Finally, Intercomm Solutions will not need to specially equip the building.

Reading 1

2 1 B 2 A 3 B 4 D 5 B 6 C 7 C 8 A

Reading 2

2 1 B 2 A 3 A 4 B 5 A 6 B

Role-play

4 *Suggested answers*
  1 [*name of contact, name of business centre*]
  2 [*your name and position*]
  3 Lease
  4 [*name of contact*]
  5 connection
  6 [*date*]
  7 Following / Further to
  8 inform / tell / notify
  9 sign / take
  10 [*date*]
  11 look forward to / are looking forward to
  12 have any questions/concerns/queries
  13 hesitate
  14 sincerely/truly (*Yours faithfully* is not used when you are writing to a named person.)
  15 [*your name and position*]

UNIT 12 Activity: Handling questions in presentations

Objectives

- To present and practise language for asking questions in presentations
- To practise making exam-style short presentations
- To practise responding to questions

Time: 30 minutes

When?: After Speaking on page 57, as it exploits both the Clock Options Express Listening and the students' subsequent presentations

Preparation: Make a copy of the activities on page 133 for each student.

It might be useful to ask students to review question forms prior to the lesson in which you do this activity.

Answers

Vocabulary

1 **2** It was very interesting.
  3 I really enjoyed your presentation.
  4 It has given us all a lot to think about.
  5 You raised some interesting points.
2 1 d 2 c 3 b 4 a 5 e 6 g 7 h 8 f
3 1 say 2 Are 3 explain/say 4 telling 5 have 6 is/was 7 arrive
  8 based

UNIT 13 Activity: Intercultural advice

Objectives

- To introduce lexis for describing cultural differences
- To practise using advice exponents when giving guidance on cultural norms in the students' own country

Time: 30 minutes

When?: Either as a warmer for the unit or after *A company meeting* Exercise 4, which includes a Speaking activity on local customs. This activity would also work very well as a warmer for Unit 24, which has a cross-cultural theme.

Preparation: Make a copy of the activities on page 134 for each student.

This activity introduces some common lexis for describing different behaviours, then looks at an example of one type of business culture, the USA. When reading the text about the USA, point out the different structures used for giving advice (*be sure to …*; *make sure you …*; *avoid …*; *never …*; *you should …*, etc.); further examples of their use could be elicited and practised before the Writing activity.

Answers

Getting started

2 1 d   2 a   3 c   4 b

Reading

Suggested answers

Doing business in the USA

On arrival, be sure to greet everyone in a friendly manner; it is common to **shake hands with** people; **hugging is reserved for very close friends or for family. You don't need to** offer your business card with both hands; using one hand **is normal and some people even throw it on the table.** In business, English will generally be used, but remember that Spanish is now more common in some cities. Avoid telling jokes in business situations **when you don't know the other people – like everywhere, some** Americans can be very serious.

For business lunches in restaurants, the host will expect **to pay the cost.** If you are lucky, you will be invited to your host's home. This is **an honour,** so **behave politely, especially if there is something you don't want to eat.** Always take **a gift,** but **it doesn't have to be expensive.**

In work, Americans are very punctual and work long hours. You should dress conservatively, and men **often** have to wear a tie. Expect meetings to be long, as Americans like to discuss everything in great detail before making decisions, although money will usually be the key factor. People are **sometimes very direct with each other,** and silence is **uncommon,** as people like **to say what they think.**

Finally, you need to confirm everything in writing. Signed contracts are critical, and so lawyers are very important figures in American business.

UNIT 14 Activity: Networking

Objectives

- To give extended speaking practice in the context of networking and making small talk

- To practise language for social situations

- To practise writing skills in an exam-style task

Time: 20–30 minutes

When?: This activity could be used after the Reading section of Unit 14, as it links well with the theme of this section, or after the networking activity on page 68 to give more extended practice of the skill.

Preparation: Make a copy of the activities on page 135 for each student. Make and cut out enough copies of the role cards on pages 136–137 to give each student a role card.

Set up the networking activity by inviting students to discuss their experiences of networking and any problems they have had or any tips they can share for success. If there are more than eight students in the class, divide the class into two (or more) 'events'.

Put them into pairs to do the matching exercise (Exercise 1), stressing how useful it will be for the role-play. Check the answers, correcting pronunciation and drilling where necessary.

Go through the background information for the role-play (Exercise 2). Tell students that they will be attending the party and that they need to meet as many other participants as possible in the time they have.

Give out the role cards and allow students time to read them and ask any questions. Check that everyone understands their role and remind them about the aims of the activity, i.e. to meet as many people as possible and, even more importantly, to try and find someone with whom they have a potential business interest in common (either to co-operate on something or to supply a product or service). Remind students that they can introduce people as well, once they have met a few of the others. There is some overlap between roles, so students have to listen and explain things carefully in order to find the right person from the group.

At this stage, you could quickly review the language from Exercise 1 so it is fresh when they start the role-play.

When everyone is ready, begin the activity, possibly with a very brief 'welcome to the conference' speech. If there is a slow start, consider participating yourself to provide an example of how to act. If students look like they are spending too long with one person, instruct everyone to change partners.

At a suitable time, end the activity and see how many people have met a potential business partner. Ask them to explain why they think this person would be a suitable partner. For those who haven't found a partner, go to Exercise 3 and ask them to explain to the class what kind of partner they are looking for. Ask the other students if they have met anyone at the party who might be able to help. If they have, they should introduce the two people and have a quick conversation to find out if they are the right person. Tell them to report back to the class on the result.

Finally, hold a quick review to see who can remember details about other students – *Who's this? What does he/she do? Where is he/she staying?* etc.

Answers

Role-play

1 1 b   2 d   3 f   4 c   5 a   6 e   7 h   8 g
2 *Suggested matches*
   AB CD EF GH (although students may be able to justify others)

UNIT 14 Case study: Conference Centre

Objectives

- To give exam-style practice in multiple-choice cloze, editing/error correction and business writing

- To practise information-sharing in the context of telephoning

Time: 90 minutes

When?: Best done at the end of the Student's Book unit, as it ties together many of the themes of that unit

Preparation: Make a copy of the activities on pages 138–139 for each student. Make enough copies of the information on page 140 to give each Student B.

It is worth discussing why companies choose to have conferences in particular countries and what problems this may present. If students are not from China, find out what experience or knowledge they have of China and/or Shanghai. Refer to the Unit 13 activity on cultural differences (see page 90) for some areas to discuss. If students are Chinese, find out what they know about Shanghai and what cultural issues may be important when doing business in China.

Preparation for the telephoning task will take 10–15 minutes. Remember to give the additional information sheet to Group B students.

The final writing task could be set for homework if time is short.

Answers

Reading 1

1 B 2 A 3 C 4 D 5 D 6 B

Writing 1

Sample answer

To: Sales Staff
From: Mariano Fellini
Subject: Annual Sales Conference

You are invited to attend the Annual Sales Conference which will take place this year in Shanghai at the Radisson Blu Hotel Shanghai New World on 1–3 April.
Please make your own travel arrangements to the conference.
We will reimburse your plane ticket and other travel expenses to fly business class.
I look forward to seeing you at the conference.

Best regards

Reading 2

2 ✓ 3 and 4 do 5 the 6 to 7 ✓ 8 to 9 therefore 10 so 11 making 12 great

Writing 2

Sample answer

Dear Keiko
I'm delighted that you will be attending the conference. Your accommodation has been booked at the Radisson Blu Hotel Shanghai New World, overlooking People's Park. It has been booked as you requested from 29 March to 4 April to give you time to see Shanghai before the start of the conference. Thank you also for your kind offer to host a Japanese evening. We would like to take advantage of your generosity and suggest the evening of 2 April. It should be a great experience for our delegates, especially in the centre of Shanghai.
I attach a provisional conference programme with a list of the conference social events. As you will see, I have added the Japanese evening to the list. I very much look forward to seeing you at the conference.

UNIT 15 Activity: Speeding up meetings

Objectives

- To use meetings and problem-solving language to discuss a meetings-related issue

- To practise paraphrasing

- To give reasons justifying answers and opinions

Time: 20–30 minutes

When?: Best done between the *Talking about meetings* listening and the final meeting in the Student's Book, as it would be a good opportunity for students to practise language from the listening before they start the final, larger-scale meeting

Preparation: Make a copy of the activities on page 141 for each student. Make and cut out enough copies of the role cards on page 142 to give each student a role card.

This activity is intended to be a lively look at the problem of wasting time in meetings. This should be a topic relevant to both students in the group with work experience and pre-service students, who should be keen to learn more about the business world in practice. The ideas involved could potentially be adopted for future role-play activities in the rest of this book or the Student's Book.

The Galbraith quotation at the start of the activity should lead in to a discussion of students' own experiences of meetings, both positive and negative, before going on to the role-play.

Be sure to invite comments on the numbers quoted, as students may dispute them from their own experiences.

The role-play will need around ten minutes' preparation time, as students need to be confident of the meaning of their role cards. Make sure this stage is monitored closely and offer help where needed. Check that all groups have agreed on a chair and that the person selected is clear on their role.

Make sure students realise that the idea of the meeting is for participants to put some of their ideas into practice during it.

As the instructions mention, the meetings should be completed as quickly as possible, but nothing must be omitted. Double-check this at the end.

The writing activity can be set as homework if time is limited.

UNIT 15 Case study: Agrodist

Objectives

- To give exam-style practice in editing and error correction
- To practise meetings and negotiations language from the Student's Book
- To practise summarising
- To give reasons justifying answers and opinions

Time: 60–90 minutes

When?: This case study would work best in a follow-up lesson to the Student's Book unit.

Preparation: Make a copy of the activities on pages 143–144 for each student. Make and cut out enough copies of the role cards on page 144 to give a role card to each student.

Tell students that this case study is based on a true story, although the names of the people and the companies have been changed.

This activity brings together a number of business skills from the Student's Book, including meetings language and negotiation techniques and language (see Unit 8), so ensure that students are aware that they need to be using these resources during the meeting.

Remind students to meet, greet and introduce each other at the start of the meeting.

Allocate at least 15 minutes' preparation time before the meeting, providing help wherever necessary.

The final discussion point could be prepared for by dividing the class into those who think that profits are the main priority of business and those who agree with the idea of an ethical dimension. Allow them time to formulate their arguments before a formal debate.

Answers

Reading

1

name of your company	Marazon
brief description of company's activities	produces and exports large agricultural machinery
company's reputation	high quality, competitively priced
terms of agreement with Agrodist	• exclusive three-year dealership • three of each machine to be supplied at a time (one to be kept in showroom) • Agrodist to set the price • 10% commission on mark-up to be paid to Marazon

2 1 there → here 2 discovery → discover 3 none → any
4 While → When 5 it → them 6 Although → However
7 a → the 8 ✓ 9 to → at 10 that → than 11 ✓ 12 theirs → their
13 was → had 14 ✓ 15 This → These 16 would → should
17 one → other

UNIT 16 Activity: Business travel game

Objectives

- To use future tenses to discuss future predictions
- To give reasons justifying answers and opinions

Time: 40–60 minutes

When?: This activity could be used at any time during the Student's Book unit, although it might work best around the section on corporate private jets.

Preparation: Make one copy of the rules and Culture-clash cards on page 145 and the game on page 146 for each group of four or five students. Cut out the Culture-clash cards. Ensure that each group has a die and that each student has a counter.

You may have to act as referee in this game. You will need a die for each group of four or five students and a counter for each student.

The aim of the activity is to get students using some of the language they might need in travel situations. It might be a good idea to run through some useful language for functions such as polite requests and offers beforehand. Check what language is required before students attempt the task and hold a quick refresher of anything you think they may have problems with.

After the game, run a quick follow-up session where you elicit language for some of the situations encountered. Write it up on the board so students can note it down in their books. You could run through the culture-clash cards and discuss the answers, especially if not many were used in the actual activity.

Answers

Suggested answers

1 I'm very sorry, but I have catch a plane at three o'clock. Would you mind if we finished in a minute?
2 Could you call me a cab/taxi to the airport, please?
3 The airport, please.
6 Did you **pack** these bags **yourself**?
8 Can I have [a cappuccino], please?
9 Black/White with(out) sugar, please.
10 Sorry, but I think I'm sitting there / but that's my seat.
11 I'd like a mineral water. / No, thanks, I'm fine.
14 I'm staying at the Regency Hotel. Here's the address.
16 Yes. I have a reservation in the name of [*your surname*].
19 Could you recommend a good restaurant near the hotel / a good local restaurant, Italian if possible?
20 Good **afternoon/evening**. Table **for one**?
21 Yes, I'd like / Can I have the chicken soup to start, then / followed by the steak.
23 Can I have the bill (UK) / the check (US), please?
25 Good morning. My name's [*your name*]. I have an appointment with Mr Peters.
26 Yes, please. / I'd prefer [coffee], if you have any.
27 Good morning, Mr Peters. I'm [*your name*]. / My name's [*your name*]. Pleased/Nice to meet you. (*How do you do?* is possible, although becoming old fashioned.)
29 What a beautiful day! / This is my first time in [New York]. It's an amazing place.
30 Thank you for a very interesting meeting. Are you free for dinner tonight? (*more informal*) / I'd like to invite you to be my guest for dinner tonight. (*more formal*)
31 Could you tell me the way to / tell me how to get to the Regency Hotel, please?
33 I'd like to check out, please.
34 Can I have a (single/return (BrE) / one-way/round-trip (AmE)) ticket to [*place*], please?
36 Do you mind me opening / Would you mind if I opened the window?
37 Can I give you / Would you like a hand with that? / Can I help you with that?
38 This is [*your name*]. I'm on the train now and I should be there / arrive (around) four o'clock.
40 Is this seat free/taken? / Is anyone sitting here? / Do you mind if I sit here?
41 Thanks, but I'm afraid I have to get to the airport / to catch a plane. Next time, perhaps?
43 Give **my regards** to Tony.
45 Do you have these in a [45]?
47 **Good/Nice/Pleasant / How was your** trip?
    Very good/interesting/successful, thanks.

UNIT 17 Activity: Traditional marketing vs. social media marketing

Objectives

- To improve speaking and discussion skills
- To practise problem-solving and presenting/exchanging information
- To develop students' vocabulary range

Time: 45–60 minutes

When?: This activity is best done after the Felicity Bannerman listening on page 80, after the four reading passages on page 82, or as a follow-up after the Student's Book unit is finished.

Preparation: Make a copy of the activities on pages 147–148 for each student.

This activity allows students the opportunity to express their views on and experience of social media in contrast to more traditional types of marketing. It is intended to be a mini case study. Some of the detail on social media marketing is deliberately vague, as the situation is developing rapidly, and dating is always a possibility with this type of material. The aim is to draw in elements of earlier units, such as the contrast with traditional marketing and promotion (Units 5 and 6), meetings language (Unit 15) and negotiations (Unit 8).

When discussing the two opposing views of traditional marketing, make sure students are able to express their views using language from previous units and that they give reasons for their ideas and opinions, as this is an important exam skill.

The role-play activity involves forming and reforming groups, so make sure that there is adequate space for this and that your instructions about who is in each group, A and B, are clearly understood. The activity ends when the class votes on who had the best ideas for a combined marketing strategy.

Answers

Vocabulary

1 c 2 f 3 a 4 e 5 b 6 g 7 h 8 d

Role-play

3 *Possible strategy*

1 Establish a strong online presence that includes a regularly updated website (including a blog), Twitter and Facebook as a minimum, although there may be other options in your country.
2 There are online tools to help you manage all your social-networking profiles from one site. Spend 20 minutes twice a day reviewing and responding to messages, sharing articles, starting dialogues with interesting people, and tracking topics important to your business.
3 Begin integrating interactive media into your traditional marketing initiatives. Offer 'Like Us on Facebook and receive a 20% discount on your next course' in your radio and TV ads (although TV is probably not an option for a school), implement a QR code in your next print advertisement that directs customers to your website or Facebook page.
4 Training is vital to becoming more efficient and effective with your digital marketing.

UNIT 18 Activity: Greening the office

Objectives

- To widen the topic of the green office (as covered in the Student's Book)
- To practise presenting and defending an argument
- To develop vocabulary for describing environmental issues

Time: 40 minutes

When?: This activity could be used to help students in the Writing activity, *Reducing waste*, on page 86, although it would also be useful after the Reading, *The green office*, on page 84.

Preparation: Make a copy of the activities on page 149 for each student.

This activity extends the theme from *The green office* (see page 84 of the Student's Book) to include another set of ideas that might be adopted to make the workplace more environmentally friendly. Some of the ideas should already be familiar to students, both in- and pre-service, but a number of common misconceptions are included to make the activity more engaging.

Students should work in small groups of three or four to discuss their ideas. It is important that everyone takes turns to present a point and that students take notes, as they will need them when they form new groups for the final stage, agreeing on a shortlist of ideas.

Finally, give feedback on each of the points (as in the key), pointing out the misconceptions mentioned.

Answers

Vocabulary

1 e 2 c 3 a 4 h 5 g 6 b 7 d 8 f

Role-play

1 It is always best to switch off your computer when you finish work for the day. It is not true that running a computer uses less energy than switching one on. It costs around $5,000 per year to run 100 computers continuously.
2 Low-energy bulbs *are* more efficient if you don't keep switching them on and off, but only if you're out of the room for less than 15 minutes. Otherwise, switch them off.
3 Undoubtedly, car pooling is a greener option. The convenience factor varies.
4 The pollution figures are correct. In fact, 25% of car journeys are less than 1.5km long.
5 Consider replanting with plants that tolerate dry conditions.
6 Both are true. Figures vary, but making a new car uses energy equivalent to driving over 35,000km.
7 Trick question! They are both true, but paper cups are made from a renewable resource so are slightly greener. The best option is to use your own cup or mug.
8 The figures quoted are generally true, although a lot depends on the energy efficiency of the building.

UNIT 19 Activity: Managing change

Objectives

- To extend the theme of change from the Student's Book into a personalised exercise in problem-solving and advice-giving
- To practise using advice exponents and asking future questions

Time: 30 minutes

When?: As a warmer or as a closing activity for the Student's Book unit

Preparation: Make a copy of the activities on page 150 for each student.

The aim of this activity is to give students the chance to discuss personal experiences of change, whether in work or studies, making it suitable for both pre- and in-service students.

Before the class begins the main activity, there is a short discussion on attitudes to change. Check whether students have any similar sayings to the one in the introduction in their own language(s). You could also introduce the saying 'Variety is the spice of life'.

It might be a good idea, especially with weaker classes, to demonstrate Speaking Exercises 2 and 3 by presenting a (real or imaginary) scenario which the class can analyse using the template before moving on to the advice-giving stage. Feed in language as necessary.

When it comes to the students doing the activity, make sure they are clear that their example can be either a current one *or* something from the past, where the outcome is already known – but that if it is the latter, they must not say so until after the activity is finished and that they should describe it as if it were current, using present tenses.

Students could be told for homework to think about a situation to discuss in Speaking Exercises 2 and 3.

UNIT 19 Case study: Fendara SL

Objectives

- To give students more work and background on the benefits of flexible working conditions
- To practise presenting information and justifying suggestions
- To practise writing proposals
- To highlight differences between reports and proposals

Time: 40 minutes

When?: Since the final outcome of the study is for students to write a proposal, it is probably best done after you have finished work on the unit (which focuses on writing reports).

Preparation: Make a copy of the activities on pages 151–152 for each student.

Use the quotation from Herb Kelleher to lead in to the topic of putting employees first and how this can affect working practices. Make sure students are clear on the situation at Fendara by asking individuals to paraphrase the information on the company at the beginning of the reading task.

As students work on the task of summarising the three companies, monitor and be ready to help with any problem language.

The writing task could be done for homework.

As reports and proposals have very similar formats and styles, this may be a good opportunity for you to remind students of the similarities and differences between the two types of writing task.

Answers

Reading

1 1 Chart 1 shows changes in staff turnover from 2010 to last year and illustrates the problem that staff turnover has risen by 6% during this period.

Chart 2 shows changes in recruitment costs per worker over the same period, and the problem that these have increased from €30,000 to €35,000.

Chart 3 illustrates the reasons why staff are leaving.

  2 The problem is that most find better conditions elsewhere, while childcare problems and pay are a significant factor. Retirement is a normal occurrence, rather than part of the problem.

2 1 Brite Paints
  2 Manufacturing
  3 50
  4 tight labour market, recruitment difficulties
  5 flexible working hours to combine with family commitments – tailored to individual requirements, flexible job routines
  6 CHF7,000 in job advertising costs, lower recruitment costs
  7 staff retention, all work and hours covered, larger skills base

  1 Vienna Electronics
  2 Manufacturing
  3 1,700
  4 improving employee loyalty and performance
  5 Staff can request: flexible working, paid adoption leave, helpline service, reduced hours, term-time working and career breaks
  6 €45,000 for each employee who leaves the company
  7 Reduction in staff turnover, improved performance, staff see benefits of working for company

  1 Guangzhou Engineering
  2 Manufacturing
  3 50
  4 more contented workforce, improved performance, higher efficiency, increased competitiveness
  5 Staff must work 1,770 hours per year, maintain core hours, and work when there is a production peak. Otherwise they can choose when to work. Time can be taken for sickness, etc.
  6 not given
  7 as above, and better teamwork

Writing

Sample answer

Proposal on changes to working practices at Fendara SL

The purpose of this proposal is to recommend changes to working practices with reference to costs, HR issues and benefits to staff.

Background

Fendara's staff turnover from 2001 to last year has risen by 6%. At the same time, recruitment costs per worker have increased from €30,000 to €35,000. There is also a serious problem with staff retention. People are leaving because they find better conditions elsewhere, and there is dissatisfaction with childcare and pay.

How working practices should change at Fendara

Following a study of the practices of three other manufacturing companies, Brite Paints, Vienna Electronics and Guangzhou Engineering, it is clear that we must improve flexibility in working hours. It is suggested that we calculate a core number of working hours and then allow staff to tailor their schedules to their own individual requirements, with time off for personal reasons, such as childcare or sickness.

Effects on HR

The changes above could reduce staff turnover by up to 50%, based on the research carried out, and this in turn would mean we would need to recruit only 14–18 new staff per year, instead of the current 30–35.

Financial effects

It is estimated that we could save around €500,000 on recruitment costs alone, with a potential boost to turnover of 8–10%, as less time would be needed for training new staff.

Benefits to staff

The changes proposed will keep the majority of staff happy and raise staff morale and productivity, as staff will feel more loyalty to the company.

UNIT 20 Activity: Outsourcing survey

Objectives

- To give students the opportunity to discuss their personal opinions on the topic of outsourcing
- To practise presenting statistics
- To practise report writing

Time: 30 minutes

When?: This activity would work well after *Getting started* and before the reading *When should we outsource?*.

Preparation: Make a copy of the activities on page 153 for each student.

The aim of this activity is to give students the opportunity to discuss their attitudes and opinions to the various aspects of outsourcing by carrying out a survey of the other members of the class.

The activity may be quite challenging for students with no working experience. If you have a class with a mix of people with and without working experience, it would be a good idea to avoid giving Box A to inexperienced students.

Once the class has been grouped appropriately, take them through the instructions, emphasising the importance of making accurate notes, which they will need to refer to when presenting the results of their surveys and when writing the reports.

Students may need to be reminded about how to refer to statistics, so it might be useful to do a quick refresher on the board.

The report could be set for homework, but be sure to discuss how it could be organised (refer back to previous examples of report structure).

UNIT 21 Activity: Good customer service?

Objectives

- To introduce the topic of good customer service
- To practise modal verbs for speculating and making deductions

Time: 30–40 minutes

When?: This activity is best done after the Speaking and before the Listening *Encouraging customer loyalty* on page 101.

Preparation: Make a copy of the activities on pages 154–155 for each student.

The activity begins with a discussion of students' own experiences, both good and bad. It is an opportunity to feed in language which will be useful in the second part of the activity, e.g. *they should(n't) have.*

In the second part of the activity, students discuss five examples of fairly typical customer-care situations and have the opportunity to discuss what they think happened, what the consequences could be for the company and ways the company could have turned the situation around.

The activity concludes with a writing exercise (which could be done on computers if available) in which students present their ideas about two of the situations and post them on the walls so that the rest of the class can read and evaluate them.

Answers

Reading and discussion

3 a – 2 – i
  b – 3 – ii
  c – 1 – iii

Writing

Sample answers

d Dear ......
  As you may know, a local company ordered some sandwiches from us for a lunchtime meeting. Unfortunately, we then received another, larger order from another client and prioritised that. Because of this, we failed to meet the first order, and the clients were not satisfied with our service. They might never use us again and our competitors will benefit.
  We should telephone the client immediately and apologise. We should also send the company free sandwiches and chocolates before lunch tomorrow.

e Dear ......
  We have just completed the new website for ABC Ltd, and the client has complained that some people have said the site looks 'ugly'. All the changes to the site were made at the client's instruction, despite our objections.
  The client will probably now not recommend us to other people, but this might not be a disaster, as they do have a reputation as a difficult client.
  We should make one final attempt to meet the client and explain patiently and carefully what the problem is and how it can be fixed. I think we should always do our best to give clients what they want, but there are limits. There is a saying that the customer is always right, but sometimes it's just not true.

UNIT 22 Activity: Designing a customer communication competition

Objectives

- To introduce the topic of customer communications as a lead-in to the unit in the Student's Book
- To practise language for decision-making and problem-solving

Time: 40–60 minutes

When?: This activity is best done as a lead-in to the Student's Book unit.

Preparation: Make a copy of the activities on page 156 for each student.

This activity introduces the idea of effective customer communications. The aim is to get students to design a competition in which the entries will provide their company with useful information on how their customers feel about the company's communication with them. This could take the form of likes and dislikes (leading to changes in communications strategy) or suggestions for making improvements (the company should adopt new or better means of communications based on suggestions received). Probably most students in the class will never have done anything like this before, but even pre-service students will have had experience from a customer's point of view and should be able to exploit this experience in the activity.

If you can find a genuine example of such a competition, you could use it as an example when setting up the activity.

Guide the groups carefully through the instructions, ensuring that they understand that they are designing the competition for their company and that they are clear on the aims of the competition, i.e. to get information that their company can use to improve communications with their customers. Each group should work separately so they all come to the competition entry stage fresh.

If time is limited, the competition design could be done in class and the entries done as homework, with the advantage that more entries will be generated.

Once the winning entry/entries for each competition have been decided and announced, you could post the different competition entries around the class so students have a chance to look at and compare the other competitions.

UNIT 23 Activity: An email of apology

Objectives

- To complement the topic of customer correspondence by introducing the topic of letters of complaint

- To practise editing and error correction

- To extend students' range of expressions for letter writing

- To practise writing skills

Time: 40–60 minutes

When?: This activity could be done at any time after the Reading *An email from a dissatisfied customer* on page 108.

Preparation: Make a copy of the activities on pages 157–158 for each student.

This activity looks at the topic of emails of apology. It is worth pointing out that this is a common area for Business Vantage/BULATS and that for every complaint email there should be a corresponding apology. As the Student's Book focuses on letters from businesses giving information to customers and on complaints to companies from customers, this activity is a natural follow-on which introduces and gives practice in apologising to customers.

Begin by discussing the students' personal experiences of complaining. Steer the discussion in the direction of how companies can handle complaints and why they might write a letter or email of apology. Invite students to give personal examples of apologies they have received and link this with question 2 (*Should companies be grateful when customers complain?*) to generate some discussion of what makes an effective apology, before looking at the Reading task.

Remind students that the Reading task is a typical exam task and briefly discuss strategies for this type of task. Exercises 3 and 4 in the Reading task develop language for writing letters of apology which could be used in the Writing task. Again, discuss strategies for dealing with this type of task and remind students about the importance of including *all* the handwritten notes in their answers.

The actual writing could be set for homework.

Answers

Reading

1 The points from Getting started Exercise 2 which were mentioned are: a, b, c, d, f and g.
2 1 it 2 ✓ 3 is 4 ✓ 5 However 6 occurred 7 So 8 to 9 ✓
   10 time 11 the 12 which
3 1 We very much regret the inconvenience that it has caused you.
   2 I am sorry for the annoyance this has caused.
   3 The damage may have been due to …
   4 Could you please keep …

Writing

2 *Sample answer*
   Dear Mr Castle,

   Incorrect and late delivery of equipment
   Thank you for your email about the mistakes in the delivery of equipment to the Berlin area. We do apologise for the inconvenience this caused you.
   The mistake which occurred was entirely our fault. This was because two different but similar orders which were received simultaneously in our warehouse were mixed up. The equipment which we should have sent to you was sent to Edinburgh, and the equipment for Edinburgh was sent to you.
   We completely understand how this mistake will have affected your costs, and on this occasion we shall not be invoicing you for the equipment which we eventually supplied.
   As a valued customer of TopTen Leasing, we hope you will continue to hire our equipment. Once again, we very much regret the inconvenience caused.

   Yours sincerely,

UNIT 24 Activity: Business gurus game

Objectives

- To review language from throughout the Student's Book

- To practise speaking skills, including exam Speaking tasks

Time: 60+ minutes

When?: This activity can be done at any time, but would make a suitable finale for the final class.

Preparation: Make a copy of the game on pages 159–160 for each group of three or four students. Ensure that each group has a die and that each student has a counter.

This activity reviews topics from throughout the Student's Book. The game requires friendly co-operation among students for scoring, so it may be worth encouraging them not to be too competitive! You may have to spend a lot of time refereeing.

Note that the game extends over two sheets; students will need both sheets side by side. Make sure that each group playing has someone who can time the speakers. As you monitor the activity, make a note of any errors made and any problem squares where students struggled to answer and use this to run a post-activity language feedback session.

The training budget

Getting started

1 To what extent do you agree with these statements?

1   The staff in each department should decide what training they need.
2   All training should help the business to become more profitable.
3   You get what you pay for in training, i.e. good training, like good education, tends to be expensive.
4   Training is an essential part of every company's activities.

2 Discuss each point above with a partner.

Vocabulary

Match the expressions (1–8) with the definitions (a–h) from the *CALD*.

1	social media	a	the arrangements and tasks needed to control the operation of a plan or organisation
2	programming	b	classes or training to practise and improve skills, especially when you have not used them for a long time
3	administration	c	ways of communicating and sharing personal details or information using the Internet or mobile phones
4	a refresher course	d	lists of things provided or work done, together with their cost, for payment at a later time
5	invoices	e	when someone writes software for computers
6	security threats	f	producing or using original and unusual ideas
7	a patent	g	something (or someone) likely to cause danger or difficulty, e.g. to a computer network
8	creativity	h	the official legal right to make or sell an invention for a particular number of years

Role-play

The computer games company you work for has to consider requests for external training courses from different departments for the next quarter. You have been asked to help make decisions about these requests. You have $150,000 to spend on staff training.

In small groups, work together to decide how to spend the budget. Each person in the group should represent a different department of the company.

When making the decision, think about:

- which types of training will be most useful for the company
- how to allocate money for training to each department
- how each department should decide who can attend training courses.

Use the information on the next sheet to help you decide.

department (+ staff numbers)	training needs	training course offered	total cost
Finance & Administration (10 staff)	The new financial software the company bought last year is still causing problems with paying invoices.	a three-day software training course	$10,000
Sales & Marketing (8 staff)	The department must improve marketing through social networking sites.	a one-day social media marketing training course	$5,200
IT Support (6 staff)	The company has experienced problems with hackers trying to access new games before they are released.	a four-day network security training course (Participants learn how to analyse IT security threats and protect the company's systems and data.)	$13,200
Creative (ideas for new games) (12 staff)	Staff are complaining that they are running out of ideas for new games.	a two-day creativity training course to improve ideas generation and development	$6,000
Programming (21 staff)	As 3D games become more popular, training is needed to learn the latest techniques.	a 250-hour online course in 3D programming	$130,000
Legal (2 staff)	It is more and more important to protect the company's legal ownership of its games software.	a refresher course to bring staff up to date with the latest developments in patent law (one day per month for one year)	$16,000

Writing

Following your meeting, you have been asked by the Managing Director to write a proposal recommending how the training budget will be spent in the next quarter.

Write a **proposal** for the Managing Director.

Include:

- which training courses the company should spend money on
- why those training courses were chosen
- what benefits you expect the company to gain from this training
- any other points which you think are important.

Useful language
to help you organise the proposal

Proposal for training

Introduction
The purpose of this proposal is to recommend which ...

Which training courses?
I suggest the company should spend money on the following training courses: ...

Reasons for choosing training courses
I recommend these training courses for the following reasons:
- Course 1: Training for ...
  This course will help staff in the ...... department to ...

Benefits of the training courses for the company
The main benefits to the company will be improved ...

Responsibilities and relationships at work

Getting started

Work in pairs. In each pair of statements, which one is closest to your opinion? Discuss with your partner.

1 I enjoy responsibility.
  I prefer others to take responsibility.
2 I work best in a team.
  I prefer to work individually.
3 I enjoy creative tasks.
  I prefer routine work.
4 I don't like too many rules.
  I prefer to follow procedures.
5 I love dealing with a crisis.
  I prefer a quiet life.

Vocabulary

Four people are describing jobs or working relationships in their companies. Work in pairs to complete the texts by adding a preposition in each gap to complete the verb + preposition collocations in bold. One gap does not need a preposition.

1 In my company, the HR department **is responsible** .... recruiting new staff. They **are** also **in charge** .... organising training courses for staff. The Director of HR **runs** .... the department. As a director, she **reports** .... the CEO.
2 I used to work in Sales and Marketing, the department which **deals** .... new customers and **takes care** .... any enquiries from potential customers.
3 Last month, I transferred to Client Services and now I **look** .... existing customers. Personally, I **report** .... the General Manager – Client Services is one of his responsibilities. I'**m** also **responsible** .... **the** Accounts Manager if money is involved, say in giving refunds to a client.
4 Like most people, I have to **liaise** .... colleagues from a variety of other departments, although this is only an informal relationship. It's always a good idea to know what's going on in a company.

Reading and discussion

Work in groups of three. For this activity, you will need a blank piece of paper or a computer with PowerPoint.

Your teacher will give you some cards with information on them about people working in a particular company.

Follow these instructions.

1 Take a card and, in your own words, present the information on the card to your partners.
2 Your partners should decide which job from the list below is being described on it. Write the answer next to the job. Tell your partners if they are correct.
3 Take turns to describe the jobs until all the cards have been used.
4 Together, use the information to construct the company organigram on your paper or computer.

1	CEO	*a*
2	Marketing Director	....
3	Financial Director	....
4	General Manager	....
5	Production Director	....
6	Marketing Manager	....
7	Sales Director	....
8	IT Support Manager	....
9	Senior Sales Manager	....
10	Plant Manager	....
11	Accounts Manager	....
12	Catering Manager	....
13	Production Manager	....
14	HR Manager	....

Writing

- Work in pairs. The manufacturing company from the previous sections has decided that it needs to reorganise its structure to make it more efficient. You have been asked to help decide what changes could be made.
- Discuss the situation together and decide:
  - which departments could be reorganised
  - how these changes could benefit the company
  - what problems could arise.
- Write a report for the Board of Directors, explaining your ideas.

Reading and discussion
Job descriptions

a This person ...
- runs the company on a day-to-day basis.
- deals directly with all senior managers.
- is responsible to company shareholders.

This is the CEO.

b This person ...
- is in charge of computer maintenance.
- deals with technical problems.
- is a colleague of the Catering Manager.

This is the IT Support Manager.

c This person ...
- is in charge of all bookkeeping.
- takes care of financial records.
- is responsible for invoicing and for collecting payments.
- is responsible to the Financial Director.

This is the Accounts Manager.

d This person ...
- takes care of infrastructure issues.
- looks after building maintenance.
- liaises with all managers regarding these matters, but reports to the CEO.

This is the General Manager.

e This person ...
- is in charge of everything to do with the manufacturing process.
- liaises with other managers regarding raw materials and equipment.
- reports to the CEO.

This is the Production Director.

f This person ...
- is responsible for feeding the workforce.
- runs the canteen.
- is responsible to the General Manager.

This is the Catering Manager.

g This person ...
- is in charge of sales strategy.
- liaises with the Marketing Director over promotional activities.
- deals only with very important customers.
- reports to the CEO.

This is the Sales Director.

h This person ...
- runs the manufacturing facilities.
- deals with equipment problems.
- liaises with the Production Manager over buying new equipment.

This is the Plant Manager.

i This person ...
- is responsible for implementing sales strategy.
- looks after the Regional sales teams.
- reports to the Sales Director.

This is the Senior Sales Manager.

j This person ...
- is in charge of promotional strategies.
- is responsible for the marketing budget.
- liaises with the Production Director over pricing issues.

This is the Marketing Director.

k This person ...
- runs the production line.
- is responsible for meeting orders on time.
- looks after the factory workers.
- liaises with the Plant Manager over equipment problems.

This is the Production Manager.

l This person ...
- runs marketing and advertising campaigns.
- deals with advertising agencies.
- liaises with the Sales Department.

This is the Marketing Manager.

m This person ...
- is in charge of dealing with banks.
- liaises with the CEO on financial strategy.
- is responsible for producing the annual budget.

This is the Financial Director.

n This person ...
- is in charge of recruitment.
- deals with training issues.
- takes care of staff welfare.
- liaises with the Accounts Manager over salary matters.

This is the HR Manager.

Management culture

Getting started

Discuss these questions in pairs.

1   Do you think all companies need managers?
    Why? / Why not?
2   What are the different responsibilities of
    (a) managers and (b) their staff?

Speaking

1   **Work in pairs. Find out your partner's opinion on these points.**

    A good manager …

    1   lets staff call him/her by their first name.
    2   doesn't just tell staff what to do, but explains why and asks them for suggestions.
    3   is available to discuss any problems or suggestions his/her staff have.
    4   lets his/her staff work without pressure from him/her, but is available if they need help.
    5   gives credit to staff who do good work or make an extra effort to do something.
    6   tries to give extra responsibility to any staff who want it.
    7   likes his/her staff to learn business skills which are not normally their responsibility.
    8   tries to organise extra training for any staff who want it.
    9   makes sure his/her staff know what their company's aims and targets are.
    10 gives his/her staff regular updates on their company or department's performance.
    11 has regular meetings with staff to discuss how everyone can improve and develop.

2   **Write the number of each point from Exercise 1 in the right place on the line below. For example, if your partner's answer to point 1 is *always*, write *1* on the right-hand side of the line.**

    never   sometimes   always

3   **What sort of manager is your partner? Present the results of your survey.**

    Answers mostly *always*: You have, or prefer, a more democratic, consultative style of management where the opinion and satisfaction of staff is important.

    Answers mostly *never*: You have, or prefer, a more autocratic, directive style of management, and believe that the role of managers is to manage and the role of workers is to work as directed by their manager.

    Answers mostly *sometimes*: You have a mixed style of management. There are occasions when you like to take charge, but you also think that your staff can sometimes think independently, make decisions and have good ideas about the company and how to do things.

4   **Discuss these questions in pairs.**

    1   If you are in work and a manager, is your management style typical of your company?
    2   Do you think managers in your country are generally more autocratic or democratic?
    3   Which management style, autocratic or democratic, do you think would be most effective in the short term or long term? Why?
    4   Are you surprised, pleased or disappointed by your result in the questionnaire in Exercise 2? Explain to your partner.
        I'm very surprised. I thought I was more democratic as a manager.
    5   What do you think is the biggest influence on people's management style? Is it the manager's own personality, the people he/she works with, the kind of company he/she works in, or the culture of the country he/she lives in?

Body language in interviews

Getting started

Discuss these questions.

1 Just how important is your body language in a job interview?
2 What advice about body language and general appearance would you give someone going for an interview in your country?

Reading

1 Study these pictures of different features of body language. How would you interpret them? Would they create a good impression in a job interview in your country or culture?

1 Crossed hands	2 Rubbing your nose	3 Leaning back in your chair	4 A confident handshake	5 Crossing your arms
6 Making eye contact	7 Mirroring	8 A 'dead fish'	9 A confident smile	10 Professional dress

2 Match the pictures in Exercise 1 (1–10) with these comments (a–j), made by a UK-based body-language expert. Use a dictionary to check any vocabulary you need.

a In the US or Western Europe, a handshake like this will immediately put the interviewer off you.

b Try not to do this for too long – it could seem that you are challenging the interviewer, which is not a good idea – about ten seconds is long enough. You should do this regularly throughout the interview.

c Gestures like this suggest that you are not being entirely honest – also something to avoid in negotiations – or that you're unsure or simply a little uncomfortable with the situation.

d Most people are aware that this posture is a sign that you feel uncomfortable or that you are being defensive, rather than open and interested.

e If you do this, you could appear too relaxed and casual and give the impression that the job isn't that important to you.

f Although this isn't really body language, your appearance matters. Besides, jeans and a T-shirt probably don't fit the dress code in most companies.

g It is sometimes possible to establish rapport with an interviewer by something called 'mirroring' – echoing their posture – but don't overdo it, as an HR professional will probably know much more than you about these techniques.

h The face is a key indicator of how confident we feel. Looking worried or unhappy will always give a negative first impression.

i Time to leave. Make sure this is done just as confidently as it should have been when you arrived.

j This shows the person is under control and calm. Waving your arms about could look unprofessional or uncertain in some cultures, but it could show commitment or interest in others.

Speaking

1 Discuss these questions in pairs.

1 Are the comments in Exercise 2 above true for your country? Why? / Why not?

2 Can you add any advice on body language in job interviews in your country? What should or shouldn't you do?

2 Work in groups of three. A law firm is offering temporary summer jobs to students doing office administration.

Student A: You are the interviewer. Prepare some questions to ask the candidates. Then interview each of the candidates in turn.

Student B: You are interested in the job. Think of some ideas to use in your interview. While Student C is being interviewed, make notes on his/her body language and give some feedback at the end.

Student C: You are also interested in the job. Think of some ideas to use in your interview. While Student B is being interviewed, make notes on his/her body language and give some feedback at the end.

Hello Holidays

Read this job advertisement from Hello Holidays.

Hello Holidays

We are a leading player in the international holiday market, specialising in holidays for young, single people aged 18–33. We organise a wide range of adventure holidays for people of different nationalities and cultures, where they have the opportunity to mix and have fun together.
Our aim is to promote international integration and understanding through shared experiences.

Currently, we are planning to open a new office in your country with the intention of bringing our products to a wider public.

We are recruiting the following posts:

Office Manager

Sales Manager

For further details, please phone Maria Rabenda on 0121 584 39920, ext. 322 during office hours.

You should divide into two equal-sized groups and follow the steps on the sheet that your teacher will give you.

Group 1:   You represent the Human Resources department at Hello Holidays. You will have to go through the various stages of recruiting new staff.

Group 2:   You are applicants for jobs with Hello Holidays. You will have to go through the various stages of applying for and being interviewed for a job.

Group 1

1 Read the job information below and decide together how to complete the missing details. When you are ready, each of you should answer a phone call from one of the applicants in Group 2, where they will ask you for details about one of the jobs.

Office Manager: job details

- In charge of managing a busy office with a staff of ....
- Job responsibilities: supervising accounts, keeping information systems up to date.
- Must have administrative and secretarial skills, be familiar with leading software programs.
- Salary: ....
- Benefits: ....
- Qualifications: ....
- Experience: ....

Sales Manager: job details

- Will be head of an enthusiastic sales team of ....
- Responsible for presenting new products, finding customers, meeting sales targets.
- Must have a background in sales, good people skills, familiarity with the travel and holiday market.
- Salary: ....
- Benefits: ....
- Qualifications: ....
- Experience: ....

2 Work in pairs. Do the Writing task outlined in this memo. Use the Useful language box below to help you. When you have finished, exchange your letters with someone from the other group.

Memo

From: Human Resources Director
To: Human Resources Assistants
Subject: Recruitment interviews

14 October is the most convenient day to hold interview boards for the posts of Office Manager and Sales Manager. Please write an email to the job applicants inviting them for interview. Inform them that:

- length of interviews will be approx. 1 hour
- travel expenses will be paid
- if 14 October is inconvenient, they should phone for an alternative day
- interviews to be held at a local hotel (details to follow).

Many thanks

Useful language

I am writing to invite you to an interview for the post of .... on .... [day] at .... [time].
The interviews will be held at ...
The interviews will take approximately ...
If you are unable to attend, ...
We look forward ...

Group 1 continued

3 Work in pairs. Match phrases 1–12 with phrases a–l to form possible interview questions.

1 This job will involve a lot of travelling.	a for successful teamwork?
2 We have a number of applications for this job.	b in ten years' time?
3 Which do you think is more important for a job of this type:	c in your free time.
4 What would you like to be doing	d job satisfaction in your current position?
5 What things in your present job are you	e qualifications or experience?
6 What things give you the most	f with difficult people?
7 Tell us what you enjoy doing	g Why should we choose you?
8 What do you think is important	h Will this be a problem for you?
9 At some times of the year, when we are very busy,	i you might be required to work long hours. Would this be a problem for you?
10 What appeals to you about	j this post?
11 Do you have any experience of dealing	k about this company?
12 What do you know	l particularly good at?

4 Prepare to interview candidates. Write four or five extra questions you would like to ask candidates for the jobs. Remember to tailor the questions to the job. Choose four or five of the questions from Exercise 3 to ask as well.

5 Interview each candidate in turn. Ask each of them between eight and ten questions. When you have finished, work with the other people in the group and decide:

- which were the best answers to each question, and why
- who is the best candidate for each job, and why.

Report back to the rest of the class.

6 Each of you should phone one of the candidates to tell them if they have been successful or unsuccessful in their application. Choose language from this Useful language box to help you.

Useful language

I'm ringing from Hello Holidays in connection with the .... job you applied for.
I'm happy/sorry to say that your application has (not) been successful (on this occasion).
Are you still interested?
We'd like you to start in a month's time. Is that still OK?
We had a very strong field of candidates.
However, we'll keep your details on file in case something else comes up.
Thank you for your interest.
We wish you luck in the future.
We're looking forward to working with you.
Many congratulations!

Group 2

1 You should each choose one of the jobs mentioned in the advertisement and prepare some questions to find out some details about the job, e.g. *What's the starting salary?* When you are ready, 'telephone' someone from Group 1 and note down the details.

2 Write a brief email, applying for one of the jobs. Include these details:

- age
- occupation
- reasons for wanting the job
- why you are suited to the job

Start your email like this:

> Dear Mr Smith,
>
> I am writing to apply for the post of …

If necessary, use the letter on page 19 of your Student's Book as a model.

3 Work in pairs. Match phrases 1–12 with phrases a–l to form possible interview questions.

1	This job will involve a lot of travelling.	a	for successful teamwork?
2	We have a number of applications for this job.	b	in ten years' time?
3	Which do you think is more important for a job of this type:	c	in your free time.
4	What would you like to be doing	d	job satisfaction in your current position?
5	What things in your present job are you	e	qualifications or experience?
6	What things give you the most	f	with difficult people?
7	Tell us what you enjoy doing	g	Why should we choose you?
8	What do you think is important	h	Will this be a problem for you?
9	At some times of the year, when we are very busy,	i	you might be required to work long hours. Would this be a problem for you?
10	What appeals to you about	j	this post?
11	Do you have any experience of dealing	k	about this company?
12	What do you know	l	particularly good at?

4 Prepare for the interview. Work in pairs and discuss how you would answer the questions in Exercise 3. When you do the interview, the interviewers will ask you some of these questions and some others.

5 You will be interviewed for the job you applied for. When you have all finished, decide:

- who you think did the interviews best
- how you could improve your interview technique.

Report back to the rest of the class.

6 Respond to the phone call telling you whether you have been successful or unsuccessful in your application.

Cool hunters

Getting started

Discuss these questions in pairs.

- Where do you get your ideas from about what clothes to wear?
- Are you a fashion leader or fashion follower?
- How do you think trends in fashion begin?

Reading and vocabulary 1

1 Match each of the words/expressions (1–4) with the correct definition (a–d).

1	trendsetter	a	having or using ideas, beliefs, etc. which are accepted by most people
2	innovator	b	a person, organisation, etc. that develops new fashions, especially in clothes
3	mainstream	c	one of the first users of a given company, product or technology, especially in fashion and art
4	early adopter	d	someone who introduces changes and completely new ideas

2 Read this description of the fashion market from an interview with Sami Logan, who runs a market research company. What type of people do you think *they* and *them* are (age, gender, etc.)? Why?

INTERVIEWER: How does a trend spread?

SAMI LOGAN: It looks a bit like a triangle in shape. At the top, there are the **1** .... , which make up only about two or three per cent of the population. They're the ones who come up with something nobody's done before. Below them are what we call the **2** .... , which represent around 15 per cent of people. What they do is take up some of the ideas from the **3** .... and claim them as their own ideas. The next category is the **4** .... We're not exactly sure how many of them there are – probably a similar number to the innovators – but they form the layer above the **5** .... , or mass market, which is about 80 per cent of the population. And what this group does is adapt what the **6** .... are doing and make it acceptable enough for mass consumption. That's when the **7** .... recognises it, goes with it and finally kills it – that's the way fashion works.

3 Complete the description in Exercise 2 with the correct form of the words and phrases from Exercise 1. You can use some words and phrases more than once.

Speaking 1

In pairs, discuss:

- which of the categories Sami describes is closest to you
- why you think mass consumption 'kills' a fashion trend
- which part of the 'triangle' fashion companies and advertisers might be interested in, and why.

Reading and vocabulary 2

1 Discuss these questions in pairs.

1 Is it easy for fashion companies and advertisers to understand the minds of teenage customers? Why? / Why not?

2 If not, how can they get useful information about teenagers?

2 Read this article from a business website in the USA.

"Cool Hunters"—Next Big Job?

by Sarah Rohner

What is a "cool hunter"? Is there such a thing? Do people get paid to do this?

Yes!—Indeed you do and, if you are one of the best, you can charge $20,000 or more per company you help. I learned this information in my Advertising class at SIUe* from a video we watched called "The Merchants of Cool." The main idea of "The Merchants of Cool" is to make teens the advertising focus, because they have the most **disposable income** and they are an estimated 32 million strong in numbers.

In the movie, several big brand-name companies, such as Sprite and MTV, do **extensive** research to find out what **makes teens tick**. The research showed that teens are a **stubborn** demographic, but do respond to one thing—the concept of being "cool." Being cool is what teens are focused on and what teens will spend their money on.

This leads to a new profession called "cool hunting." Cool hunters do major research on teens, by observing, surveying, and even taking pictures of them to study. Once they have the knowledge of what is "cool," they can sell their information and consult companies.

Two of the best-known cool hunters are Dee Dee Gordon and Sharon Lee. These two female researchers created the website "Look Look" to sell their cool-hunting research. Companies can **subscribe** to the website for $20,000! Gordon and Lee are now very successful Look Look consultants.

I think cool hunting sounds like a very interesting new profession. I have never heard of it before, but I can definitely see the usefulness of the research. I believe if you are in public relations that you do use a version of cool hunting, because you have to stay on top of what the new and **hot** commodity [is]. Maybe someday cool hunting will be a popular skill that people will add to their public-relations **résumés**.

* Southern Illinois University Edwardsville

3 Match the expressions on the left (1–7) with the correct definition on the right from the *CALD* (a–g).

1	disposable income	a	describes someone who is determined to do what they want and refuses to do anything else
2	extensive	b	to pay money in order to receive a product or use a service regularly
3	what makes someone tick	c	the money which you can spend as you want (not including taxes, food and other basic needs)
4	stubborn	d	new, exciting and very fashionable
5	subscribe	e	a short written description of your education, qualifications, previous jobs and personal interests, used when you are trying to get a job (AmE)
6	hot	f	covering a large area; having a great range
7	a resumé	g	the reason you behave as you do

4 Answer these questions about 'cool hunters' in your own words.

1 Why is the teen age group so important to advertisers?

2 Why are teenagers sometimes a difficult market for companies to sell to?

3 How can 'cool hunters' help large companies attract the teen market?

4 Does the writer think that cool hunting is a good profession to join? Why? / Why not?

Speaking 2

Discuss these questions in pairs.

- Do you think you would make a good cool hunter? Why? / Why not?
- Could every kind of company use this kind of research? Why? / Why not?

Publicity stunts

Getting started

Work in pairs and look at this dictionary definition, then answer the questions (1–2) below.

> **publicity stunt** something that people or companies do in order to attract attention

In 2005, someone at electronics company Sony suggested the following publicity stunt: graffiti artists would spray-paint pictures of their new PlayStation Portable games console at locations around New York City.

1　Should the Marketing Manager have agreed to this idea? Why? / Why not?
2　What do you think the result was? Choose the most likely outcome, A or B below. Explain your answers to the class. To help you, think about whether it would be successful in your country.

A　Most people hated the idea. Nobody liked seeing more graffiti, and many thought they were exploiting the graffiti artists in a poor attempt to look cool. It was a disaster.
B　Most people loved the graffiti, which was praised as street art. Many thought they were giving the graffiti artists an opportunity to show their work. Sony looked cool. It was a great success, and sales rocketed.

Speaking

1　Work in small groups. Below are real-life examples of publicity stunts carried out by various companies. In each case, imagine you are the marketing team of the company in question. Discuss the pros and cons of the suggested stunts and decide whether your team would give them the go-ahead.

product	stunt
1 sun visors	Offer to give $4 million to Mount Rushmore in exchange for the chance to put one of your sun-visor products (plus logo) on each of the presidents' heads. Let the media know about this offer and stress how you will also be helping to preserve the monument for the nation.
2 fruit juice	To give the company a fun image, change the managers' titles? The CEO will become Chief Entertainment Officer; the Chief Technology Officer will be renamed Chief Tasting Officer. Also throw a big party with a Hawaiian theme and give away free sunglasses and free product samples.
3 cars	To get fans interested in your new car, give them a preview of the design by putting photographs on your Facebook page. To get the ball rolling, ask managers from the company to write a few positive comments.
4 cat food	Make a reality TV show for cats. Get ten cats from animal shelters. Build a special house with webcams for people to watch what these cats get up to. Every Friday, one of the cats is voted out (which actually means put up for adoption and receive a year's supply of the cat food you are promoting).
5 fast food	Offer a free chicken meal to customers through a celebrity's website. Customers can download a voucher, print it and take it to any outlet.
6 hot dogs	The hot dogs are a low-price brand. To stop people being suspicious of the quality of such cheap hot dogs, hire people dressed as doctors to stand in front of the restaurants eating hot dogs.

2 Your teacher will give you a sheet saying what actually happened in the cases on the previous sheet. What could the companies who failed have done to avoid their marketing disasters? Discuss in small groups and then present your ideas to the class.

Think about:
- why the disaster happened
- whether the disaster was predictable
- what alternatives could they have used.

Writing

1 Work in pairs. Nathan's Hot Dogs (example 6 on the previous sheet) is a good example of low-cost marketing. You work for a marketing magazine. Your magazine has a special page where you try to give advice to readers with marketing problems. You have received this letter from a reader.

> Dear Problem Page
>
> I own a small retail business selling bicycles. I want to get some publicity for my store, but I don't have enough money for advertising. Can you help?
>
> Best wishes
>
> Laura Paolucci

Write a reply to Laura Paolucci.
- Suggest a way of getting publicity cheaply.
- Say why your idea would be successful.
- Explain any risks involved.

2 Read your answers to the rest of the class. Vote on who had the best ideas.

Speaking Exercise 2

What were the results?

These are the actual companies or products.

1 **Proshade:** Success…
The National Park Service didn't accept their offer, but the company received lot of free publicity. One journalist said it was obviously a publicity stunt, 'but I'll write about it anyway'.

2 **Maui Beverages:** Success
After changing the job titles and holding the party, the company got a lot of positive publicity in the media, and annual sales went up by more than 50%.

3 **Honda:** Failure
The campaign was for the new Crosstour car. The fans were not impressed, and their Facebook page was soon full of negative comments. Fans soon realised that the only positive message was from a Honda manager.

4 **Meow Mix:** Success
Meow Mix's Marketing Director gave a lot of interviews, and the brand became associated with a good cause: animal welfare. Sales rose sharply.

5 **KFC:** Failure
KFC offered the vouchers on Oprah Winfrey's website. Because there was no limit, four million people printed vouchers in the first week. There were mini-riots at some branches and, most importantly, not enough chicken. Eventually, the President of KFC went on a TV show to apologise and promised to honour all vouchers. In the end, 10.5 million coupons were downloaded, and America consumed $42 million worth of free food.

6 **Nathan's Hot Dogs:** Success
In 1915, with signs that said 'If doctors eat our hot dogs, you know they're good!', Nathan was able to generate the growth that lead to a 'hot-dog empire' and Nathan's becoming a household name.

MyOfficeChef

Getting started

Discuss these questions in pairs.

1 How important is lunch as a meal for people in your culture?
2 Are lunchtimes for working people in your country changing? How?
3 What kind of lunch do you usually have – a proper meal, or just a quick sandwich? Why?

Reading

1 Read this information about a catering company.

A working lunch should still be a good lunch

At MyOfficeChef, we are dedicated to supplying you with a wide range of delicious hot meals, sandwiches, salads and executive corporate lunches. We use only the finest and freshest ingredients, locally produced where possible. Your food is made in the morning by our team of skilled chefs and delivered to your workplace exactly when you want it.

Whether it's lunch for one or a working lunch for a crucial meeting, it will be delicious, be exactly what you ordered and arrive on time, every time or your money back.

Extract from MyOfficeChef's website

The men behind MyOfficeChef are Paolo Nugnes (known to everyone as Papa), a chef of over 25 years' experience, and his friend Michel Dubois, a former financial analyst, who decided to move into catering after being made redundant during the last recession.

As working hours increase and office staff find themselves having less and less time for lunch, the two spotted an opportunity to provide an at-your-desk food-delivery service. Other companies were already active in this field, but from personal experience, Michel knew the quality of the food was often poor and over-priced.

After a slow start, their company, MyOfficeChef, has gained a word-of-mouth reputation for high standards, reasonable prices and punctual delivery – vital for the busy office worker. MyOfficeChef now supplies around 1,200 lunches per day to businesses in central London, employs 20 full-time staff and turns over £2.5m per year.

Now eating at your desk or *sur la pouce* (literally 'on the thumb') has taken off in Paris, and Michel, a Parisian by birth, wants to get in on the act. Papa Nugnes has similar ambitions for opening in his home town of Milan, Italy.

In London, where both men live and have plenty of contacts around the city, getting started still took time. Opening operations in France and Italy will be much more difficult, and effective promotion will be the key to success. With that in mind, Paolo and Michel have decided they need help and have approached IMS (International Marketing Services), a marketing consultancy service, to obtain advice.

2 Without looking at the text again, decide whether these statements about MyOfficeChef are true (T) or false (F). If they are false, correct them.

1 Paolo Nugnes and Michel Dubois are both chefs.
2 Their company was the first to open a food-delivery service.
3 Their company did not succeed immediately.
4 They became successful due to effective advertising.
5 Their turnover is £20m, and they supply nearly 1,000 lunches per day.
6 They plan to open businesses in other European cities.
7 Their approach to marketing will be the same in their new operations.

3 Work in pairs and check your answers by looking at the text again.

4 Complete this letter of enquiry from Paolo Nugnes and Michel Dubois to IMS by choosing the best alternative – A, B, C or D – for each gap.

Dear Sir or Madam

We are a **1** .... express catering company based in London, delivering hot and cold food to offices and other businesses **2** .... in the City of London. Your consultancy has been **3** .... to us by one of our clients, Sleaford Publishing Ltd.

We are in the process of expanding our operations into Paris and Milan and we would like to **4** .... a consultancy to give us advice on marketing and promotional strategy.

If you are interested in working with us, please contact me at the above number to arrange an **5** .... meeting where we can discuss our expansion plans, and you can **6** .... your services and your fees.

I look forward to hearing from you.

Yours faithfully

Paolo Nugnes and Michel Dubois

---

1 A regular	B typical	C medium-sized	D middling
2 A operating	B conducting	C running	D producing
3 A informed	B recommended	C advised	D given
4 A commission	B compensate	C outsource	D lease
5 A open	B initial	C advance	D introduction
6 A tell	B inform	C relate	D outline

Vocabulary

Match these words and phrases from the information in Reading Exercise 1 (1–6) with their definitions (a–f).

1 over-priced	a	something which costs more than it is worth	
2 to move into	b	promoted by recommendations from existing customers or users	
3 word-of-mouth	c	to lose your job for economic reasons	
4 to get in on the act	d	to start to work in a new area of business	
5 made redundant	e	the opinion people have about whether something is good or bad	
6 reputation	f	to become involved in something that someone else has started	

Speaking

1 Work in pairs. You are employees of International Marketing Services. You have been asked to prepare some ideas for promoting MyOfficeChef in Europe to present to the company's owners. Discuss the situation together and decide:

- what would be the most effective ways to promote the business
- what the unique selling points of this business are
- what the main market(s) would be
- how this company would fit into the existing catering market
- what problems MyOfficeChef might have establishing the company abroad (e.g. existing competitors).

Do not tell your colleagues your ideas yet.

2 Some of your colleagues at IMS came up with four other ways of promoting MyOfficeChef. Read their ideas (A–C) below. Which type of promotion does each statement (1–5) refer to?

1 Examples of this take almost any form.
2 This is a good way of establishing customers' belief in your products.
3 Customers are given the chance to learn how the products are created.
4 The product can often advertise itself.
5 Companies must be careful who they try this method with.

A **Demonstrations** Demonstrations are an option to show customers how your product is made and establish your credibility. One example is holding cooking demonstrations twice a week, featuring chefs from the company. Recipe cards are even given out. Demonstrations have also worked well for companies selling products associated with them.

B **Free gifts** A premium is a gift of some kind that reminds your customer of you and your service. There are thousands from which to choose: coffee mugs, baseball caps, and just about anything that can be engraved, printed on or decorated with your company name and phone number. If you have a restaurant, give away a drink with each meal.

C **Free trials or samples** Giving potential customers a sample is an excellent way to attract attention and make a positive impression. It often makes as much sense spending your marketing and advertising budget on giving out your products instead of buying advertisements, especially if cash is tight. The key is to give samples to the target market, i.e. delicious snacks to hungry consumers. Most people appreciate the opportunity to try the product, and hopefully many will like it enough to buy it.

3 In pairs, combine your own ideas from Exercise 2 with anything you like from A–C. Use these ideas to prepare and present a marketing plan to representatives of MyOfficeChef (the rest of the class). At the end, vote for which marketing plan would be best for MyOfficeChef.

To prepare your marketing plan, think about:

- who or what the target market is
- how to reach that target market (e.g. types of promotional activities and advertising)
- the possible competition and how to differentiate yourself from that competition
- your budget
- the time frame (how long the process will take).

Writing

Write a summary proposal of your promotional ideas to send to MyOfficeChef.

Location, location, location: which stand is best?

Speaking

1 Work in pairs. You have been made responsible for booking a stand for your office furniture company at the London Contemporary Design Show. Discuss and decide together what makes a good location for a stand.

Consider the following:

- the importance of 'footfall' – how many people will be walking past per hour?
- who your neighbours will be
- noise
- your competitors

2 Study the floor plan your teacher gives you. In pairs, decide which stand would be your first choice, and why.

3 Change partners and compare your ideas. Decide who has the best suggestion.

4 Work in groups of three. Your teacher will now give one of you an information sheet. Listen and consider each new piece of information. Does each piece of information make you change your mind about which stand to choose? Make a final decision and explain it to the rest of the class.

Writing

You have decided to write a short email to your manager, telling him what you have arranged for the trade fair. Write about:

- which stand you chose
- why you chose that stand
- how you will attract visitors to your stand.

Information sheet

- Read each piece of information out to your colleagues. Discuss the information and decide if it affects the decision you made on which stand to choose.
- Do not read the next piece of information until you have finished discussing the previous one.
- You can change your opinion as often as you like, but you must make a final decision at the end.

1 The more sides a stand has, the more visitors it can accommodate at a time.

2 People who have just arrived are not always ready to start seriously studying what's on offer.

3 Loading or unloading exhibits or stock can be noisy, and visitors might not hear your sales pitch.

4 Apart from the exit, there is one place every visitor will probably visit during the day, but you don't want a stand too near that, do you?

5 Competition in business is a good thing, but not always in trade fairs.

6 If you want good Chinese food, visit Chinatown. People apply the same principle when looking around a trade fair.

7 Visitors who are lost are probably more interested in getting some help finding their way around than looking at product samples.

8 Hungry or tired people aren't usually interested in looking at stands.

9 People sometimes feel a bit trapped if they are stuck in the corner.

Floor plan

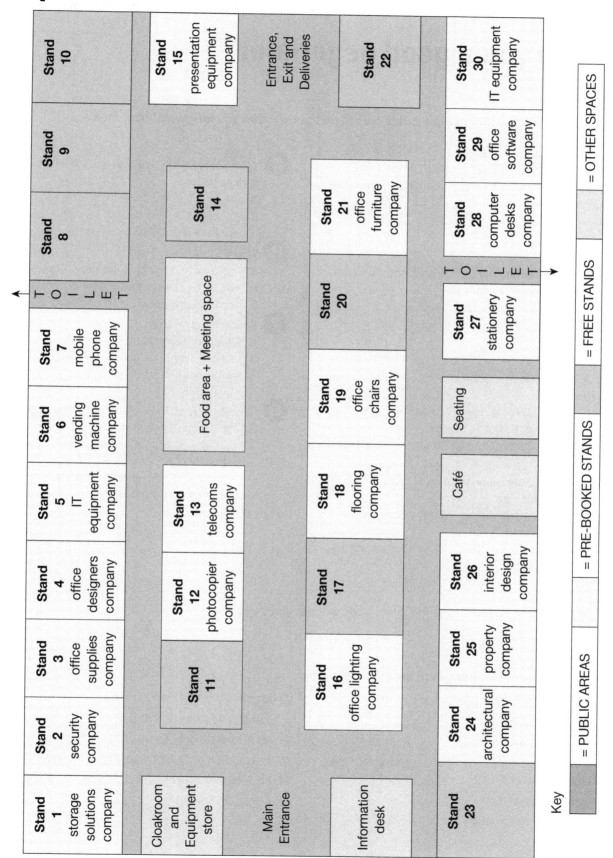

Quiz: Are you a good negotiator?

Reading

1 Work in pairs. Discuss your answers to this quiz to find out whether you are good negotiators.

1 When I negotiate, I try to get what I want, but I also try to make sure the other side leaves the table happy too.
A never
B sometimes
C always

2 What sort of relationship do you look for with the people you're negotiating with?
A It helps if I like them as individuals.
B I try to keep personal feelings out of my working life.
C They're the enemy: I have to defeat them.

3 How soon do you like to get down to business when you're negotiating?
A It depends on the people I'm negotiating with.
B Straight away – time is money.
C Once I've taken time to get to know my opposite numbers.

4 In negotiations, I'm more successful if I …
A set my sights high.
B am ready to compromise when we can't make progress.
C break off the negotiation when I really don't like the deal on offer.

5 When negotiating, who usually presents their demands first?
A me
B my opposite number
C We take it in turns.

6 When I negotiate, I am …
A aggressive, though it's not my normal character.
B the same as I normally am.
C a bit more aggressive than usual.

7 Before a negotiation, I …
A prepare thoroughly.
B make a few brief notes.
C get on with other work and in the negotiation, I play it by ear.

8 What's your attitude to honesty in a negotiation?
A I'm scrupulously honest at all times.
B I'll tell a lie if it helps me get what I want – all's fair in love and war.
C I never actually tell a lie, but I might keep quiet about something if it's to my advantage.

2 Calculate your score by looking at the sheet your teacher gives you.

Vocabulary

Find words or phrases in the quiz which mean the following.

1 concludes the negotiation (question 1)
2 start working (question 3)
3 fix high objectives (question 4)
4 reach an agreement which involves accepting less than you wanted (question 4)
5 stop, interrupt (question 4)
6 what you want from the negotiation (question 5)
7 improvise (question 7)
8 completely (question 8)
9 start immediately (answer 3)
10 your lowest acceptable position (answer 4)
11 be a lot more successful than you (answer 8)
12 direct (answer 8)

Quiz scores

1 A 2   B 8   C 4

If you're negotiating with someone who you're going to have a long-term relationship with, it's a good idea to make the other side happy, too – the classic win–win situation. But there are often times when you're negotiating with someone you're never going to see again, so you might as well get as much as you can and not worry about the consequences for the other side.

2 A 8   B 0   C 1

There's more to life than work and making money. Personal relationships do matter, and there's no point in going around making enemies unnecessarily.

3 A 8   B 2   C 6

You have to adapt to the people you're working with. In some cultures, business people like to get to know you before doing business with you, and you have to respect this. In other cultures, business people like to get straight down to work, and perhaps to relax together afterwards.

4 A 8   B 4   C 4

All studies of negotiation technique show that negotiators get more if they have high expectations. However, negotiation, by its nature, requires flexibility and the ability to compromise. On the other hand, if the deal they offer is below your bottom line, you shouldn't be frightened of breaking off the negotiation: you run a business, not a charity.

5 A 2   B 8   C 3

Knowledge is power. Find out as much as possible about what your opposite number wants before you say anything – you may be able to manipulate the negotiation to your advantage.

6 A 2   B 8   C 8

Be yourself and you'll do just about everything in life well.

7 A 8   B 4   C 0

We're all busy people, but negotiating is an important part of the job, and the better you prepare, the better you'll do it. It's surprising just how many business people go into meetings and negotiations with little or no previous preparation.

8 A 3   B 5   C 8

This is a difficult one: we all like to think that honesty is the best policy, but if you get a reputation for scrupulous honesty at all times, other negotiators are going to run rings around you. On the other hand, if you get a reputation for lying, no one will want to negotiate with you because they won't trust you – the best policy is really to keep quiet rather than reveal sensitive information or tell an outright lie.

If you scored 45–64
You're clearly a great negotiator: you've thought about it a lot and you've had plenty of practice. You should make plenty of money for your company and for yourself.

If you scored 29–44
Negotiating can be one of the most stressful areas of business, but it's something that almost anyone can learn to do. So why not do a course?

If you scored 15–28
Negotiation is a business skill which can be learned by going on courses and with practice. With plenty of time and hard work, you can become very successful at it.

A letter to a franchiser

Getting started

Work in small groups and answer this question.

Which of these types of franchise might interest you?

- a fitness club
- a shop
- a hair and beauty salon
- something else

Vocabulary

Match the words (1–6) with their definitions (a–f).

1	proven	a	clients who use the service again
2	comprehensive	b	complete
3	praise	c	continuing
4	repeat business customers	d	expression of approval
5	ongoing	e	help
6	assistance	f	shown to work

Reading

You have seen a website advertising Petpals franchises (see below). You have printed it out and written some notes on it. Read it and decide whether these statements are true (T) or false (F). Correct the false ones.

1 Before starting this franchise, you will have to write your own business plan.
2 This franchise looks after other people's animals when they cannot do it themselves.
3 The franchise provides accommodation for pets when their owners are on holiday.
4 The franchiser offers to teach franchisees how to run their business better.

Writing

Write a letter to the franchiser to find out more about the possibilities of taking out a Petpals franchise in your country. Use all your handwritten notes.

Say why I'm interested

Initial investment?

What turnover/ profits in first year?

Work: when/ how many hours?

What training?

The Petpals Plan for Business Success

Firstly, thanks for your interest in the Petpals business franchise opportunity.

Petpals is the first nationally recognised professional pet-care franchise. Its proven franchise management skills have created the Petpals Plan for Business Success. This scheme is now being opened up internationally to allow pet lovers worldwide to take advantage of our unique services.

With a pet industry worth over £200 billion worldwide, there is an urgent need for an internationally recognised, professional, trained organisation to allow both working and holidaying pet owners to have a more flexible lifestyle.

At Petpals, we provide a comprehensive service of pet care that has had the praise and support of the nation's pet owners, as well as pet professionals.

The Petpals' flexible and friendly approach has helped thousands of pet owners. The growing number of happy repeat business customers demonstrates that pet owners can go to work, have a holiday, visit friends, take short breaks, have a day off in the certain knowledge that their pet will be exercised and loved in their own environment.

Due to the success of and demand for its franchise operations, Petpals has opened a dedicated education centre for our existing Petpals Club Members, as well as providing ongoing support and assistance to new franchisees.

adapted from www.petpals.com

Business start-up game

Rules

Play in groups of four or five.

You need a die for each group and one counter for each player.

1 Take turns to throw the die and move to a square.
2 Follow the instructions on the square.
3 Explain the meaning of the word(s)/phrase(s) in bold to the other players. If you explain the word(s)/phrase(s) correctly (according to the other players or your teacher), you get 10 points.

4 If another player has already landed on the square and explained the word(s) in bold, you can't earn the points.
5 Follow any other instructions on the square (e.g. *Miss a turn*).
6 You needn't throw the exact number to reach **Finish**. The first player to reach **Finish** gets 100 points. The second player gets 60 points. The third player gets 30 points.
7 When the third player reaches **Finish**, the game ends. The winner is the player with the most points.

START			
1 Your **market research** consists of asking your friends and family if they think your business idea is a good one. *Miss a turn.*	**2** You spend several days **cold-calling** potential customers to see if they would buy your product. *Go forward to 6.*	**3** You've spent a couple of weeks investigating **the competition**. *Go forward to 10.*	**4** You haven't done any market research because your **intuition** tells you your idea is a good one. *Return to START.*
8 You've spent several months **testing people's reactions** to your samples. *Go forward to 12.*	**7** You've spent all your **savings** by using a market-research firm. You're still waiting for their report. *Return to START.*	**6**	**5** When you ask for a **start-up loan**, your bank asks to see a more detailed business plan. *Miss a turn.*
9 You've found an **angel investor**. Unfortunately, he wants a 50% share in the business. *Return to 6.*	**10**	**11** Your family is prepared to **put up the finance**. *Go forward to 15.*	**12**
16 You've been given a **business development grant**. *Go forward to 20.*	**15**	**14** You've just **quarrelled** with your business partner. *Miss two turns.*	**13** You've decided not to **raise finance**. You're going to build up the business little by little. *Go to 20, then miss a turn.*
17 You've opened your offices in the city centre. A good location, but your **rent is prohibitive**. *Go back to 10.*	**18** You've decided to run your business from your spare bedroom until you can **afford** somewhere better. *Go forward to 20.*	**19** You've spent all your start-up finance on a **state-of-the-art computer**. *Go back to START.*	**20**
24 Your suppliers have just **gone bankrupt**. *Miss two turns while you find new ones.*	**23** Your assistant has just found **a better-paid job**. *Miss a turn while you find a replacement.*	**22** The building inspectors say that your **premises** are not safe. *Go back to 15.*	**21** The telephone company will take two months to **install a broadband connection**. *Miss a turn.*

25 Your business is growing steadily but well **by word of mouth**. *Go forward to 29.*	**26** You've done a **mail shot** to hundreds of potential customers. Most have gone in the bin without being read. *Go back to 20.*	**27** Your **banner ads** on various websites have created some interest. *Go forward to 31.*	**28** The regional TV station has done **a piece** about you. *Go forward to 31.*
32 Your nephew spent last Saturday **handing out leaflets** in the street. *Go forward to 35.*	**31**	**30** Your old boss wants you back. She offers you twice your previous salary plus some excellent **perks**. *Miss a turn while you think about it.*	**29**
33 Your business is growing fast. You need to **take on** new staff. *Go forward to 35.*	**34** You've spotted another **gap in the market**, but you'll need more finance. *Go back to 12.*	**35**	**36** Your partner has disappeared with all **the cash**. *Go back to 10.*
40 Your **profits** are up 200%. *Go forward to 48.*	**39** Interest rates on **mortgages** have gone up. *Go back to 35.*	**38** You've just **landed** an excellent new contract. *Go forward to 50.*	**37** You've been expanding too fast and have run into **cashflow problems**. *Go back to 35.*
41 Supplies have been interrupted due to **a transport strike**. *Miss a turn.*	**42** Your website is attracting hundreds of **hits** and plenty of new customers. *Go forward to 50.*	**43** Your assistant is off on 16 weeks' **maternity leave**. *Miss a turn while you take on a temporary replacement.*	**44** The tax inspectors want to check that you've been paying all your **VAT**. You have! *Go forward to 50, then miss a turn.*
48	**47** Sales doubled in **the first quarter**. *Go forward to 55.*	**46** A competitor has opened up in the same street and is **undercutting your prices**. *Go back to 35.*	**45** You have been named 'Young **Entrepreneur** of the Year'. *Go forward to 55.*
49 An American **multinational** offers you $10 million for your company. *Accept and go to FINISH.*	**50**	**51** You have decided to set up as a **limited company**. *Miss a turn due to paperwork.*	**52** There is a fire in your office and you have to **claim on insurance**. *Miss two turns while you do the paperwork.*
FINISH **56** You're suffering from stress due to **overwork**. *Miss a turn while you take a holiday.*	**55**	**54** A bright new **graduate trainee** is making your company prosper. *Go forward to 55.*	**53** You urgently need **to invest in new equipment**. This will be expensive. *Go back to 31.*

Location bingo

Getting started

Discuss this question in pairs.

What makes a business park attractive to companies?

Think about the location, the environment in and around the building(s), the facilities and anything else you think is important.

Vocabulary

Match the expressions (1–10) with their definitions from the *CALD* (a–j).

1	laid out	a	land that was in a very poor condition, but has been improved so that it can be used for another purpose
2	motorway	b	an area especially next to a building or road designed to look like natural countryside
3	extensive	c	a calm, pleasant place with lots of trees in the middle of somewhere busy
4	reclaimed urban land	d	planned, designed or organised
5	a leafy oasis	e	electricity produced in a way that protects the environment, for example by using wind, water or the sun
6	at a premium	f	a group of people who travel together, especially to work or school, usually with a different member each day
7	green energy	g	a wide road built for fast-moving traffic travelling long distances
8	car sharing	h	a group of people working together for one particular purpose
9	a dedicated team	i	a higher than normal price for something
10	landscaped	j	covering a large area

Speaking

Work in groups of four.

Student A: You are looking for premises on a business park for your company. You have a list of requirements (see separate sheet).

Students B–D: You represent different business parks and are hoping to offer Student A suitable office space in your park. Information on your business park is on the card your teacher will give you.

Listen to each requirement in turn. If you think your park fits this requirement, tick (✓) the relevant box. If you tick all the boxes, shout 'Bingo!' and the game ends. Your answers will then be checked against the list of requirements, so make sure you are confident before you tick a box.

Student A

Company representative

This is your list of requirements for the premises you want for your company. Present them one by one to your colleagues. If they ask any questions for clarification, you can answer them, but don't discuss them any further. When someone shouts 'Bingo!', check their answers carefully, with the help of all the other people in the group, to be sure they are correct. If they are wrong, someone else has the correct card and you need to find it to end the activity.

Checklist for new business park premises

- We need a temperature-controlled environment for some of the equipment we use.
- Our company has a strong environmental record, and we want our new premises to reflect this.
- The working environment must be pleasant, as we believe this motivates staff.
- We want a say in the way the offices are laid out.
- Our staff work hard and need the chance to do their shopping conveniently. Several have small children.
- We need to entertain clients regularly. Some of them have expensive tastes.
- We have 62 staff. Two-thirds of them drive to work.
- We require flexible leasing agreements and would expect some form of discount if we sign an extended contract.
- We are looking for somewhere with excellent transport links – road, rail and air (as we have a number of international clients).
- Property is not our expertise, so we want as much help with organising this move as possible.

Student B

You represent Green Lanes Business Park.

This is what your business park offers:

- There is a cycle network around the park with cycle paths to the nearest train station 1 km away. ❑
- There is enough space available to make it possible to extend the buildings if a company grows. ❑
- There is parking for 30 cars. ❑
- There are two supermarkets and a number of family-style restaurants on the park Your staff can keep fit in our dedicated leisure centre. ❑
- Flexible leases available from 1 to 25 years. ❑
- All offices can be fully air-conditioned. ❑
- You can be on the motorway in less than half an hour, and at an international airport in under two hours' drive. ❑
- Our office buildings are surrounded by open spaces, water and trees. ❑
- The layout of the offices has been designed by award-winning architects. ❑

Student C

You represent **Oasis Business Park.**

This is what your business park offers:

- Choose your own office interior designs from our extensive range of options. ❑
- The business park is a fantastic example of reclaimed urban land. Formerly an industrial site, it is now a leafy oasis in the city. ❑
- We offer (at a slight premium) a green energy option to everyone. ❑
- The excellent transport infrastructure means that you have rail connections with destinations all over the country, including the main international airport 45 minutes away. ❑
- In this part of the city, there is no shortage of shops and entertainment. Everything from a simple sandwich bar to a gourmet meal is within walking distance. ❑
- In keeping with our green philosophy, we offer a car-sharing policy to all companies on the park. ❑
- Fully negotiable leases with longer-term discounts ❑
- Our expert team will work closely with you to organise the interior design and construction of your offices just the way you want them. ❑

Student D

You represent **Arbor Business Park.**

This is what your business park offers:

- All offices are fully air-conditioned as standard. ❑
- There is parking for 44 cars. ❑
- An on-site wind turbine means we supply 50% green energy. ❑
- The interior layout of the offices is tailor-made for the clients. ❑
- We offer dedicated development and project management teams to make sure you get the office you are looking for. ❑
- Our office buildings are set within beautifully landscaped grounds. ❑
- There is a full range of amenities in the park, including retail outlets, restaurants to suit every budget, a sports centre and two childcare providers.❑
- We are less than 2 km from the nearest motorway, 4 km from a mainline rail station and only 40 minutes from a regional airport (which is a 30-minute flight from the main international airport). ❑
- Minimum six-month lease, no maximum; 12 months' lease for the price of 11 on contracts over five years. ❑

Finding a new office

Background

You work for Intercomm Solutions, an IT support company providing services to other companies, such as systems maintenance, installation of hardware and software, network upgrades and troubleshooting. The company has been extremely successful recently, and the Board has decided that the time has come to think about opening a second branch in another region. New staff will be recruited, and Intercomm is seeking office space for about 30 staff at first. The first question is whether it should choose to buy or to lease the new office space. Currently prices for commercial property are depressed, and rents are also low.

Speaking

1 Work in pairs. Discuss this question.

Is it usually better to buy or lease office space? Why?

Consider the following:
- how long you plan to remain in the location
- trends in commercial property prices (vs. rental prices)
- infrastructure requirements (e.g. specialised requirements for certain companies).

2 Now look at information that your teacher will give you. Use it to decide whether Intercomm Solutions should buy or lease office space. Give a reason for your decision.

Reading 1

1 Read this article, from a website giving advice to small businesses, about what to consider when negotiating a lease for a new office. Ignore the gaps in the text. Does it mention any of your ideas from the discussion? What extra information did you discover?

Leasing contracts for small businesses

The majority of companies need to lease workspace. If you are lucky enough to run a growing business, you could have to find room for extra staff or 1 .... production. Leasing contracts are often a serious monetary 2 .... for a firm. Despite this, many executives put their name to contracts that 3 .... their company to a long-term lease while apparently never negotiating its contents.

As soon as you locate the perfect location for the business, the owner usually gives you a ready-made blank contract which appears to be the real thing and calls this his so-called 'standard' leasing contract, implying that the leasing contract had already achieved an ideal form, having been 4 .... in stone many long years ago.

This contract is certainly drawn up to benefit the owner. There is no such thing in law as a 'standard' lease. 5 .... of the appearance of the leasing form, no matter how official it might appear, it's your duty to discuss the lease thoroughly, point by point, if necessary.

How successfully you're able to agree on amendments to the terms of a lease 6 .... on the amount of pressure you can bring to bear. Is another firm 7 .... to sign the lease? Has the vacant space opposite been like that for long? What sort of rent are you willing to offer? Be honest with yourself: if Apple and Samsung are ready to get involved in a 8 .... war over the location you've set your heart on, none of your talents as an ace negotiator will come to anything.

 Business Benchmark Upper Intermediate Teacher's Resource Book © Cambridge University Press 2013 **PHOTOCOPIABLE**

2 Read the article again and choose the best word – A, B, C or D – to fill each gap.

1	A risen	B increased	C grown	D raised
2	A commitment	B promise	C assurance	D duty
3	A connect	B tie	C unite	D attach
4	A put	B made	C placed	D set
5	A Apart	B Regardless	C Despite	D Although
6	A banks	B counts	C depends	D trusts
7	A contesting	B participating	C competing	D rivaling
8	A bidding	B tendering	C proposing	D bargaining

Reading 2

Work in pairs. After some research, Intercomm Solutions narrowed its options down to two possible locations. Read the information below and discuss your first impressions of each one with your partner.

A

Holmepoint Business Centres

Holmepoint Business Centres offer a wide choice of exceptional offices to let, all with a full range of support and maintenance services. They are designed for all kinds of small to medium businesses, are fully equipped and can save you money.

Thanks to our convenient leasing agreement, you can stay as long as you like or leave with just a month's notice. You can control your spending with our straightforward monthly fee, and benefit from a whole array of extra business benefits such as dedicated meeting rooms.

Why not take a look at our range of current locations and future developments and find out why we're different.

B

Low-cost offices at the International Commerce Centre

Our inexpensive offices are perfect, value-for-money accommodation in these difficult economic times.

We are situated close to the town centre, within easy reach of the country's main transport networks.

Services include ...
- 24-hour access
- 24-hour security teams
- on-site parking
- personal signage
- postal services

Rents include ...
- maintenance
- heat, light and power
- cleaning
- waste disposal
- buildings insurance

Role-play

Intercomm Solutions has arranged preliminary meetings with representatives of the two potential new sites in order to discuss their requirements. Divide into three groups.

Group 1:   You represent **Intercomm Solutions**. (This group should then sub-divide into two.)

Group 2:   You will represent **Holmepoint Business Centres**.

Group 3:   You will represent the **International Commerce Centre**.

1   **Initial meeting**

Half of the group from Intercomm Solutions will meet the representatives of Holmepoint, and the other half will meet the representatives of the International Commerce Centre. Study the role cards you will be given. When everyone is ready, hold the meeting.

2   **Assessment**

The representatives of Intercomm Solutions should now re-group and compare their notes from the preliminary meetings and prepare for the next stage – the negotiations.

The representatives of Holmepoint Business Centres and the International Commerce Centre should spend some time thinking about what they have learned from their meetings with Intercomm Solutions and use this to help their preparations for the next stage.

3   **Final negotiations**

All representatives should meet as in Stage 1. During this meeting, you should try to negotiate the terms and conditions of a possible lease. At the end of the negotiations, the representatives of Intercomm Solutions will meet to decide which offer is best. They will then notify either Holmepoint Business Centres or the International Commerce Centre, by email, of their decision.

4   **The decision**

Once the representatives of Intercomm Solutions have made their decision, they should write to the winning business centre to tell them the good news. Complete the numbered gaps in the email below using up to three words. Work in groups of three, with one person from Intercomm Solutions, one from Holmepoint and one from the International Commerce Centre. Do not complete gaps 1 or 4 until you have checked your answers.

To: **1** ....

From: **2** ....

Subject: **3** ....agreement

Dear **4** .... [*name of contact*]

I am writing in **5** .... with our meeting on **6** .... [*date*] to discuss the leasing of office space in your business centre.

7 .... our discussions, we are pleased to **8** .... you that we would like to **9** .... a lease on the terms agreed at our meeting, starting on **10** .... [*date*].

We **11** .... moving into our new premises and hope this is the beginning of a long and fruitful business relationship.

In the meantime, if you **12** .... , please do not **13** .... to contact me.

Yours **14** ....

15 .... [*your name and position*]

Now you can reveal the winning business centre! Complete gaps 1 and 4 above.

Role cards

Holmepoint Business Centres

You should begin the first meeting with a very brief presentation of your business centre.

Business is not very good at your business centre (this is confidential) and you have several empty offices available from 40m² up to 500m². Your company is keen to fill these as soon as possible because empty offices give a bad impression to potential clients, so remember to be flexible in your discussions.

Leases

- You do not have a standard lease, but you can make concessions for longer-term leases (three years +).
- Rent is currently $350 per workstation and is reviewed on an annual basis.
- Tenants may want to make alterations. This is acceptable, but only with your written permission, and clients must pay for it.
- The premises must be returned in their original condition.
- Clients may upsize or downsize (move to bigger or smaller offices) in the Business Centre if space is available, but rents will have to be renegotiated.

Other

- Each office includes 10 parking spaces. Extra spaces may be rented.
- High-speed internet access, security patrols, cleaning and maintenance are included.
- Heat, light and power are paid for on a client-by-client basis.

The first meeting is an information exchange only. Listen to the other side, ask any questions you wish and make notes. This is NOT a negotiation. The negotiation will happen in the second meeting.

The International Commerce Centre

You should begin the first meeting with a very brief presentation of your business centre.

Business is great at the moment, and you only have two empty offices available – one of 300m² (25 workstations) and one of 500m² (40 workstations). Several companies are currently interested in these offices.

Leases

- Your standard leases are six months, 12 months or 36 months.
- Rent is currently $320 per workstation and is reviewed on a six-monthly basis.
- Any alterations to the premises must be agreed in writing before the client moves in, or when the lease is renegotiated.
- The premises must be returned in their original condition.
- There is unlikely to be any chance of moving to bigger or smaller offices in the Commerce Centre, as space is limited. If it were possible, the rent would be renegotiated, and there would be a 5% administration fee.

Other

- Each office includes one parking space per workstation.
- High-speed internet access, security patrols, cleaning, maintenance, heat, light and power are included in the rent.
- Repairs and breakages must be paid for by the client.

The first meeting is an information exchange only. Listen to the other side, ask any questions you wish and make notes. This is NOT a negotiation. The negotiation will happen in the second meeting.

Intercomm Solutions

Negotiating the best possible lease can save your company enough money to hire more employees or to spend on promotion, so getting a good deal is vital. If you don't get what you are looking for, you might want to consider leasing office space with the other company.

You have the following requirements (but can be flexible):

Space: 400m² for approximately 30 staff, including a reception area and a main meeting room for up to 10 people.

Parking: 20 parking spaces (probably 10 people will use public transport)

Cost: maximum $300 per workstation per month ($108,000 per year for 30 staff)

Facilities: All the standard facilities of a serviced office, such as high-speed, Wi-Fi-enabled internet access, on-site security, cleaning, maintenance, and heat, light and power to be included in the rent.

The lease

You want:

- two years with an option to renew
- the option to cancel the lease with two weeks' notice
- no rent increases during the first three years (inflation-linked increases if you renew the lease)
- the right to make alterations or improvements with the landlord's agreement
- the option to take over additional space in the building *at the same rent* if your business is successful and wants to expand. This will save a lot of the time and effort of moving again.

The first meeting is an information exchange only. Present your requirements, ask any questions you wish and make notes to share the information with your colleagues. This is NOT a negotiation. The negotiation will happen in the second meeting.

Additional information

Should Intercomm Solutions buy or lease?

Consider purchasing a property if you:

- plan to stay in it for ten years or more
- think you can get the property at a discount price, or if the market is rising and you'll make money from capital growth in the value of the property when you sell
- are in a specialised industry (e.g. manufacturing or science-based) that has unique infrastructure needs. Investing in equipping a building to suit your needs means you'll want to own the results.

Handling questions in presentations

Getting started

Discuss these questions in pairs.

1 When making a presentation, why is it important to tell the audience when you want them to ask questions?
2 When making a presentation, how do you prefer to schedule audience questions? Which of these do you prefer to say? Why?
   a *If you have any questions, I'll be happy to answer them at the end of my presentation.*
   b *I'll be happy to answer any questions you have at any time.*
3 How do you feel about asking questions during or after presentations? Why?
4 What would motivate you to ask a question at the end of someone's presentation?

Vocabulary

1 **Unscramble these sentences for thanking a speaker.**
   1 for / you / the / talk / thank *Thank you for the talk.*
   2 very / was / interesting / it
   3 I / your / presentation / enjoyed / really
   4 has / it / us / all / to / think / about / a / lot / given
   5 raised / you / points / some / interesting

2 ①22 **To make things easier for the speaker, it is helpful to be clear what part of your presentation your question refers to. Listen again to the presentation about Clock Option Express. Match these sentence beginnings (1–8) with an appropriate ending (a–h). More than one match may be possible.**
   1 At the start of your presentation, …
   2 In the section on advertising, …
   3 In the introduction, …
   4 In your conclusion, …
   5 Early in your talk, …
   6 Near the end of the presentation, …
   7 On your [last] slide, …
   8 I was interested in what …

a … you said you needed £500,000.
b … you referred to your market research.
c … you suggested that advertisers would be happy to pay premium rates.
d … you mentioned investing in Clock Options Express.
e … you pointed out that nothing similar is currently on the market.
f … you said about the market potential of your products.
g … you described your financial requirements as 'modest'.
h … you showed us some figures on costs.

3 **The questions below could be used at the end of a presentation. Complete them using the verbs in the box in the correct form. More than one answer might be possible.**

arrive	base	be	be	explain	have	say	tell

   1 Could you .... a little more about that?
   2 .... you sure that is true?
   3 Can you .... why that is?
   4 Would you mind .... me the reasons for that?
   5 Do you .... any figures for that?
   6 Who exactly .... responsible for that?
   7 How did you .... at that figure?
   8 What are those figures .... on?

Speaking

Work in pairs. Repeat your short presentation from Unit 12 (the company or organisation you work for; a product or service you know well; the town you live in), but make sure you are working with a different partner this time.

As you listen, note down something your partner says so you can ask a question about it at the end. Use the language from the Vocabulary section above.

Thank you for the talk. I really enjoyed it. Near the end of the talk, you mentioned a new airport near your town. Could you say a little more about that?

Intercultural advice

Getting started

1 **Work in pairs. Which of these reactions (a–c) best describes your reaction to situations 1–4 below?**

   a Offended – that's quite rude or impolite behaviour.

   b Neutral – I wouldn't do that, but it's not rude.

   c Positive – it could be describing my country.

   1 After the sixth meeting with my overseas client, he still calls me Mr Ortiz.

   2 When I arrived for a meeting, it was not in a private office, and my host took several phone calls during the meeting. Other people interrupted the meeting every few minutes.

   3 A potential client told me it would be 'difficult' to agree to the price I was offering. I later discovered 'difficult' means 'impossible'. Why couldn't he just say that?

   4 Once we were driving to a meeting. In the middle of nowhere, we came to a stop sign. There was no traffic for miles, but he still stopped!

2 **Read this information and match it to the situations (1–4) in Exercise 1.**

   a In **monochronic cultures**, people prefer to do things one at a time and believe there is a time and a place for everything. **Polychronic cultures**, however, are happy doing a number of things at the same time.

   b **Time-plentiful** cultures like to do business based mainly on trust. **Time-limited** cultures don't have enough time to develop this level of trust and so develop other systems to replace trust (such as strong rule-by-law).

   c In **high-context** cultures, people tend to be less direct in the way they communicate. In **low-context** cultures, they are much clearer in meaning: *no* means *no*.

   d **Cultural norms** affect our understanding of a situation. In one culture, continuing to be formal may mean we do not like or we distrust the other person, whereas in another culture, it is a mark of respect.

3 **Which of the descriptions in Exercise 2 apply to your country?**

Reading

Read this text, which gives advice to people visiting the USA on business. Can you find any incorrect information in it? If you think something is not true, try to correct it.

> **Doing business in the USA**
>
> On arrival, be sure to greet everyone in a very friendly manner; it is common to hug people you like. Make sure you offer your business card with both hands; using one hand or throwing the card on the table are considered disrespectful. In business, English will generally be used, but remember that Spanish is now more common in some cities. Avoid telling jokes in business situations, Americans can be very serious.
>
> For business lunches in restaurants, the host will expect you to share the cost. If you are lucky, you will be invited to your host's home. This is a rare honour, so be careful how you behave. Never refuse any food you are offered and always take an expensive gift— perfume, for a female host, is a good choice.
>
> In work, Americans are very punctual and work long hours. You should dress conservatively, and men have to wear a tie. Expect meetings to be long, as Americans like to discuss everything in great detail before making decisions, although money will usually be the key factor. People are polite, and silence is common, as people like time to think.
>
> Finally, you need to confirm everything in writing. Signed contracts are critical, and so lawyers are very important figures in American business.

Writing

A colleague from an overseas branch of the company you work for is coming to work in your country for six months. You have been asked to write to your colleague, giving cultural advice to help him during his stay. Use the Reading text above as an example.

Write to your colleague:

• explaining how people behave in social situations in your country

• describing what to expect in business situations.

Give a presentation of your ideas to the rest of the class.

Networking

Role-play

1 Work in pairs. Match the two halves of the sentences or questions to make useful expressions for the networking activity in Exercise 2.

1	Marek, there's someone …	a	… in your free time?
2	Natalie, I'd like to introduce you …	b	… you should meet.
3	Mr Chung, have you met …	c	… people here?
4	Do you know many …	d	… to Francisco. I think he might be able to help you out.
5	So, what do you do …	e	… like your hotel?
6	How do you …	f	… Alex Kaufmann? You might have something in common.
7	What line of business …	g	… first time in Moscow?
8	Is this your …	h	… are you in?

2 You're at an international conference in Moscow, and it is the reception party the night before the conference begins – a perfect networking opportunity. Study the role card your teacher gives you. Mingle with the other guests and introduce yourself, make small talk, try to find business and non-business interests in common. As you get to know people, introduce them to other people, especially people they may have something in common with. Use your real name. Your teacher will tell you when to stop.

3 How's your memory? If you didn't manage to find your perfect business partner, perhaps someone else in the class could introduce you to the right person. During their conversations, they might have heard something useful. If you think you can introduce two people who might be able to work together, now is the time.

4 Introduce your possible new business partner to the rest of the class, saying why you think you could work together.

Role cards

A

company and position	Director of International Projects, Cygnet Civil Engineering
hotel	The Hilton – very comfortable – a short walk from here
knowledge of city	first time here
likes and dislikes	You like travel and learning about food in other countries. You dislike cold weather – you prefer the beach!
networking information	You're looking for someone who can help with raising finance for a construction project in Germany (a leisure centre). Keep an eye out for any financiers.

B

company and position	Senior Partner, Sokolov & Partners, law firm
hotel	none – resident
knowledge of city	moved here four months ago
likes and dislikes	You like skiing and good food; you dislike Moscow traffic.
networking information	You are also on the board of a couple of Russian banks which are looking for business opportunities abroad. Maybe someone here is interested.

C

company and position	Partner, Carter and Raine, law firm
hotel	The Hilton – you're not pleased with your room – too noisy
knowledge of city	third visit
likes and dislikes	You like music (especially opera) and skiing. You aren't very interested in travel, as you spend about four months of the year away from home anyway.
networking information	Your company is seeking office premises in Moscow – you might be opening a new branch here next year if you can find the right opportunities.

D

company and position	Investment banker, Mizuko Finance Group
hotel	The Bristol – beautiful, but too far from here
knowledge of city	first time here
likes and dislikes	You tend to be too busy with work to have many interests.
networking information	A Russian business contact of yours is a specialist in commercial property and construction. You're having dinner with him tomorrow evening.

E

company and position	banker, PSR Bank, Spain, based in Madrid
hotel	The Royal – very modern, beautiful, but you would prefer somewhere more traditional
knowledge of city	second time here (But only quick business trips, so you don't know much about it.)
likes and dislikes	You like swimming, tennis and winter sports. You dislike being so busy!
networking information	Your bank lost a lot of money in the recession, funding a huge retail development in Madrid. You now plan to concentrate on export finance – it receives government assistance in Spain.

F

company and position	CEO of Herthaus, a supermarket chain
hotel	The National – only 200 metres from Red Square
knowledge of city	fourth visit (You know the central part and some good restaurants.)
likes and dislikes	You love cultural activities – music, art and books – but dislike sport.
networking information	Your supermarket chain imports fruit and vegetables from Spain, Portugal and Italy, but many banks are now careful about lending to producers in those countries.

G

company and position	Director, Chocolaterie du Frey, a Swiss chocolate producer
hotel	The Sheraton Palace – OK, typical business hotel
knowledge of city	second visit
likes and dislikes	You like travel and the arts, you don't really like winter sports (unusual for a Swiss person).
networking information	Your company is a high-class confectionary manufacturer and you are always on the lookout for new sales opportunities. Demand is falling in the more exclusive retail outlets – perhaps it is time to look at the mass market.

H

company and position	CEO of Delahaye Group, an international retail company
hotel	The Metropole – great location, only five minutes from the ballet
knowledge of city	You've been several times before for business and culture.
likes and dislikes	You love the ballet and are interested in art – Moscow has some excellent galleries. You prefer to visit in the summer because you dislike the cold.
networking information	As a major international retail chain, you are interested in three things: new product lines, new premises and, finally, contacts in the world of finance who can help with your international expansion plans.

Conference centre

Reading 1

Read this email from your boss. Choose the best word below – A, B, C or D – to fill each gap.

The Board of Directors has given its **1** .... for this year's sales conference to be
2 .... in Shanghai, China. Please find a suitable conference **3** .... The
conference details are as follows:

- Number of delegates: 350–400
- Dates: Friday 1 April – Sunday 3 April
- Facilities required for six plenary meetings and up to five smaller meetings at any one time
- Number of **4** .... speakers: six

Remember that delegates will **5** .... sales staff, agents and distributors from all
over the world. For many of them, this will be their first visit to Shanghai, so we want
it to be a memorable occasion. Please find a conference centre which can organise
6 .... outside the main conference as well.

Let me know what you come up with.

Thanks

Francesca

1	A permission	B approval	C order	D acceptance
2	A held	B set	C celebrated	D met
3	A place	B premises	C venue	D gathering
4	A invitation	B visiting	C outside	D guest
5	A consist	B contain	C constitute	D include
6	A actions	B events	C occasions	D happenings

Speaking

1   You have found a number of conference centres on the Internet, but how are you
    going to choose the one which best suits your purpose? Work with a partner and
    make a list of the things you will want to find out when you phone the various centres.

2   Divide into two groups.

   Group A: You are going to phone the **Radisson Blu Hotel Shanghai New World** in
   Shanghai, China. Prepare a list of questions you would like to ask. When
   you are ready, work with a partner from the other group and role-play the
   telephone call.

   Group B: Study the information sheet that your teacher will give you.

Writing 1

Write an email to all sales staff in your company to tell them about the annual sales conference. You should:

- mention where and when the conference is being held
- ask them to confirm their attendance
- request them to make their own travel arrangements to the conference flying business class (to be reimbursed by the company).

Write 40–50 words.

Reading 2

Read this email from your distributors in Kyoto, Japan. In most lines, there is one extra word. Write the extra words in the spaces. Some lines, however, are correct. If a line is correct, write a tick (✓).

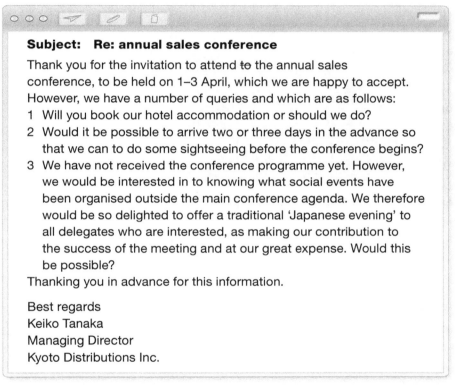

Subject: Re: annual sales conference

Thank you for the invitation to attend ~~to~~ the annual sales	1 ..to..
conference, to be held on 1–3 April, which we are happy to accept.	2 ....
However, we have a number of queries and which are as follows:	3 ....
1 Will you book our hotel accommodation or should we do?	4 ....
2 Would it be possible to arrive two or three days in the advance so	5 ....
that we can to do some sightseeing before the conference begins?	6 ....
3 We have not received the conference programme yet. However,	7 ....
we would be interested in to knowing what social events have	8 ....
been organised outside the main conference agenda. We therefore	9 ....
would be so delighted to offer a traditional 'Japanese evening' to	10 ....
all delegates who are interested, as making our contribution to	11 ....
the success of the meeting and at our great expense. Would this	12 ....
be possible?	

Thanking you in advance for this information.

Best regards
Keiko Tanaka
Managing Director
Kyoto Distributions Inc.

Writing 2

1 Work in small groups. Discuss what your answers should be to each of the questions in the email.

2 Write an email to Keiko Tanaka with your answers.

Group B

You work as sales assistants for the **Radisson Blu Hotel Shanghai New World** in Shanghai, China. You will have to deal with a telephone enquiry about the centre. Study the leaflet below and be prepared to answer any questions. If you are asked about prices, get the caller's details and tell him/her that you will fax or email a quote to them.

The Radisson Blu Hotel Shanghai New World

Conveniently located in downtown Shanghai, the Radisson Blu Hotel Shanghai New World, with its unique glass dome, is an icon of the Shanghai city skyline, and the perfect choice for the business and leisure traveller.

The Radisson Blu Hotel Shanghai New World offers 953 square meters of fully air-conditioned, flexible function space to suit all needs. With creative catering options, a comprehensive audio-visual service and experienced staff, your event is sure to be a success.

Conference facilities: The Grand Ballroom can accommodate up to 400 delegates. Divisible into three, the ballroom also provides flexibility for smaller groups and functions.

Meeting rooms: For smaller events, there's a choice of 10 private meeting rooms, each seating between 8 and 20 guests.

Meeting facilities:

- audio-visual equipment
- high-speed, wireless Internet
- LCD projector/screen, DVD player, PA system and screen
- a full range of support services, including IT specialists, photographers, secretaries, translators and couriers

Accommodation

The Radisson Blu Hotel Shanghai New World has 520 well-appointed guestrooms, including 91 suites and a Presidential Suite. All rooms feature large work areas with complimentary high-speed broadband internet access, both cable and wireless.

Dining choices include the revolving restaurant 'Epicure on 45' on the 45th floor, the 'Sky Dome Bar' on the 47th floor, Western and Chinese restaurants and the Lobby Bar

Email: newworld@radisson-nw.com

Speeding up meetings

Getting started

Meetings are indispensable when you don't want to do anything.
John Kenneth Galbraith, economist (1908–2006)

Discuss these questions in pairs.

1   Do you both agree with the above quotation? Why? / Why not?
2   How do you feel about meetings – when do you enjoy them / not enjoy them?
3   What purposes do meetings serve?
4   When are meetings essential?
5   What causes time-wasting in meetings?
6   In what other ways can meetings be frustrating?

Role-play

In a recent US survey, managers claimed that 90% of meetings were a waste of their time. As most managers spend at least 10–15 hours per week in meetings, ways need to be found of speeding up meetings so managers waste less time. You are going to participate in a meeting about holding quicker meetings.

1   Form groups of four and appoint someone to chair the meeting.
2   Study this agenda.

Agenda

1   Presentation of proposals for making meetings quicker
2   Discussion of proposals
3   Recommendations for future meetings
4   Any other business

3   You will be given a role card with proposals for point 1 on the agenda. Before you get this from your teacher, hold a two-minute brainstorming session to think of some ideas of your own. The chair should make a note of these ideas to include in the discussion.
4   In the meeting, each person should present their proposals, *in their own words*, on how to make meetings quicker. Use the information on your role card to help you.
5   The group should discuss each proposal, rejecting any you do not like. You must give reasons for your decisions and opinions. Remember to include any ideas from Step 3 above.
6   Finally, the group should agree on one or more ideas which the company can use in all future meetings.
7   See who can finish their meeting quickest without missing out any of the points. When everyone has finished, the chair of each meeting should present a summary of your discussion and conclusions to the rest of the class.

Writing

Write an email to all members of staff about your ideas for making meetings shorter.
- Say what the new rules are.
- Explain how they will work.
- Say when the new rules will begin.

Role cards

Student A Your idea is to hold all meetings standing up – no chairs or even tables, so participants don't get too comfortable. Suggest that *this* meeting is held standing up to try it out. (But should there be any exceptions to this system?) Also, you think small talk at the beginning of the meeting should be banned.	**Student B** Your idea is that everyone who wants to speak must have a time limit of one minute. You can say a lot in a minute, so why not? The chair of the meeting should time each speaker and tell them when their time is up. Why not try it in *this* meeting? Also, you think serving tea and coffee in meetings should stop. It just delays things.
Student C Your idea is that only items on the agenda can be discussed at a meeting. The agenda should be decided the day before and emailed to everyone. Too many things are added in the AOB (any other business) part, and nobody is really prepared for them. Suggest cancelling AOBs today! Also you think nobody should be allowed to bring mobile phones to meetings. It would make people keen to finish quicker.	**Student D** You are going to chair this meeting. Make sure everyone speaks and that nobody dominates the discussion. Personally, your idea is to stop having meetings altogether – they never achieve anything, and most decisions can be made by managers alone – that's what managers are for. You have an important announcement to make in Any Other Business. The company is considering making some staff redundant, and you have only just discovered this.

Agrodist

Reading

1   Read this information and complete the table below.

You work for Marazon, a company which produces large agricultural machines for use on farms and in agricultural warehouses. The machines have a reputation for high quality, while at the same time being competitively priced. As a result, your machines have become brand names on farms and in agricultural businesses in many parts of the world.

Recently, you decided to break into the Polish market, and last year your company signed a contract giving an exclusive three-year dealership to a distributor of agricultural machinery, Agrodist SP ZOO, based in Kraków in southern Poland. Under the terms of your agreement, Agrodist were initially to be supplied with three machines of each type: one for the showroom and the others for sale to customers. Agrodist could set the Polish price, but they would pay Marazon a commission of 10% on their mark-up.

name of your company	
brief description of company's activities	
company's reputation	
terms of agreement with Agrodist	

2   One of your sales staff went to Poland last week and visited Agrodist in Kraków. Directly after his visit to the showroom, he sent this email to head office. In most lines, there is one word which is wrong. Write the correct word in the gap on the right. If the line is correct, put a tick (✓).

To: **Marketing Director and Export Sales Director**
From: **Pau Catalá**
Subject: **Agrodist SP ZOO, Kraków**

I visited our distributors ~~there~~ in Kraków last Friday as agreed.
I was surprised to discovery a number of anomalies during my visit.   1 *here*
1 Agrodist do not have none of our machines in their showroom.   2 ....
   While I asked them about this, the reason they gave me was that   3 ....
   they had sold it all. This must be true, because they immediately   4 ....
   placed an order for three more of each. Although, prospective   5 ....
   customers do not have an opportunity to see a product in the   6 ....
   showroom, as agreed.   7 ....
2 When I looked to their price list, I saw that they have been selling   8 ....
   the machines at a higher price that the one they are declaring to us,   9 ....
   i.e. they are not paying us the full 10% commission on the mark-up.   10 ....
3 I visited one of theirs customers near Kraków, only to discover that   11 ....
   Marazon's logo was been removed from the machine and replaced   12 ....
   with Agrodist's logo.   13 ....
This three points are in clear breach of our three-year renewable contract 14 ....
with Agrodist, and I believe that urgent action would be taken. On the   15 ....
one hand, the good news is that they are selling plenty of our products.   16 ....

Regards   17 ....
Pau Catalá

Role-play

1 Work in groups of four. You are the senior Sales and Marketing team. Hold a meeting to discuss what action you should take with regard to Agrodist. Here is an agenda for your meeting.

AGENDA

1 Machines in the showroom
2 Commission
3 Company logo
4 Sales
5 Action to be taken

2 Work in different groups of four. You have decided to have a meeting with the directors of Agrodist in Kraków.

Students A and B:	You should take the parts of the Export Sales Director and the Marketing Director of Marazon.
Students C and D:	You should take the parts of the Managing Director and the Marketing Director of Agrodist.

Your teacher will give you your instructions.

Speaking

Work in groups and discuss this question.

Which is more important in this case: ethical behaviour or maximising profits?

Role cards

Students A and B

Directors of Marazon

Before the meeting, work together and decide your strategy for the meeting, based on what you decided in Exercise 1.

You need to consider what actions you want Agrodist to take to meet the terms of your agreement; what action, if any, to take against Agrodist if they do not agree; and what concessions you are prepared to give Agrodist in order to achieve an agreement. You do not really want this relationship to end, as it is proving a profitable one.

Students C and D

Directors of Agrodist

Prepare for the meeting with the directors of Marazon. Base your strategy on these points.

You recognise that you have been in breach of contract, but:

- you have exceeded sales targets set by Marazon
- although you have been selling at a higher price than the one you declared to Marazon, Marazon has been receiving more commission than it expected
- you have been replacing Marazon's logo because Agrodist is a more recognised brand name in Poland, and this is therefore a logical way to boost sales.

You are not worried if Marazon threaten you with legal action. You have many other suppliers. However, you are ready to agree to all their demands as long as they agree to reduce the commission to 5%, though this is also negotiable.

Business travel game

Rules

Play in groups of four or five.

You need a die for each group and one counter for each player.

1 Take turns to throw the die and move to a square.
2 Follow the instructions on the square.
3 If you perform the task correctly (according to the other players or your teacher), you get 10 points.
4 If another player has already landed on the square and explained the word(s) in bold, you can't earn the extra points unless you can think of an alternative expression.
5 If you land on a *Culture clash* square, you have to pick a card and give it to the person next to you, who will ask you a question. Answer the question correctly for 10 points.
6 You needn't throw the exact number to reach *Finish*.
   The first player to reach *Finish* gets 100 points.
   The second player gets 60 points.
   The third player gets 30 points.
7 When the third player reaches *Finish*, the game ends. The winner is the player with the most points.

Culture-clash cards

Culture clash! **Q:** True or false? In Japan, the most important person in a meeting sits nearest to the door. **A:** False. They usually sit furthest from and facing the door. If they were correct, tell them to go forward to the next blank space.	**Culture clash!** **Q:** If you have a delicious meal in a restaurant in Beijing, how much should you leave as a tip? **A:** Nothing. Tipping is not common in most Asian countries. If they were correct, tell them to go forward to the next blank space.	**Culture clash!** **Q:** True or false? Everyone uses first names in business in America. **A:** False. It is very common, but only call an older person, or someone more senior, by their first name if they invite you to. If they were correct, tell them to go forward to the next blank space.	**Culture clash!** **Q:** True or false? In the Middle East, it is considered impolite to take phone calls in meetings. **A:** False. For an Arab business person, it is rude not to take the call. If they were correct, tell them to go forward to the next blank space.
Culture clash! **Q:** True or false? In Russia, major decisions tend to be made in formal meetings of senior management. **A:** Generally false. Formal meetings are often held to confirm decisions which have been made elsewhere. If they were correct, tell them to go forward to the next blank space.	**Culture clash!** **Q:** In Switzerland, how important is small talk before a meeting? **A:** Not very important. People usually prefer to keep their business and personal life separate, so there is little small talk prior to starting a meeting. If they were correct, tell them to go forward to the next blank space.	**Culture clash!** **Q:** True or false? Shaking hands when meeting someone is acceptable all over the world. **A:** True. Although some countries have their own traditions, such as bowing in Japan, globalisation means that shaking hands is commonplace. If they were correct, tell them to go forward to the next blank space.	**Culture clash!** **Q:** True or false? In China, a formal meal to celebrate a business deal can be up to 30 courses long. **A:** True. Avoid finishing everything, as this means you are still hungry and more food will be served to you. If they were correct, tell them to go forward to the next blank space.

DAY 1 You're in a meeting at another company. You need to go straight to the airport to begin a business trip as soon as the meeting ends. The problem is, the meeting is taking forever. Go to Square 1.

1 START This is an important client. End the meeting, explain the situation, but be polite!	2 You need a taxi to the airport. Perhaps your host can help. What do you say?	3 Get in the taxi. The driver says *Where to?* How do you reply?	4	5 You can't find your passport. Go back one space.	6 At airport security, they ask you a question: *Did you ...... these bags ......?* Complete the gaps.	7 **Culture clash!** Take a card, give it to the person next to you and answer the question.	8 You have some time to kill. Order a coffee.
16 You arrive at the hotel. The receptionist says *Can I help you?* What do you say?	15	14 One of your bags is missing. Go to the desk and explain where you're staying so they can deliver the bag later.	13 There is a huge queue at immigration Miss a turn.	12 **Culture clash!** Take a card, give it to the person next to you and answer the question.	11 The flight attendant says *Can I offer you anything to drink?* How do you reply?	10 You board the plane and head for seat 10F. Someone is already sitting there. What do you say?	9 The person making your coffee says *How do you like it?* What do you say?
17 Your room is not ready yet. Go back two spaces.	18 **Culture clash!** Take a card, give it to the person next to you and answer the question.	19 You're hungry. Call reception and ask for information on local restaurants. You like Italian food.	20 You find a nice Italian restaurant. A waiter says *Good .... Table ....?* Complete the gaps.	21 In the restaurant, the waiter says *Are you ready to order?* Chicken soup, then steak sounds good. What do you say?	22 Your food takes a long time to come, so the restaurant offers you a free dessert. Go to square 24.	23 You want to pay for your dinner. What do you say to the waiter?	24
32	31 You decide to walk back to your hotel (The Bristol), but you get lost. Ask someone for directions.	30 You have had a successful meeting with Mr Peters. Thank him and invite him to join you for dinner this evening.	29 Time for some small talk. Make a comment about the weather or the city you're in.	28 **Culture clash!** Take a card, give it to the person next to you and answer the question.	27 Your client, Mr Peters, arrives. You have never met him face to face before. Introduce yourself.	26 Your client, Mr Peters, is late for work. His PA offers you some tea while you wait. What do you say?	25 **DAY 2** You arrive at the client's offices to meet Mr Peters. Explain who you are and what you want to the receptionist.
33 **DAY 3** It's time to leave your hotel. What do you say at reception?	34 Off to the train station to buy a ticket to your next destination. What do you say to the ticket seller?	35 **Culture clash!** Take a card, give it to the person next to you and answer the question.	36 It's very hot on the train, but the windows are all closed. What do you say to the other passengers?	37 One of your fellow passengers is having trouble lifting a heavy bag. Offer to help.	38 While you're on the train, call your next appointment. Leave a message on her voicemail explaining where you are and when you'll arrive.	39 The train arrives early. Go to square 42	40 You decide to go to a café for a coffee. There is only one empty seat. What do you say to the person in the next seat?
48 **FINISH** HOME AT LAST!	47 The company driver picks you up. What does he ask you? Complete the gap: *...... trip?* How do you reply?	46	45 In the airport shop, you see a beautiful pair of shoes. They are too small. What do you say to the shop assistant?	44 **Culture clash!** Take a card, give it to the person next to you and answer the question.	43 As you're leaving, your host asks you to say hello to one of your colleagues for him. Complete his request: *Give ...... to Tony.*	42	41 Another successful meeting. Your host invites you out to celebrate. Unfortunately, you have a plane to catch. What do you say?

Traditional marketing vs. social media marketing

Getting started

Discuss this question in pairs.

Is traditional marketing dying?

Think about the advantages and disadvantages of traditional marketing compared to social media marketing. Consider cost and the numbers and type of people reached.

Reading

1 Work in pairs. Read these extracts from an online forum for discussing the question above.

Is traditional marketing dying?

With social media gaining in popularity for marketing messages, do you think traditional marketing will now disappear? Will traditional marketing survive?

> **Answer This Question**

Jake Hodge, High Altitude Hardware

Yes, it is. The Internet means **your audience is now highly fragmented**, difficult to reach and easily able to **collect opinions, reviews and ratings from peers** – people they trust more than you as a **vendor**. The audience can consume information and media when, where, and how they want to – companies no longer control this. What we should really do is build great products and then have conversations about them with our customers.

 Reply

Dennis Scheyer

Absolutely not. You still have to **build a brand**, and while social media is definitely a vital part of that these days, you can only say so much in a 140-character Tweet. Many Facebook and Twitter users do not respond positively to commercial messaging – they even **block the messenger** or remove them as a friend. The key is to **make the message fit the medium**. Be sure to hire someone who understands these options to design your message.

---

2 Explain the words and phrases in bold in Exercise 1 in your own words. Cover the Vocabulary exercise below before you start. When you have finished, do the Vocabulary exercise.

Vocabulary

Match the words (1–8) with their definitions (a–h) from Cambridge dictionaries. Were your answers to Reading Exercise 2 correct?

1	fragmented	**a**	measurements of how good or popular someone or something is
2	reviews	**b**	someone who is selling something
3	ratings	**c**	consisting of several separate parts
4	peers	**d**	a method or way of expressing something
5	vendor	**e**	people who are the same age or who have the same social position as you
6	brand	**f**	reports that give an opinion about something
7	block	**g**	a type of product made by a particular company
8	medium	**h**	prevent something from happening or succeeding

Speaking

Discuss these questions.

1 Which reply do you agree with most? Why?

2 Do you think traditional marketing has a future in the internet age? Why? / Why not?

Role-play

A medium-sized language school, with 400–500 students and ten full-time teachers, wants to boost student numbers through more effective marketing, but has a limited budget. Currently, marketing is done through their website and through mailing brochures in response to telephone or email enquiries, although brochures are expensive to print. It also advertises in local newspapers in the month before the school year begins. The Director of the school is also interested in making more use of social media.

1 Divide into two groups.

Group A: **Traditional marketing**
Your task is to think of ways the language school could promote itself through traditional marketing methods.
Brainstorm some ideas. Think about what the most effective traditional marketing methods are for a business of this size (print, radio, TV) and whether any new or unusual ways of marketing might be worth trying.

Group B: **Social media marketing**
Your task is to think of ways the language school could promote itself through social media.
Brainstorm some ideas. Think about:
- how best to communicate with potential students
- which media to use
- what you can do through social media to generate interest in the school
- how to avoid being blocked by users.

2 Form pairs, one from Group A and one from Group B. Share your ideas and make comments.

3 Go back to your groups, A and B. Your task now is to produce a combined strategy which will include elements of both traditional and social media marketing.

Here are some areas to consider:
- What will your online presence be in future? (e.g. website only, website plus social networking site, or something else?)
- How will you manage this online presence? (e.g. who will be responsible for managing social-media profiles, issuing updates, responding to messages, sharing ideas and information and so on, and how often will they do this?)
- How can you link your online presence with traditional marketing? (e.g. get customers to join your social networking site to receive a 20% discount on their next course)
- Will there be any training needs? (e.g. digital marketing courses or tutorials)

4 Nominate someone from each group to present your ideas to the rest of the class. Which group had the best ideas?

Greening the office

Getting started

Work in groups of three. You all work in the administration department of a medium-sized company. It is a typical office, with about 80 staff, 100 computer terminals, several meeting rooms and is located in a building with a small garden area outside. The management is looking at ways of saving money through being more environmentally friendly. What would you suggest? You have two minutes to come up with some initial ideas.

Vocabulary

Match these words or expressions (1–8) with their definitions (a–h) from Cambridge dictionaries.

1	efficient	a	an action which saves money at the beginning, but which, over a longer period of time, results in more money being wasted than being saved
2	rechargeable	b	to send out a noise, smell or gas
3	false economy	c	able to be filled with electricity so that it can work again
4	car pooling	d	vehicles with engines that use both petrol and electricity
5	congestion	e	working or operating quickly and effectively in an organised way
6	emit	f	clean, especially in order to prevent disease
7	hybrids	g	a situation where there is too much traffic and movement is made difficult
8	hygienic	h	a group of people who travel to work together, usually in a different person's vehicle each day

Role-play

Work in small groups. Your company has decided that it needs ideas from staff about how to make the office more environmentally friendly. Discuss each of the proposals on the right and decide whether they would be good practices for the office staff to adopt. Take turns to ask the questions and keep a note of your group's final answers. Some staff opinions for and against each proposal have been included to help your discussion, but they might not be true!

1   **Staff should always switch off their computers and printers at the end of the day.**

Yes – switching off a computer prevents energy being wasted overnight and at weekends.

No – it takes more energy starting up a computer than it does running it.

2   **Use low-energy bulbs and switch off the lights every time you leave a room.**

Yes – lighting represents the majority of energy use in most companies.

No – low-energy bulbs are more efficient if you don't keep switching them on and off.

3   **Set up a car-pooling scheme for employees.**

Yes – traffic congestion costs $40bn in fuel and time in the US alone.

No – it's too inconvenient.

4   **Insist that all staff walk to all appointments within 1.5km of the office.**

Yes – cars emit 90% of their pollution in the first 1.5km.

No – it's a nice idea, but what about in the winter or when it's raining?

5   **Stop watering the grass outside the company offices. Let nature look after it.**

Yes – it's extremely wasteful and unnecessary to water grass.

No – It's bad for the company image if visitors see nothing but dead grass when they arrive.

6   **Buy new company cars, especially hybrids, to replace older, less efficient models.**

Yes – new cars are much more fuel efficient.

No – making a new car causes more pollution than keeping older cars on the road.

7   **Use paper cups instead of plastic cups in the company coffee machines.**

Yes – paper is easier to recycle and less polluting to make.

No – plastic cups are more hygienic and can also be recycled.

8   **Turn down the heating to 21°C in winter. In summer, open the windows.**

Yes – a 1°C cut in heating saves 10% in cost.

No – people will be less productive if they are cold, and this will cost us more.

Form new groups and share your ideas with the new members. Find at least four ideas you can all agree on, then tell the rest of the class. Your teacher will give you some feedback on each of the points 1–8.

Managing change

A change is as good as a rest.
English saying

Getting started

Discuss these questions in pairs.

1   Do you agree with the saying above? Why? / Why not?
2   Do you think change is always a good thing in study, work or business situations? Why? / Why not? Give examples to support your views.

Speaking

1   Work in groups of three. Think of a problem in your work or studies where a change is necessary or would be an improvement. This could be a current situation where you would like to see a change OR a past situation where a change happened and the results are known (it is important that you do not tell your colleagues which at this stage, so use present tenses to describe it).

2   Present your problem to your two colleagues and explain what you would like to achieve. Your colleagues should follow the steps in the next column to find out more about the problem and take notes to help you with ideas for solving it. Your presentation should take one minute only.

Organising change

1   How do you know what elements of the situation require change? (And should any parts of the situation be left unchanged?)
2   Are there any other people who also have an interest in the results of any change? (If not, go to 6)
3   Have you considered the best way to involve these people in the decision-making process?
4   How can you be sure that they really do support your change ideas?
5   What will you do if they think any change is a bad idea?
6   What are the first priorities for?
7   How will you manage disputes between the various parties involved?
8   What will be the best way for you (and any other parties involved) to supervise and check the change(s) as they happen?
9   What will be a successful outcome for you?
10 How will you make certain that the changes you have made will work long term?

3   Once everyone in each group has presented their problem, spend a few minutes thinking about what advice you could offer each person on solving it. Take it in turns to present your ideas to the person seeking help. Each person will receive two sets of advice. Now discuss how to reduce ideas to a short-list of the best four or five.

If your problem was one from the past and there was a real outcome, you can now tell your colleagues what *really* happened. Were their ideas similar to what actually happened?

Fendara SL

Getting started

Read this quote and discuss in small groups to what extent you agree or disagree with Herb Kelleher. Give reasons for your answers.

'Herb Kelleher, CEO of Southwest Airlines, rejects the conventional notion of putting the customer first. At Southwest, employees come first, in the belief that a company with happy and productive workers will have happy, paying customers.'

Reading

Fendara SL is a medium-sized hi-tech engineering company located near Verona in northern Italy. The company has 147 employees, of which 86 are shopfloor workers. Factory work is organised in three shifts, from 6 a.m. to 2 p.m., 2 p.m. to 10 p.m. and 10 p.m. to 6 a.m.

In recent years, they have seen their staff costs spiral due to rising salaries, higher training costs and the difficulty of recruiting and retaining skilled workers, particularly for the night shift.

1 You are managers at Fendara. Recently, the HR department presented you with the charts below. Work in pairs and answer these questions.

    1 What do the charts show?
    2 How do they illustrate Fendara's problems?

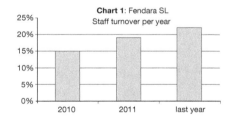

Chart 1: Fendara SL
Staff turnover per year

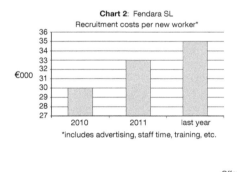

Chart 2: Fendara SL
Recruitment costs per new worker*
*includes advertising, staff time, training, etc.

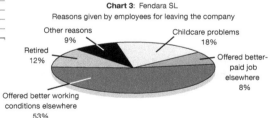

Chart 3: Fendara SL
Reasons given by employees for leaving the company

Other reasons 9%
Childcare problems 18%
Retired 12%
Offered better-paid job elsewhere 8%
Offered better working conditions elsewhere 53%

2 You have decided to investigate flexible working practices as a way of reducing staff turnover. Work in three groups, with each group studying one of the companies on the next sheet. Take notes under these headings for the company you have studied.

    1 Name of company
    2 Sector
    3 No. of employees
    4 Reasons given for introducing flexible working
    5 How their flexibility works
    6 Cost savings from flexible working
    7 Other benefits from flexibility

Speaking

1 Work in groups of three, with one student from each of the groups in Reading Exercise 2. Hold a meeting to discuss changes to Fendara's working practices. You should:

- each present your findings from Reading Exercise 2
- discuss the advantages and disadvantages of introducing a flexible work system
- produce an action plan for changes to working practices in the company.

2 Present your action plan to the whole class, and discuss the pros and cons of each.

Writing

Write a proposal, outlining your recommendations or changes to working practices at Fendara SL. If you wish, use the proposals in the Writing reference on page 122 in the Student's Book as a model.

In your proposal, you should include information on:

- how working practices should change at Fendara
- the effects on HR (recruitment, staff turnover, etc.)
- the financial effects (costs, turnover, etc.)
- how the changes will benefit the staff (motivation, work–life balance, etc.).

Brite Paints

Sector: Manufacturing
Location: Zurich, Switzerland
Employees: 50

The waiting list is constantly growing of people wanting to join Brite Paints in Zurich, attracted by the company's positive approach to work–life balance issues. In a very tight labour market, where recruitment is difficult, Brite is saving on advertising costs – some CHF7,000 over the last 12 months – as its reputation for flexible working spreads. Staff retention is excellent, and many wait to retire rather than leave to go to another job, again saving valuable recruitment money.

Chief Executive Simon Hofmann is convinced that the company's flexible working practices are critical to this high level of staff retention and recruitment, and offers different packages to meet individual staff requirements.

The workforce is ethnically diverse, with many more women than men, and the work–life balance policies reflect this mix. Hours can be adjusted to fit in with family commitments, and flexible job routines have been introduced, both within and across departments, to make sure all work and hours are covered. This has led to an increase in the skills base and so widened the company pool of resources.

Vienna Electronics (VE)

Sector: Manufacturing
Location: Vienna, Austria
Employees: 1,700

Flexible working has had a positive impact on employee loyalty and improved performance at VE. Importantly, a significant reduction in staff turnover has been seen since the launch of their flexible working program three years ago. Previously, people who wanted to work only in term time, for example, would have moved to a competitor; now they are staying with SE. According to the HR Director, 'People are our greatest asset at SE, and with an estimated €45,000 cost for each employee who leaves the company, our flexible compensation and benefits package aims to reinforce a culture of flexibility and commitment to our company.'

Recent initiatives include a standard request process for flexible working, paid adoption leave, a childcare and eldercare helpline service, reduced hours and term-time working for employees, work–life resources online and a career-break pilot scheme.

Employee reaction has been very positive, and the re-packaging of existing benefits into the work–life framework has shown staff – both actual and potential – the benefits of working for the company.

Guangzhou Engineering

Sector: Manufacturing
Location: Southern China
Employees: 50

Changing to annualised hours has maximised efficiency at steel manufacturer Guangzhou Engineering. Its 50 staff are contracted to work 1,770 hours a year, with a reserve of 160 hours to cover sickness, medical appointments, rework and peak production.

Working hours are determined by customer demand, with the only requirement that teams deliver products to the customer on time and to high quality. As long as the core hours are maintained, operatives can take an afternoon off to spend with their family. Because of this improved work–life balance, employees feel valued and trusted, paying dividends for the company in terms of a more contented workforce.

'The difference in performance has been incredible,' says CEO Zhongye Zhu. 'Efficiency leapt up beyond all our expectations. Our teams are now not only facing in the same direction; they are focused correctly and all pulling together … We can now compete with anyone worldwide.'

'Ninety-eight per cent of the most successful organisations in the world work in teams. They provide an effective framework within which to introduce flexible working patterns,' says Bao Chang, Managing Director.

Outsourcing survey

You are going to conduct a class survey to find out people's attitudes to issues connected with outsourcing.

Instructions

1 Divide into three groups.
2 Each group should choose one of the three boxes (A, B or C) containing questions.
3 First, ask the people in your group the questions and note down the statistics.
4 Next, ask the people in the other two groups and note down the statistics.
5 When you have collected all the answers, work together in your group and draw charts to illustrate the statistics.
6 Present your group's findings to the rest of the class.
7 Write a short report based on your findings in the survey.

A

1 Which of these things do you think is most important when considering whether to outsource activities (choose two)? Please give reasons.

- reducing exposure to risk
- reducing costs
- increasing productivity
- skills not available in-house
- activity better handled by specialist company
- other (please specify)

2 Which activities in your company (or a company you know well) could be outsourced or are already outsourced? Please give reasons.

- IT activities
- back-office activities*
- recruitment
- customer services, including call centre
- production
- security
- cleaning
- other (please specify)

* Back-office activities are activities which do not involve contact with customers, e.g. payroll, bookkeeping, stock control, etc. Front-office activities would include customer services, sales, etc.

B

1 Where would you prefer to outsource? Please give reasons.

- in your own country/region
- offshore/overseas

2 Which of these criteria do you think is most important when choosing a specialist supplier of a) IT services; b) back-office activities*; c) customer services? Why? (choose from this list)

- low wages/costs
- talented professional workers
- high level of technical ability
- ability to speak your language
- ability to speak your customers' language(s)
- reputation of company
- other (please specify)

* Back-office activities are activities which do not involve contact with customers, e.g. payroll, bookkeeping, stock control, etc. Front-office activities would include customer services, sales, etc.

C

1 If you were a manager, which of these issues would worry you most about a decision to outsource offshore? Give reasons.

- bad publicity for your company
- political reactions to your decision
- loss of jobs inside your company
- managing the change within your company
- organising communications with the service provider
- measuring the quality of the service provided

2 If you had to reduce staff levels as a result of outsourcing, which of the methods below would be best? Give reasons.

- offering voluntary redundancies or early retirement to any staff who wish to take them
- selecting the workers you no longer require and making them redundant
- employing a specialist agency to find jobs for staff in other companies
- through natural wastage (i.e. waiting for people to retire or leave when they want to)
- redeploying staff to other jobs inside your organisation
- other (please specify)

Good customer service?

Getting started

1   Discuss this question in pairs.

When was the last time you experienced poor customer service from a company? Compare your experiences. You should say:

- what you wanted from this company
- why the customer service was poor
- what you think the company should have done to improve the situation.

2   Describe an example of excellent customer service you have experienced.

3   What could the company you described in Exercise 1 learn from the company you described in Exercise 2?

Reading and discussion

1   Work in small groups. Look at these examples of real-life customer service problems and decide what order you would put them in, from most to least serious, and why.

a   A customer comes into your store to buy a washing machine. The customer wants advice on which model to buy, but they are served by a new member of staff who is not familiar with the products the customer is looking for. After spending ten minutes trying to help the customer, the customer becomes frustrated and leaves the store.

b   Your company has set up a new telephone helpline to deal with customer enquiries. Customers have to listen to recorded instructions and press buttons on their telephone keypad to be directed to the relevant information. Customers have begun to complain about the system: there is nobody to speak to; they are always being disconnected before they have found out what they want; and it's costing them money.

c   Your company's website is proving a great success, but recently there have been problems with customers complaining that their emails are not being answered for up to three days. When you investigate, you find that these cases involved staff having to consult their superiors or people in other departments before they could deal with the customer.

d   A company planned a lunch meeting with some important clients. The company's administrative assistant ordered sandwiches from your catering company, which you agreed to provide. In the meantime, you received a larger order from someone else and prioritised that. The meeting ended without sandwiches being provided.

e   Your website-design company put together an attractive looking website for a new client and even gave him a discount on the price. The client ordered some changes to the design. Your company objected to the changes because they ruined the appearance and functionality of the website. The situation became heated, but you finally made the changes. When the site was finished, the client asked you why people said it looked ugly.

2   Work in pairs. Look at problems a–c in Exercise 1 again. With your partner, briefly discuss what the consequences could be, and what possible solutions each company could have tried.

3 Match situations a–c in Exercise 1 with these possible consequences (1–3) and with an appropriate solution (i–iii).

1 It is not a good example of customer care, although the customers were at least not completely forgotten. The risk is that ignoring a customer makes them less likely to recommend you to their friends. If you do it regularly, they could go elsewhere.	i Make sure staff have the correct training. Telling the truth only makes things worse. If someone is in this situation, they should know what to do, which is to say that they will find someone to help them. That at least shows you're going to help them.
2 This is an example of poor product knowledge, which should be covered in training. Letting someone who doesn't know about what you offer serve a customer, is a big mistake. If you've just started with the company, it's not good enough to use that as an excuse. Customers don't care, they just want help and information. If they don't get it, they won't come back.	ii Consider reducing the number of stages to navigate and make real people easier to reach. It's more expensive, but could retain customers more effectively. You could even use this in your marketing – *ring us and chat to a real person.*
3 This technology does keep costs down, but problems arise when there are too many levels of automation or technical problems and there is nobody to help. It's a serious issue, because customers may stop calling or even choose to use a company where they can speak to another person.	iii When something can't be resolved immediately, you need to tell the customer what is happening and be clear how long it will take before you have an answer. They won't feel that you are ignoring them, and it would give them confidence that their issue is being taken care of and will be resolved as soon as possible.

4 Do you agree with the solutions suggested? Why? / Why not?

How do they compare with your ideas?

Writing

Work in pairs. Look again at problems d and e in Reading Exercise 1. With your partner, plan and write an email to your line manager:

- summarising one of the problems (d or e)
- explaining the possible consequences
- recommending a solution.

When you have finished, post your emails on the classroom walls. Read other pairs' emails. You should say which one has the best ideas, and why.

Designing a customer communication competition

1 Work in four groups. The retail company you work for wants to find out more about what customers *really* think about the way it communicates with its customers and, if possible, to improve that communication. Currently, your company advertises in newspapers and magazines, sends mailshots, and sometimes telephones people with special promotional offers.

In order to get customers' suggestions for better communication, the company has decided to design a competition in which customers will write in with their ideas. They will have the chance of winning a prize for the best ideas.

In your groups, you should follow the instructions below, which have been prepared by the Marketing Director:

You need to decide what:

- you want to learn from customers, for example their opinions on your company's customer communication at the moment or suggestions for how to improve it.
- customers will have to do in the competition, for example write a letter, complete a form or a multiple-choice questionnaire, or something else. This should not be too long. If it is, most customers won't bother to read it.
- prize, or prizes, you will offer to the best ideas. For example you could give a prize to *every* useful idea, or you could offer one 'grand prize' to the best idea, with smaller prizes for other ideas you use.

2 When you have decided on the points above, you should design, on a separate piece of paper, the competition the customers will see. Ask your teacher to check it for you. He or she will then make copies for you.

3 Exchange copies of your competition with another group. Each person in the group should then complete an entry to the competition. When everyone has finished, send all your entries back to the other group.

4 When you have received the entries to your competition, discuss and decide together on which one(s) will win the prize or prizes.

5 Each group should announce the winner(s) of their competition, saying what people had to do in the competition and how you chose the winner.

An email of apology

Getting started

Discuss these questions in pairs.

1 Have you ever had to write apologising about something? If yes, who did you write to, and why?

2 Which of these elements would you personally expect to find in an email of apology, and why?

   a an expression of thanks for the complaint
   b an apology
   c an explanation of the causes of the problem
   d a promise to correct the problem
   e an offer of compensation
   f another apology
   g something saying you hope they will continue as customers
   h something saying your company's products or services should be better quality

Reading

1 Read this email of apology. Which of the points (a–h) above are men tioned in it?

To:	Ann Massey
From:	Mariano Godoy, Operations Manager
Subject:	damaged shipment

Dear Mrs Massen

Thank you for your message about the damaged shipment which it was carried by   **1** ....
Wanderer's Transport. We very much regret the inconvenience that it has caused you.   **2** ....
From your explanation of the problem, I am quite sure that your request is for the   **3** ....
€700 reduction in the cost of the three computer monitors will be approved.   **4** ....
However, our investigations have revealed that the damage may have been due to an   **5** ....
accident occurred at our warehouse while the goods were being loaded for shipment.   **6** ....
So I am sorry for the annoyance this has caused.   **7** ....
Could you please to keep the damaged monitors and their packaging in the same   **8** ....
condition as you received them until our insurance company can inspect them in the   **9** ....
next three days time?   **10** ....
If all is in the order, we will reimburse you immediately. I hope this unfortunate   **11** ....
incident which will not affect your relationship with Wanderer's Transport in the   **12** ....
future.

Yours sincerely,
Mariano Godoy
Operations Manager

2 In most lines of the above email, there is one extra word. Find the word and write it in the space provided. If a line is correct, put a tick (✓) in the space.

3 Read the email again and add to the lists below:

- two more ways of apologising
- one more way of expressing causes
- one more way of requesting.

Apologising

- I do apologise for the inconvenience that this problem has caused.

    1 ....

    2 ....

Expressing causes

- This was caused by …
- This was because …

    3 ....

Requesting

- I would be grateful if you could …
- Please would you …

    4 ....

Writing

1 You work in the customer services department of TopTen Leasing (see Unit 23 of the Student's Book). Here is the email you received from Bob Castle on which your manager has written some notes. He has asked you to write a reply to the email. Discuss the following questions with a partner.

1 Which phrases from Exercise 3 above could you use in your reply?

2 How many paragraphs should your email have, and what should each paragraph contain?

2 Write the reply using all the handwritten notes.

To: Jenny Morrison
From: Bob Castle, CEO
Subject: Incorrect and late delivery of equipment

Dear Ms Morrison,

Say you regret problem. — Following our telephone conversation last Wednesday, I would like to express my dissatisfaction with your company's recent service in writing.

Last Monday, I ordered the delivery of two Yamaha Mark 5 building hoists which were urgently needed for construction work we are carrying out in the Berlin area. According to your recent letter, we understood we would have this equipment within 24 hours and so we organised our work schedules to take this into account. However, the equipment did not arrive until late on Wednesday, nearly 48 hours after placing the order, and instead of sending Mark 5 hoists, your company delivered Mark 2s, which do not meet our requirements.

Agree: our mistake —
Explain: two orders were mixed up. Say why. —

As a consequence of this, we were forced to entirely reorganise our construction teams and our building programmes until the correct equipment arrived. This involved a considerable amount of extra work and loss of time on projects where our costs have been calculated very exactly.

Say we won't charge for hoists this time. —

We have, over the years, been very happy with your service and we have recommended you to other companies working in the sector. A repetition of last week's incident would result in our having to look for other leasers, which is something we would prefer to avoid.

Hope they continue to be customers. —

Yours sincerely,
Bob Castle
CEO

Business gurus game

How to play

1 Play in groups of three or four. Each group needs one die and a counter for each player.
2 You each start with $1,000. You can either keep track of your own score, or you can appoint a 'banker' to keep everyone's score.
3 Each player throws the die. The player who throws the highest number starts, and throws the die again to move.
4 If you land on a white square, answer the question on the square. The other people in your group should decide whether you have answered the question correctly or not and give reasons for their opinion. If they do not think your answer is good enough, they can choose how much of the money to give you.
5 If the square is a TALK square, you should speak for one minute on the subject given. If you speak for less than a minute, you lose $500. You gain $200 for each main point you express, up to a maximum of four. You can use the ideas suggested in brackets. The other players will time you and count how many main points you have expressed.
6 If you land on a square that someone else has already answered, move to the square immediately after it and answer the question for that square instead – no one wants to listen to the same talk again!
7 The game ends when everyone reaches the end of the board. The person who has made the most money wins.

1 You have just been appointed Training Manager for your company. Say what the duties of a training manager are.	**2** CEOs often say, 'Our people are our best asset'. Do you agree? $50 for each reason you give as an answer.	**3** Interest rates have gone down. Gain $200 if you can say how this could benefit a business.
6 Which is more important for you: job satisfaction or salary? Up to $500 for a convincing answer – your colleagues decide.	**5** What is important when choosing a new supplier? (reliability, payment terms, etc.)	**4** Your company needs a new Customer Services Manager. What qualities does he or she need?
7 It is your annual performance review. Say what business skills you would like to acquire in the next year. $200 for each skill (maximum five).	**8** What is important when writing a CV? (layout, information, etc.)	**9** Name five ways of raising money for a new business activity. $100 for each idea.
12 How can business meetings be made more successful? $50 for each idea (maximum ten).	**11** Which is more important in business: qualifications and training or experience? $1,000 for a convincing answer.	**10** Describe a business trip you have made OR Say what is important when going on a business trip.

13 What is important when preparing a mail shot? (target audience, costs, etc.)	**14** What should you do before leaving the office to go on holiday? $100 for each reasonable action.	**15** What is important when assessing staff performance? (setting targets, providing training, etc.)
18 What mistakes do people make when giving presentations? $50 for each mistake (maximum ten).	**17** What is important when making a business presentation? (clear structure, illustrations and handouts, etc.)	**16** Do you think companies should consider the wishes of staff before relocating offices? $250 for a reasonable answer.
19 What is important when deciding on a business location? (proximity to markets, skilled workforce, etc.)	**20** What are the advantages for a company of having their offices in the capital city? $250 for each advantage (maximum three).	**21** What equipment is essential in a modern office and why? $50 for each piece of equipment and the reason (maximum ten).
24 What is important when accepting an overseas posting? (living conditions, expenses, etc.)	**23** What is important when choosing an employer? (contractual terms, promotion prospects, etc.)	**22** How would you entertain foreign business visitors to your town/city? $250 for a good answer.
25 How should companies decide where to advertise? $1,500 for a good answer.	**26** What can you find out by doing market research? $100 for each idea (maximum ten).	**27** What is important when carrying out market research? (clear objectives, good questions, etc.)
30 What is important when caring for customers? (clear communications, speed of service, etc.)	**29** What factors should employers take into account when deciding employees' salaries? $200 for each factor (maximum ten).	**28** What is important when negotiating a salary increase? (inflation, productivity, etc.)
31 Do you believe that the customer is always right? Why? / Why not? $500 for a well-reasoned answer.	**32** What rules would you give customer-service staff for answering the telephone? $25 for each rule (maximum ten).	**33** What is important when preparing a brochure? (Photography, words, etc.)
36 What advice would you give to a 17-year-old who told you he/she wanted to go into business?	**35** What job would you like to be doing in ten years' time? $1,000 for a convincing, well-reasoned answer.	**34** What image does the company you work for have? OR Talk about a company you know well: what image does it have? $750 for a good answer.

Lightning Source UK Ltd.
Milton Keynes UK
UKHW052158050422
401118UK00004B/13

9 781107 632110